Praise for *Outdoor Parents, Outdoor Kids*

"An excellent beginner's guide to help parents instill in their kids a love of outdoor activities - crucial to children's emotional and physical health."
- RICHARD LOUV, AUTHOR OF *LAST CHILD IN THE WOODS*

"Trying to hip your kids to the places and sports you love best can be surprisingly hard, even not-fun. That's why Outdoor Parents, Outdoor Kids is so valuable. Packed with practical advice, but also humor - Buchanan isn't the smug expert who makes you feel like an idiot, but a buddy who's been there - it flags up the challenges you want to consider before everyone, mom and dad included, are ready to throw a tantrum, and offers frequent reminders of why it's absolutely worth the effort."
- BRAD WIENERS, EDITOR, *MEN'S JOURNAL*

"A fun and informative guide that will help families experience a lifetime of wonder in the great outdoors."
- FRANK HUGELMEYER, PRESIDENT/CEO, OUTDOOR INDUSTRY ASSOCIATION

"If you're hoping to pass on the thrill of outdoor fun to your kids, read this book. Buchanan's rich—and frequently hilarious—experiences offer essential advice to any adventure-loving parent."
- CHRISTOPHER KEYES, EDITOR, OUTSIDE MAGAZINE

"I don't know which is more challenging — summiting Everest or raising teen-agers! As Eugene Buchanan knows, preparation is the key to both endeavors, and his book will help any parent navigate the rewarding outdoor adventures that can be had with their children. This entertaining and informative book showcases how activities of all shapes and sizes can be as fun, informative, challenging and inspirational as making it to the top of the highest peak."
- U.S. SENATOR MARK UDALL, COLORADO

"A hilarious and highly informative resource that makes life easier for all parents as Buchanan shares the lessons he's learned the hard way..."
- ROYAL ROBBINS, FOUNDER OF ROYAL ROBBINS, AND AUTHOR OF *TO BE BRAVE*

* A portion of all book sales benefits the Outdoor Foundation and their efforts to grow youth participation in outdoor recreation.

D1279194

"'Go to the mountains and get their blessings,' John Muir once said. Nowadays, however, too many of us, especially our children, suffer from a Nature deficit. This wonderful book will go a long way toward remedying that."
        - KEN BURNS, FILMMAKER (ACADEMY AWARD NOMINEE)

"Outdoor Parents, Outdoor Kids is an important contribution to the work of connecting our children to the outdoors. It's imperative that we give every American child an outdoor experience so they can explore, enjoy and protect our planet."
        - CARL POPE, EXECUTIVE DIRECTOR, SIERRA CLUB

"Eugene Buchanan is the real deal. He's a gifted outdoor athlete, loving father, and decorated journalist. Outdoor Parents, Outdoor Kids combines all he knows."
        - PHILIP ARMOUR, FORMER EDITOR OF FORBESLIFE MOUNTAINTIME

"The importance of getting more kids outside has been a driving force for Kelty KIDS for two decades. For those looking to take the first steps toward a fit outdoor lifestyle, or to nurture a child's respect for the earth, Eugene Buchanan's Outdoor Parents, Outdoor Kids puts all the essentials in a refreshing new light."
        - KENNY BALLARD, PRESIDENT, KELTY/KELTY KIDS

"Our responsibility as parents is to open our kids' eyes to the world around us and beyond. Outdoor Parents, Outdoor Kids nails it perfectly on how to enable us to do just that. Buchanan is a master."
        - BILL GAMBER, PRESIDENT, BIG AGNES

"Wish I'd had this book when my kids were snuggly sized. We muddled through okay but Buchanan gives young parents what they really need: good info, superb tips, and the inspiration to head out."
        - TODD BALF, AUTHOR OF THE LAST RIVER

"In a book loaded with practical advice and hilarious anecdotes, Buchanan never loses track of the best reason for kids and parents to play together outside: Because it is fun."
        - JEFF MOAG, EDITOR-IN-CHIEF, CANOE AND KAYAK MAGAZINE

"A great read that leads the way to healthier kids and a healthier planet, written by one of my favorite writers. Fun, health, and a really cool perspective on the best ways to interact with our world. A must-read for anyone who wants healthier, happier kids right now."
        - PETER KRAY, EDITOR, SKI PRESS WORLD; FOUNDER, SHRED WHITE AND BLUE

"The ultimate support group for outdoor parenting."
        - DOUG SCHNITZSPAHN, EDITOR-IN-CHIEF, ELEVATION OUTDOORS

Outdoor PARENTS, OUTDOOR Kids

A Guide to Getting Your Kids Active in the Great Outdoors

EUGENE BUCHANAN

Illustrations by Dennis Hengeveld

THE **HELICONIA PRESS**

an Imprint of Fox Chapel Publishing
www.FoxChapelPublishing.com

© 2010, 2012 by Fox Chapel Publishing Company, Inc., East Petersburg, PA.

Written by: Eugene Buchanan
Edited by: Lori Covington
Cover photo by: Trevor Lush
Illustrations by: Dennis Hengeveld
Design and Layout by: Ken Whiting

ISBN 978-1-896980-70-6

Library of Congress Cataloging-in-Publication Data

Buchanan, Eugene.

Outdoor parents, outdoor kids / Eugene Buchanan ; illustrations by Dennis Hengeveld.

   p. cm.

Includes index.

Originally published : Ontario : Heliconia Press, 2010.

ISBN 978-1-896980-70-6

1. Outdoor recreation. 2. Family recreation. I. Title.

GV191.6.B79 2012

796.5--dc23

2011051645

To learn more about the other great books from Fox Chapel Publishing, or to find a retailer near you, call toll-free 800-457-9112 or visit us at *www.FoxChapelPublishing.com*.

Note to Authors: We are always looking for talented authors to write new books. Please send a brief letter describing your idea to Acquisition Editor, 1970 Broad Street, East Petersburg, PA 17520.

Printed in United States of America
First printing

CONTENTS

To (who else?) but my two outdoorsy daughters, Brooke and Casey. Hopefully, you'll get my grandkids out in the Great Outdoors as well...

ABOUT THE AUTHOR

A FORMER REPORTER FOR the *Denver Business Journal* and 14-year editor-in-chief of *Paddler* magazine, Eugene Buchanan has written about the outdoors for more than 25 years, from covering the X Games for ESPN.com to working for NBC at the Beijing Olympics. With freelance articles published in the *New York Times*, *Men's Journal*, *National Geographic Adventure*, *Sports Afield*, *Outside*, *Forbes Life* and other publications, his passion for traveling and writing has taken him to more than 30 countries on six continents. A Fellow member of the Explorer's Club and contributor to *Men's Journal's The Great Life* anthology, he spearheaded the Outdoor Industry Association's Outdoor Idols campaign, honoring teens' accomplishments in the outdoors. His first book, *Brothers on the Bashkaus*, was released by Fulcrum Publishing in 2007. He lives with his wife, Denise, and daughters, Brooke, 11, and Casey, 7, in Steamboat Springs, Colorado, just a block away from the Yampa River.

INTRODUCTION

"Teaching children about the natural world should be treated as one of the most important events in their lives."
—Thomas Berry

WHEN ASKED ABOUT HIS APPEARANCE on the cover of *Outside* magazine along such outdoor recreation legends as Lance Armstrong, Kelly Slater and Ed Viesturs, musician Ben Harper had only this to say: "To the people who say what the #$%& is he doing on the cover of *Outside* magazine, let me just say this: I've got four kids. Four kids is an extreme sport, period." I'm not harping on Harper. Raising kids is an extreme sport. And I only have half of his harem.

But as hard as caring for kids is, try recreating with them outside and things get even more harrowing. For Harper, a simple bike ride with the kids means possibly repairing 10 flats. Head skiing and he's packing and tracking just as many poles, skis, boots, socks and gloves. That's 40 different things, assuming his kids' socks stay on their feet. It's a lot of work, and if you think it's easy you're in for a brood awakening.

That's where this book comes in. It's designed to help parents get their kids active outside, while instilling in their brood a respect for their health and the Great Outdoors. It's for first-time parents wondering how to go about it, as well as the Harpers of the world already pursuing outdoor activities with their offspring. When adrenaline junkies go through withdrawals, they feel a need to "feed the rat." This book shows parents how to do that, while including the rugrats as well.

Doing so has several positive impacts. It brings you together as a family and keeps everyone healthier, from diaper-clad Danny on up to the gear-packing grown-ups.

More than 22 million of the world's children under the age of five are overweight or obese. This equals 13% of all children in the United States. Hand-in-hand with this, kids spend an average of 44 hours a week in front of TVs, computers and video games, and pediatricians are treating fewer broken bones today and more repetitive motion injuries. After a lackluster U.S. showing in the Rome Olympics a half century ago, even President John F. Kennedy commented on the problem. "Our struggles against aggressors...have been won on the playgrounds, corner lots and fields of America," he penned in a piece called "The Soft American" for *Sports Illustrated*. "Our growing softness, our increasing lack of physical fitness, is a menace to our security."

It's also a menace to families' health and well-being.

Fortunately, there are groups trying to help. In a survey of more than 60,000 Americans ages 6 and older, the Outdoor Foundation, whose charter is to grow youth participation in outdoor pursuits (and whose initiatives we're proud to support by donating a portion of this book's sales), found that the best way to get kids involved in the outdoors is to take them there. Ninety percent of today's active adults were introduced to their favorite outdoor activities before the age of 18. Unfortunately, participation in these activities declines with age. While 78% of kids 6-12 participate in outdoor activities, this number falls to 55% for those aged 18-24. As part of a solution, it recently launched its "I Will" campaign, challenging members of the outdoor industry to take kids outside. Even the government is getting involved. Using the campaign as a model, Secretary of the Interior Ken Salazar recently called upon every adult in the country to take a child outdoors as part of the White House's Summer of Service Initiative.

But the real burden lays with us parents. It's up to us to encourage our kids to engage in outdoor pursuits. Hopefully this book will help.

Perhaps no one has put his finger on the problem better than Richard Louv, whose best-selling book, *Last Child in the Woods*, carries the tagline, "Saving our Children from Nature Deficit Disorder." In it he reveals a host of societal costs to children not playing in nature, from diminished use of senses and attention difficulties to higher rates of physical and emotional illness. He's become a messiah, of sorts, for the movement, speaking across the country on the importance of getting youth outdoors. The outdoor industry, he maintains, understands this problem and is one group trying to fix it. Consider this book a stab at saving our children from slouchdom and couchdom.

Many of you likely already indulge your children's more conventional active pastimes—shuttling them to gymnastics, baseball, dance, soccer, football, swim lessons, tennis, piano, play dates, playgrounds, and other time-, gas- and money-consuming activities, sometimes all on the same day. Throw in the inevitable potty breaks and tantrums before, during and after, and it's a schedule as full as the average stuffed animal shelf.

Painful as all this shuttling is, it shows you're on the right track. My purpose is to help you add the world of outdoor recreation into the mix as well.

I'm no Dr. Ruth of Recreation. There are no fancy Recreating with Kids diplomas hanging on my office walls (just a handful of my kids' soccer and swimming ribbons). I'm just an average Joe Schmoe father who loves being outside with my kids and inspiring them to respect their health and the environment as much as I do.

My only certification is that I've done everything in this book with them, whether they've liked it or not. We've camped in the rain, hiked through mosquitoes, skied in the cold, rafted through hailstorms, flown over bike handlebars, and pierced ears with fish hooks. But the good times far outnumber the bad, and it's my hope that our own trials and tribulations can offer hints on how and how not to get your kids involved in these same pursuits.

To help you along this road, I've divided the book into chapters, broken down into different outdoor activities. While not every one is covered, a fair amount of those lending themselves to family participation are. There are sections on skiing, climbing, fishing, hiking, camping, backpacking, swimming, snorkeling, jogging, biking, paddling and more, all designed to help ease the learning curve of getting your brood outside. There's even a section on statistics, pointing to the importance of keeping youth active, as well as a chapter highlighting ways to shave off a little Me Time for your own sanity-saving pursuits.

This book was created with one purpose in mind: to help parents get their kids active outside. As well as creating fit, fun-loving offspring, in so doing it will hopefully also instill ethics that your kids pass on to theirs after you've moved on to that big mountain bike trail in the sky.

As Harper notes, you're going to have your hands full enough raising kids; so you might as well use every resource at your disposal to make things easier when you recreate with them. If this tome helps even one of you turn your kids on to an outdoor activity they can enjoy for life, I'll have considered it a success. And then it will be you and your children who deserve to be on that magazine cover as much as Harper and his colleagues.

A PARENTING PROLOGUE

"You will always be your child's favorite toy."
—Vicki Lansky, *Trouble-Free Travel with Children*

THERE'S A PHOTO IN A SHOEBOX SOMEWHERE (no, not on an Iphone or even a hard drive) showing my family—six kids, my mom and a buff, shirtless, dad— in a field near our house where I grew up in Boulder, Colorado (yes, the place where "the hip meet to trip" and where Mork lived). We had just finished picnicking and were all, for lack of a better term, happily recreating outside. Maybe we tossed the Frisbee. Maybe we played tag. Maybe we played Spud, that game where you throw a ball up and then try to cream your sister with it. Maybe we simply walked our dog, Boots, who had her own weight issues, in our collective, Boulder-era Birkenstocks. The point is, we were doing something together as a family outside, bell bottoms, bandanas and all.

Not that our family was obsessive about it. Other families camped, backpacked, surfed, skied, fished, rafted and whatever-elsed far more than we did. It was Boulder, after all, with more VW campers topped with two-by-four racks than anywhere else on the patchouli-oil-burning planet.

But we did enough such outings for me to take joy in passing along that outdoor ethos to the next generation, my own two kids, Brooke, now 10, and Casey, 7. From my brothers putting a snake in my sister's bike basket to discovering a ski lodge candy machine that dispensed free Big Red cinnamon gum, I remember it all. And those memories are responsible for my joy in creating similar ones for my kids.

Recreating outdoors with your family isn't difficult. But like everything else about child rearing, there are tricks to making it easier. When my daughter asks me for a combo-bowl of Cheerios and Lucky Charms, I put the Charms on top to make it look like there are more Yellow Moons and Green Clovers than there are Cheerios. You can employ similar ploys to get your family on its way to a healthier, outdoor lifestyle. Tell your kids you're going to throw rocks in a lake, not go for a hike. Say you're going for a bike ride, not to get exercise. These tricks and more can do wonders to get the recreation wheels rolling.

Doing so won't always be easy. Kids add a third dimension ~ an inter-whining variable, if you will ~ to otherwise simple activities. You'll have wind blow down your tents, forget gloves on ski trips, suffer sunburn at the beach, and endure bee stings on hikes. Along the way, you'll experience every single emotion of Snow White's seven dwarves. Your kids will be Sleepy from being tired, Bashful about trying new things, Dopey with excitement about mastering a new skill, Sneezy from catching colds, and Grumpy from temper tantrums, while you're playing Doc by bandaging scrapes and bruises. Above all, they, and you, will be Happy for life from your taking the time to instill in them a respect for their health and the outdoors.

Recreating with your kids is all about having a high tolerance for cluster-management. You'll load and unload bikes atop cars until your head is spinning like the wheels you're wrestling. But put up with it. Childhood goes around just as quickly as those spokes.

A friend's dad, whom they call Dude (yes, he's from Boulder also), provides a prime example. He regularly tortured his kids with river, climbing and backpacking trips to Kingdom Come and hopefully back, enough so that he'd likely be behind bars today. "I could never tell if all the misadventures he put us through were planned or not," says son John, now forty-seven and with two sons of his own. "We'd run out of food on day four of a ten-day river trip, but somehow get through it." Regardless, both sons are now extremely active and successful—one runs a rock-climbing wall company, and the other a backcountry products company—and are instilling the same values in their own families.

People say you should write what you know about. If that's the case, I feel halfway qualified to put this work together—much like Boulder's Ph.Ds working as waiters. I'm a self-professed "yahoo," not in the Internet sense, but in terms of outdoor recreation. Between work, chores and raising kids I try to fit in as many activities as possible. I'll kayak during lunch, mountain bike before work, and enact the powder clause when it snows eight inches or more. I know countless other parents who do the same.

I owe this lifestyle to my parents, for both a weird blend of recreational genetics and the environmental component of instilling an active lifestyle in us six Buchanan kids. That's right, there were six of us – which likely explains why they wanted us out of the house so much and expending as much energy as possible. Most of their encouragement, I'm sure, was simply to get us out of their hair. Whenever I got bored, my dad would say, "Go outside and play in the street with some broken glass." (I think he was joking.) While that might not fly with today's social services, to his credit—swerving cars and broken bottles aside—in some sort of twisted, Thoreauian way it was his way of encouraging us to go outdoors, maybe not to Walden Pond, but at least to the closest curb.

Armed with such permission, we quickly took to the outdoors. We learned the basics of climbing by scrambling up the nearby Flatirons and scaling the flagstone walls of university buildings. We got primed in paddling by inner-tubing Boulder Creek, returning with bruised butts. We built ski jumps at Chautauqua Park whenever enough snow fell. We biked to the Meadows Club and caught crawdads and small-mouth bass in the pond all afternoon. I skateboarded so much that the side of my jeans always wore through from the grip tape chafing it when hiking back uphill (it took my mom years to figure out what caused it).

The point is, we kept ourselves busy outdoors and took the habit with us as we aged.

Not all of these activities were conventional or condonable. Skitching behind cars comes to mind, as does throwing snowballs at them, followed by the subsequent Brave Sir Robin 100-yard-dash into the nearest bush to hide from irate drivers.

But we also pursued more conventional activities. I played Pop Werner football, biking to and from practice in my pads. In junior high, I competed in wrestling and gymnastics, which helped whenever Doug Weller, the state champ I had to fight for A Mat, used me as a guinea pig for such moves as the Nutcracker. I played soccer, football and baseball, and while too short for the eighth-grade basketball team, I made up for it with pick-up games at home. Top this off with games of Cream Ball during lunch, using a smashed eight-ounce milk carton as an indicator of who gets tackled, and I was lucky to gain any weight at all.

I carried this mindset to college. I worked ski patrol the same weekend I had a lacrosse game, and served a community service sentence (I won't go into the details) by cross-country skiing up Pikes Peak and helping the hutkeeper toboggan firewood back to the cabin. We also explored tunnels below campus as if they were caves, save for the laser alarms guarding the subterranean entrance to the science building and stumbling upon a crate of World War II-era Phenobarbital. The same day I groggily graduated, I hopped on a plane to Alaska to manage a rafting company.

Other components of my life likely suffered accordingly. I remember studying for my GMAT test in a Telluride, Colorado, library and seeing a Frisbee fly by the window. My scores might have soared like the Frisbee had I not put my books down and joined in. But life's too short to have it any other way, and I fully believe that recreating outdoors prolongs it.

Now that I've "matured," I pursue more standard outdoor activities. And I've learned that with kids, even a walk in the park isn't a walk in the park.

The first key is to settle down wisely. It's easier to head into the woods with kids if you live in Walla Walla, Washington, than Detroit. Live someplace where there are more striped bass than strip malls.

Another hint: follow the seasons. A change in the time of year should simply mean a change in activities, not a clamber back to the couch. Where we live in Steamboat Springs, Colorado, our options change every few months and we try to take advantage of all of them. The melting snow exposes bike paths, playgrounds, hiking trails and fishing ponds. As skis and sleds go into storage, out come the trail-a-bikes, burleys and climbing ropes. Let the seasons dictate your pursuits.

Another trick: double dip by tying an activity into a more conventional obligation. In the winter, Casey and I sometimes cross-country ski to school. In the spring, I'll pick her up on the trail-a-bike. I once even picked her up at her riverside day care in a raft, then floated four miles down to the library where we walked home.

While the jury's still out on whether memories like these will send her to a shrink or a healthy, happy lifestyle, at least they're there for her to selectively relish or ignore.

I'm the first to admit that we (or rather, I ~ no need to lump my wife, Denise, into this) have done plenty of wrong things along the way. (I'm sorry about that bike wreck, Casey, and fish hook in your thumb, Brooke.) Like mood swings fueled by Sugar Smacks, this book showcases the highs and lows of our family's outdoor endeavors. While not glorifying our mistakes, I'm also not hiding them. I'm simply exposing secrets we've learned along the way to make things easier. That way you can shake the cobwebs off your gear—and acquire mountains more for your kids—and get back to enjoying the outdoors.

Plenty of parents do far more with their kids than we do. Friends John and Inga took their kids out of school for a year-long sailing trip around the world. Ben and Lisa took their kids on a bike trip through Europe. John and Nancy have taken their kids on river trips throughout the West, and have them ski-jour behind their dogs in the winter.

Tami and Tom (who just ran Alaska's Iditarod) have their eight-year-old daughter guide dogsled trips (don't ask about how, when we turned her loose with Casey and Brooke, we saw the team emerge from a corner running full tilt sans any kids at all). It all makes me feel like asking for another potato chip.

Even more famous outdoorsy parents recognize the importance of recreating with their kids. Laird Hamilton surfs with his brood, mountaineer Ed Viesturs hikes with his, and rock climber Nancy Pritchard climbs with hers. It all makes me feel inadequate about what we don't do with ours. But every family is different. The key is doing what feels right for yours.

Whatever pursuit you tackle, the most important thing is sharing what you know. As Bobbi Connor, host of radio's *The Parent's Journal*, puts it, "When the parents have expertise in something like camping, kayaking or bicycling, it's a wonderful tradition to share it with kids. Kids might sit in front of the keyboard and screen and be happy in the moment...but they don't realize what they're losing. When kids are outdoors in any season, just connecting with nature and feeling the sunshine or stomping in a mud puddle, it gives them a spontaneous opportunity to create things and taps into a different part of them than a pre-programmed game."

The game is on now to get them off video games and into the Great Outdoors.

Chapter 1

GETTING OUT WHILE YOU CAN

"If we want children to flourish, to become truly empowered, then let us allow them
to love the earth before we ask them to save it."
—David Sobel, *Beyond Ecophobia*

AFTER MOVING TO STEAMBOAT SPRINGS, Colorado, my wife and I continued our happy-go-lucky recreational ways for seven years before that path got hit by
a landslide. That's when our daughter, Brooke, was born and we became...Recreation-
ally Challenged Parents.

Not that this prompted a visit to Recreationally Challenged Parents Anonymous—
"Uh, my name is Eugene and I'm..."—but it did affect our erstwhile selfish approach to
recreation. Gone were the days when we could agree to bike queries at the drop of a
helmet, and here for good was a new world of involving our kids (now including Casey)
in our favorite pastimes.

Doing so has been a mountain of work. It's meant carrying armloads of skis and
poles to the ski area, rigging burleys behind bikes, piling pack n' play cribs onto rafts,
and cramming kids and camping gear into our car until its mudflaps touch the pavement. It's crimped our style like a kinked bike cable, but it's been worth every extra
piece of gear we've lugged from garage to car to trail.

What we've found through all of this is that your activities and those of your kids
don't have to be mutually exclusive. In short, your rec life doesn't have to be a wreck

when children enter the picture. It changes, sure—just like your bank account, sex, tidiness, tardiness and everything else parents bemoan. But like climbing Mount Everest, all it takes is a little acclimation to get back on top of your game. A few minor tweaks and adjustments, just like that visit to the chiropractor, will get both you and your children on your way to a healthy outdoor lifestyle.

Kids shouldn't put the skids on outdoor recreation. Priorities change with parenting, sure. You'll change diapers with the same aplomb you previously reserved for placing climbing protection (the lack of which got you into parentdom in the first place), and you'll become an expert at jigsaw-puzzling bikes into the back of your car. But kids don't mean throwing your outdoor lifestyle out the car window (which is now lowered to accommodate an extra set of bike handlebars).

Perhaps nowhere is parents' fear of losing their recreational livelihood better illustrated than in the birth announcement for our daughter, Brooke. Shortly after she was born, Denise called me home from work to stage a photo for our pronouncement. When I arrived, she had piled all of our outdoor gear—from climbing ropes and tennis racquets to surfboards, mountain bikes, skis, golf clubs, kayaks and more—into a massive mound outside with a giant For Sale sign sticking out of it.

Cradling Brooke in our arms, the context of the resultant announcement was obvious: *hasta luego*, life of recreational leisure; hellooo—parenthood! While my mom thought it drew attention away from Brooke, it made a point we were determined to share. Rather than selling our gear, we vowed to continue using it and even update it to include our newborn in our pastimes. If anything, we added to the mound. We purchased burleys for our bikes, sleds for skiing, and backpacks for hiking, and slowly acquired gear for her as well. The mound grew, just as Brooke did, as she progressed from breast milk to Formula to Gerbers and finally grilled cheese.

But the photo sums up a fear many new parents face. For those who enjoy outdoor recreation, parenthood comes with a price. How do you pursue your favorite pastimes while caring for your brood? More importantly, how do you involve your children in outdoor activities dear to your heart, instilling in them a respect for their health and the environment so they can some day do the same with their kids?

From a purely self-centered standpoint, to start you have to have a base to build from, right? You're certainly not going to take your kid kite-boarding without a nominal mastery of the sport yourself. So *before* kids enter the picture, polish your own skills as much as possible. This section's not so much about recreating *with* kids, but doing so *without* them.

Don't feel guilty about it. You'll be with your brood plenty, especially if you take home anything from this book. But anyone who has changed diapers at 3 a.m. appreciates the importance of a little solo time far away from the changing room. Change those diapers often enough and you won't even have the energy for personal pursuits anymore. But it's important to keep recreation an active part of your life so you can pass on its benefits to your brood during theirs. And if you can't master this art of the solo fix, as well as being doomed to a life on the couch like so many other parenting potatoes you won't stand a chance when it comes to recreating with brood in tow.

Having kids *will* affect your recreational livelihood. If a new parent tells you otherwise, he or she is lying. How could it not, when recreation time is now absorbed by child-rearing time? If you're accustomed to hopping on the bike at the drop of a helmet and then dropping the peloton, get used to your windows becoming as short as Lance Armstrong's hair.

Before, it was easy. You could do things spontaneously. "Hey, honey!" you'd cheerfully suggest over coffee. "Let's go for a hike today." And then you'd be merrily on your way, stopping for a leisurely latte beforehand. Little Johnny Burpalot has changed things. Now you'll need that latte, and the time to enjoy it, more than ever. Because here's the thing: while you're out feeding your own rat, your spouse is at home feeding the rugrat creamed peas. And that spouse is counting the minutes with rolling pin in hand, until you return. When you do, that warm kiss on the cheek you used to get, and genuine inquiry into your activity, evaporates like spilt milk. It's replaced as quickly as a pedal crank by your little bundle of joy, deposited into your arms.

This isn't meant to scare you away from parentdom. By all means, procreate to your heart's content. Just remember the time constraints that lie ahead, and take advantage of your recreational freedom while you can. A little Me Time makes anyone a better parent.

Guys, admittedly, have an easier time cramming in recreation up to the moment of childbirth than women do. So gals, if your body's up to it, continue recreating as long as your doctor, diaphragm and desire allow. One lady friend of mine skied up until she was eight months, her belly as rounded as the moguls she was avoiding. Another kayaked up to the same point, testing both her doctor's patience and spray skirt's adhesion.

Regardless of your gender, use your child's nine-month incubation period as a last recreational hurrah of sorts. Squeeze in daily routines like they're going out of style, which they soon will be. Even try for a bigger journey, if circumstances and partners allow ~ a golf trip to North Carolina, climbing excursion to Hueco Tanks, or mountain bike jaunt to Moab.

If not for your own sake, do it for the rest of us already blessed with child.

THE GREAT ESCAPE

With my wife due in February, both of our clocks were ticking, hers as far as procreation, mine for recreation. So I did what any expectant father would do under the circumstances: I called a few buddies to go on a kayaking trip in Mexico. It would be a last rite of recreation, I figured, before paddling gave way to parenting.

Having a child, I surmised, was a rite of passage every bit as much as sticking one's first Eskimo roll. But since kayaking is a solo pursuit that usually involves traveling and a modicum of danger (as well as enchiladas afterwards), it doesn't always go hand-in-hand with raising kids. So knowing things would change like my newborn's diapers, I made the dash south of the border.

The trip's timing, of course, was as delicate as my wife's temperament. I would return, I told my expanding lifemate, on January 10—a month before her due date and in plenty of time should she experience a premature runoff. Hall pass granted, I pitched a few paddling friends on the last hurrah angle and headed to the heart of the aptly named Sierra Madre Mountains.

To help justify the time away from wife and zygote, I also vowed to polish up on the nuances of parenthood. For this, I enlisted the help of the renowned Dr. Spock and his timeless *Baby and Child Care* book. If anything could help prepare me for fatherhood as much as a boating trip to Mexico, this was surely it. Bringing it along meant exposing my jugular to my buddies, who, like wingmen the world over, are notorious for heckling the weak and wounded for far more trivial breaches of the Universal Man Code. But I was willing to risk jeers from my peers if it meant becoming a better father.

Like my wife disguising her pregnancy with maternity clothes, I tried to hide the book on the plane, sneaking it out of my backpack and stuffing it inside an in-flight magazine to serve as a cover shield. Inevitably, I was discovered. "Hey! Look who brought

a baby book!" said my kidless rowmate Dave when he glimpsed the cover. "I bet you only get ten pages read the whole trip."

Soon my remaining friends joined in from across the aisle; the heckling had begun and we hadn't even touched ground. It seemed like the whole plane was wondering what I was doing, bringing a parenting book on a guys' trip. I half expected the captain to join the fray on the loudspeaker: "Uh, ladies and gentlemen, this is your captain speaking, and even though he's on a trip with manly guy friends, please note the reading material the passenger in Seat 22C is burying his nose in." Vowing to prove my detractors wrong, I ignored their remarks and attempted to digest the good doctor's advice.

My reading plan, I quickly learned, was rather ambitious. It would take a few shuttle break-downs on the way to the river, and perhaps even one on our plane, to get through the book's 939 pages. But I resolved to power through it.

Like negotiating whitewater, it didn't take long to get disoriented—especially when I turned to the fourteen-page-long Table of Contents. Subheads such as "The Parents' Part," "Common Behavior Problems" and "First Year Feeding" soon had my head swirling as if I were upside-down in a whirlpool. But then I saw it, the first Spockism I could relate to:

"Many fathers feel they're being called on to give up all their freedom and former pleasures. Others forget their hobbies and interests. Even if they do occasionally sneak off, they feel too guilty to get full enjoyment."

Is that the way I'd feel at the top of my first rapid? Too guilty to get full enjoyment? Before I had time to answer, Dave sidetracked me by breaking out a guidebook, dangling it like the mini-carrots we'd soon be feeding our daughter. For the time being, I put Dr. Spock away.

I gave the doctor another chance after changing planes in Houston. Once again, his words struck home. "For too long fathers have gotten away with the clever ruse that they lacked the intelligence, manual dexterity and visual motor-skills to change a smelly diaper." What better way to enhance one's intelligence, manual dexterity and visual motor-skills, I reasoned, than by unselfishly pursuing your recreational pleasure of choice before practicing said maneuvers on a helpless baby? Need to polish your visual motor skills before being turned loose on a wayward diaper? Take that ski or golf trip with the fellas. I made a note to apply the skills I learned on this boating trip to my baby's bottom back home.

After landing in Tampico (which sounds oddly like the tapioca we'd soon be feeding Brooke), we bussed to Ciudad Valles, a few miles from our base camp on the Rio Micos. There, we pacified ourselves with Coronas while waiting for our pick-up. We used the time to meet the rest of the clients, getting to know one another like couples in the Lamaze class my wife and I had just finished back home. This, however, was a markedly rougher crowd. When I used my limited Spanish to say "I am happy," Jeff, a return client from Washington who had been apprised of my pending date with parenthood, saw the opening and pounced. "Yeah, well you better enjoy it," he chided. "Your life's over." Heckle session round two had begun. Naturally, I countered. "How do you know?"

I asked. "Do you have kids?" His response put an end to the subject. "Nope," he replied. "I had a vasectomy when I was twenty."

Around the fire at camp, I assessed what I was up against. The respective kid-factors of my cohorts didn't look promising. Homer, my cousin from Salida, Colorado, was the only one blessed with child. The rest were staunch birth control boaters: John: kidless; Vasectomized Jeff: kidless for life; Dave: kidless, wifeless and dogless; 21-year-old Annie: still a kid; Mike and Dion: married seven years, no kids. I wasn't going to find much sympathy from this crew.

So I retired to my *palapa* and sought advice from the venerable doctor. Glancing through such subheads as "The Reluctant Weaner," "The Important Sucking Instinct," and "Breast Engorgement Due to Plugged Ducts," I began to notice baby reminders everywhere. Outside, the lapping of the river took on the metronome of a wind-up baby swing. Mosquito netting hung down from the ceiling like a mobile. In the cot next to me was John, whose raspy breathing painted a future of coughs, colds and the croup. I could only hope he wouldn't crawl into bed with me for a snuggle.

The reminders continued the next morning as I awoke, far too early, to parrots squawking. "Better get used to it," said the snoring señor next to me, unable to resist an early morning jab. "Soon that'll be little Eugenia."

Great, I thought. Now they have the name picked out for my daughter as well.

After breakfast, we chose from a line of kayaks in a rack, pointing fingers like fathers in a nursery. The selection process evoked a not-too-flattering image of my wife. Eight months into it, she was beginning to look a lot like the playboats in front of us, skinny on the ends with a rather bulbous midsection, like the snake who swallowed an elephant in *The Little Prince*. Pushing the image aside, I piled into the shuttle rig with the rest of the group and headed for the Micos, which means "monkey." "You know... those cute, small cuddly things," said Dave from the back seat. "Like a baby with hair."

The water at the put-in was baby-bottle warm. "Might want to test it by slapping some on your arm," chided John. Dave threw the next punch, handing me a tube of Water Babies sunscreen. My only escape lay in the river. Cinching my PFD, I paddled off the first drop, severing my umbilical cord from the eddy above. As soon as I landed I wished I hadn't snipped it so soon. I also yearned for some of my wife's belly—the extra forward weight might have kept me from a flat, back-rattling landing.

Like a toddler taking a few stove touches to learn the word "hot," we ran the drop again and again, not really learning from our mistakes. Child psychologist Jean Piaget calls the first two years of development the "sensori-motor period, where infants learn by doing..." We, too, were learning by doing. When someone landed flat, everyone else leaned forward. When someone landed too far forward, everyone else leaned back. Hot. Ouch! Hot. Ouch! It was operant conditioning at its finest. If my newborn was capable of learning half as quickly, she'd be in fine shape.

On the paddle out at the end of the day, we ran into another group from Colorado, there to film a video. Their ringleader quickly explained why producer Paul Tefft wasn't with them: he was saddled down with newborn twins back home. Vasectomized Jeff pounced again. "Better enjoy it," he reminded me yet again. "You probably won't be getting out much after this, either."

Another harbinger reared itself farther downstream; just before camp we paddled up to a large stork standing in the middle of the river, his legs bent at an impossible angle. "Aren't those the birds that deliver babies to your doorstep?" asked John. "You might want to call your wife. It could be an omen." That night I borrowed the camp's satellite phone to make the call. She wasn't home.

The harassing continued that night when I took off my shorts and exposed an adult version of diaper rash. Drying the offending neoprene in front of the fire, I was target practice for Hecklers Anonymous. "Why bother?" asked Jeff. "You don't need to keep that part of your body warm any more; it's served its purpose."

To escape further barbs I retired again to my *palapa* and sought solace from the benevolent doctor. Tonight's lesson: How Human Beings Get Their Aspirations. "A man may react to his wife's pregnancy with various feelings. There can be a feeling of being left out, which may be expressed as...wanting to spend more time with his men friends." Bingo. Justification for the trip right there in black and white, both for me and any other man about to enter the plight of parenthood.

So the men I was with weren't cutting me any slack. So what? Isn't that what being out with the guys is for? I was spending "more time" with them, and had the doctor's blessing to do so. Recreation is a natural reaction to fatherhood, says the doctor. When a baby's about to enter the picture, forget dogs—Doctor Spock is man's best friend. Intrigued, I continued. The next chapter was entitled, "What Kind of Delivery Do You Want?" For my wife, it boiled down to one word: epidural. (We didn't know it would also result in a C-section when our daughter's heart rate dropped.) For selfish little old me, I was simply hoping for a painless delivery of my own off the next day's 25-foot waterfall on the Rio Salto.

I felt a few Braxton Hicks-like contractions myself at the fall's brink the next morning as my stomach tightened with nerves. Luckily, I had another Spockism to rely on: "Trust yourself...you know more than you think you do." Helping me gain the necessary knowledge was Dave, who missed his line, wet-exited his boat and swam at the fall's base. Armed with his miscalculation, I stroked for the left and sailed off into a perfect trajectory, my bow bouncing up at the bottom like a baby in a jumpy-seat. Eventually we reached the take-out, located at the brink of an 85-foot waterfall called El Meco, a cascading ribbon of white. On the shuttle home, I asked our driver what it meant. The answer shouldn't have been surprising: The Sperm.

The remainder of the week was filled with more rivers and reminders of my impending date with parenthood. Out of touch for eight days, I was nervous about how things were going back home. On our last night, I finally got through on the satellite phone and wasted no time in finding out the crucial information on everyone's mind... the Broncos would face Miami in the playoffs. Returning to the fire, I shared the news to a loud cheer.

To celebrate the playoffs, my wife not going into labor and a successful week of waterfalls, we sang and gave toasts until we all crawled to bed. The next morning, I felt better prepared for fatherhood than ever—at least for the sleep-deprivation part. I felt even more prepared when I strolled over to the campfire site, which looked like a band of toddlers had ravaged someone's living room. Chairs were overturned, clothes were strewn about and bottles lay in disarray.

After cleaning things up and saying our good-byes, we caught a bus back to Tampico and hopped on our plane. On the flight home, I again pulled out Dr. Spock, this time settling into a chapter on ear infections—an especially pertinent one since my own were hurting from time spent upside-down. "Still reading that?" interrupted Dave from across the aisle. "How far did you get?"

"Not very," I replied. But I'm sure Dr. Spock would understand.

BROOKE ARRIVES

Brooke was born a day late, on February 15. My wife didn't really want her to be born on Valentine's Day and have friends and loved ones double-dip on cards, and that subconscious thought perhaps helped delay matters. I was just glad not to be delayed on my flight home, making it back a whole thirty days before Delivery Day.

Of course, I didn't let that stop me from continuing to recreate closer to home those last few weeks. In fact, I had a sore neck from playing hockey on Valentine's Day itself, the day Brooke was supposed to come into this world (I had my cell phone on the bench, and was prepared to show up in hockey pants if need be). But I certainly wasn't going to complain about it to my wife or doctor——even after a miserable night's sleep on a hospital cot.

I felt better about my own recreation indiscretions when I found out what my buddy, Paul, did the day his wife gave birth. It was a powder day at our local ski resort, and he snuck out to snowboard a foot of fresh snow just two hours after his daughter Chloe was born. "That's great that everything worked out fine, Honey," I envisioned him telling his bed-ridden wife. "The mountain got a foot, so I'll be back in a couple of hours." That never would have flown in my house, where the recreational reins are tighter. I could only surmise that, since it was their third child, Paul's leash had been lengthened.

When we got home from the hospital, yearning for the instructions for this thing making googoo-eyes up at us from her car-seat perch on the dining room table, the recreational reality of kids began to hit home. Over the next few months, we each still managed to sneak out for short activities, but in more rigidly designated time windows. Shuttling time to the day's pursuit all of a sudden became part of our allowed time-frame. A fifteen-minute drive to and from a trailhead ate up half of an hour's recreational window. Not that the person exercising counted, but rather the person waiting at home.

We quickly learned that it's all about windows. You have to take advantage of them when you can. One friend started recreating with a fury any spare chance he had, once his daughter entered the picture. He'd wear his running shoes while rocking her to sleep so he could take off as soon as the nap took hold.

We began passing Brooke off as if she were a baton or pigskin. Our hand-offs became quarterback-to-fullback smooth. There was no time for fumbles or misunderstood plays. And certainly no baton drops like those that besieged the U.S. Olympic Track Team in Beijing. When your opening arose, you sprinted for it. My wife would come in the door from a ride and have Brooke in her arms before her bike shorts even came off, while I'd be riding out the mud room and down the front stairs. The meter was running.

That spring, I learned another lesson: mountain bike trips to Moab, skiing forays to the San Juan Mountains and kayaking road trips all but dried up. The problem: they were all-day or longer adventures, not just the hour-or-so quickie. They weren't conducive to passing the babysitting baton. The ability to take those kinds of excursions had evaporated like the snow on our local mountain, feeding the now-roaring river.

I knew the issue would surface. I'd seen the recreation windows of other friends with kids dwindle down to nothing. "Just wait," they said whenever I tried to rally them away from their families. "You'll see." Now the creamed-pea-covered tables had been turned.

I penned a letter about my plunge into parenthood for the paddling magazine I edited at the time. *"My plunge into fatherhood doesn't mean I've completely hung up my paddle,"* it read. *"It's just a minor affliction, like a tweaked shoulder, that should only set me back a couple of months. Besides, as luck would have it, it's a poor water year in Colorado, meaning it's a good year to have a kid. And rest assured that my new Family Man role won't mean gear reviews on 10 Top Pacifiers and skills on riverside diaper-changing techniques. Sleep deprivation might cause more typos, but content will remain status quo. Proof lies in this issue's Gear department, which includes a review of sit-on-tops (for paddling, not potty-training) and portage packs (for canoes, not kids). So even though fatherhood is a big commitment for a dyed-in-the-polypro paddler, we'll still get your paddling juices flowing as freely as my baby's spittle. And I've already realized a hidden benefit of bringing another being to life. Three weeks after she was born, I put Brooke's name on the list for a Grand Canyon permit. According to the National Park Service, her turn will come in the year 2014."*

After a few weeks of turning down calls, I got up the gumption to ask my spouse if I could rally out for something a little longer than a half-hour jog. I'd bring the issue up, combining a well-practiced sales pitch from the publishing industry with the look of the saddest of lower-lip-drooping puppies. "Puhleeeease?" I'd whine to an ensuing glare that told me not to press matters.

So while friends embarked on road trips, I remained Local Boy, pedaling between Pampers and running when not dealing with runny noses. Instead of biking until sunset, I'd return home at a reasonable, Ward Cleaver hour.

And here's the thing: I didn't mind missing out on the fun the childless were having at all, or that my skills and fitness deteriorated along with my free time. Fatherhood, I learned, is a much better barometer of life's success than how quickly I can mountain bike up Emerald Mountain. But there's also a happy medium. For sanity and health's sake, everyone — husbands and wives alike — needs some time to get their pulse rates up like those of a kid throwing a tantrum. Like climbing or riding a bike, the trick is finding the right balance.

FREEDOM POINTS

For my wife and me, our recreation life has boiled down to two words: freedom points, and the accumulation and appropriation thereof. These two small words virtually control our recreational existence. We've come to worship them as much as anything, except what we're using them for to escape: our children.

Though you won't find them in Webster, Wikipedia or parenting books, freedom points are an unofficial record of who spends more time with the kids when. And this, of course, leads to the more important converse of who gets to recreate when.

It's a simple barometer, or tally sheet, between you and your spouse. If you've squeezed in three runs during the week while your spouse is home raising Arizona, it's probably her turn to get off the couch. No one that I know of really keeps track of them with ledgers and spreadsheets and things, or even a list taped to the fridge, but

that doesn't mean they don't exist. And it doesn't mean that deep down, both parents aren't keeping score.

The math is simple: you earn them by staying home with the kids and you spend them by recreating. Unless your better half is working, shopping (for the good of the team, not just for fun) or otherwise contributing to the family, they accumulate any time you're stuck watching the kids solo. Watch the kids for two hours while your spouse is joy-riding, and you've earned the unofficial right to do the same.

You can also earn them while both you and your spouse are watching the children together, but it has to go above and beyond the normal call of duty. Spend the weekend playing Dora games and you have a good case for sneaking out during the week. Any judge would grant you that, especially one with kids. You can also accrue them for other family-friendly duties like visiting the in-laws, mowing your sister-in-law's lawn, or doing a special favor for your wife, like helping pick out drapes and matching sheets for the guest bed—especially if you're doing so with kids in tow. "Come on," you can plead to the highest of courts. "I went with you to Bed, Bath and Beyond. Can't I go for a quick ride?"

Just don't expect an in-kind trade. You don't get equal rec time for every hour spent caring for your brood. Most of that caring is expected. Redemption ratios vary with personalities, relationships and even past recreation infractions. And every family has different exchange rates. It's like exchanging currency when you have a weaker dollar. You never get quite what you put in.

Points earned, their redemption follows an unspoken law of supply and demand. If they're there, it's your right to use them. If the supply's run dry, then so have your chances of recreating, at least until the stockpile has been replenished.

This brings up their expiration. Unfortunately, they have a finite redemption period, much like exercising a stock option. This usually lasts no more than a week or two. Don't fall prey to expiration loophole. You can't come back a few months after a particular child-sitting stint and say, "Remember when I watched Brooke that afternoon? Well, I want to climb Denali." Use it or lose it applies as much to freedom points as it does to other things in a relationship.

Like stocks, you also don't realize a profit from accrued points until you redeem them. You have to cash them in, and realize the full cost basis of when you acquired them.

They're like sick days at work. If you don't use them, they don't carry over. They simply disappear. And they certainly don't grow interest. Try that argument and watch out for the rolling pin.

When it comes time to spend them, maximize their value. It's not like playing the slots in Vegas, mindlessly seeing your stockpile shrink. There's a knack to it. The key lies in efficient spending. You earned them fair and square, so don't squander them. Don't burn them waiting to pick up a friend who's operating on a more lackadaisical, kidless time schedule. Your meter's running. Don't let them dissipate while waiting for someone else's misplaced car key.

You'll find yourself a better team player because of it. You'll ask at the bike trailhead if someone has a pump. You'll unload boats off someone's car—and make sure they have the shuttle key—to expedite getting to the river. You'll retrieve a friend's lost ski on the slopes because your time is ticking. You'll learn to match every tick of the clock with a stroke of the paddle, pedal of the crank, or stride of the foot.

Another trick: don't dilute your investment doing something you could just as easily do with kids in tow. If you're exercising a coveted hall pass, don't hike the same trail you normally stroll with your child, or bike the same path you routinely ride with your burley. Go someplace different, try something new.

Also, don't waste points on something you could've done anyway without spending them. If your wife normally lets you jog a few times each week, don't take the same jog when you have points to spend. That's like spending birthday money on your mortgage. It's going to get done anyway. Use them on something you otherwise wouldn't have time for. Don't burn them biking to work.

An example: After visiting my South Dakota in-laws twice within six weeks, my wife gave me the go-ahead for a four-day mountain biking trip. I didn't spend these hard-earned points biking local. I used them for a road trip with friends.

If your spouse is ever away with the kids, you can even score the coveted freedom point freebie. But only if you take advantage of it. You can't bank these free points for later. The lesson can be learned from mice. When the cat is away, get out and play. If your family is gone, don't fix the gutter unless you absolutely have to. Do that on a weekend when everyone's home (best yet, double down by fixing it while watching the kids, knocking off a chore and earning points).

You can also fit in rec time without redeeming points, like jogging during lunch or biking to work. Your defense: you're away from family at work anyway, so why should it count against you? Another option: attend a conference coincidentally held at a ski area or golf resort.

You can also get creative, earning points while you recreate. Once, when it was my turn to watch Brooke, I pawned her off on a babysitter and went for a bike ride. I was technically watching her, thus gaining points for later, while squeezing in a ride at the same time. It cost money, sure, but technically gave me a twofer (though it was a tough sell to the jury back home).

Tactic #26: encourage your spouse to take your child along during his or her outing, freeing you up for a non-kid activity of your own. "Oh, you're going jogging?" you innocently ask. "Why don't you take Sweet Pea in the jogger for some fresh air?" Then you high-tail it out of there for a win-win recreational window. Of course, then your spouse is recreating while watching the kid, scoring a twofer of her own, perpetuating the vicious cycle.

While these tricks work with one child, the game changes when Kid #2 enters the picture. For us, that transpired when Casey was born. We were now on man-on-man coverage instead of zone D—a complete overnight change in our defensive scheme. Points became even more precious and we kept better track of them than ever. While one of us was working out, the other was getting worked over. Every spare second counted. We timed our bike rides so we got to day care at exactly 5:29 p.m., with only a minute to spare until tardy fines began. Add more kids to the mix and free time evaporates exponentially.

The point-counting gets trickier, also. Watch an only child and you technically earn points for it. Have a second kid and just watch one of them and now you're only breaking even. You have to watch both kids to put free time in the bank.

This is when you start micro-analyzing things, like when the actual point-earning and/or point-spending time starts. Once, while on a ski trip to Canada, my wife docked me the full eight days, while I felt it only constituted six (the day there and back were only partials). Plus, I only skied on five. She won, of course, but it was worth the contention.

Another time, we went on a family vacation to an all-exclusive retreat in Puerto Vallarta that my wife won in some sales contest. She said it would be the most sedentary vacation I'd ever taken (if you call drinking umbrella drinks sedentary). We were just an hour away from great surfing, but I buttoned my lip and stayed happily at the beach and buffet. Besides, by being Family Man so diligently, I figured I was earning points at the same time, just like shopping for drapes, and I counted how I would spend them while building sand castles on the beach.

Bottom line: it's an uphill battle for the person recreating, one that can get as complicated as you let it. Does the meter start running at the trailhead, or the moment you leave home? The sooner you can resolve these issues, the sooner you can each be on the road to recreation.

ARTISTRY AT WORK

If there's anything this chapter shows, it's that just as recreating with kids is an art form, so, too, is recreating without them, and the best artists go to creative extremes with their canvas to achieve the desired results.

In truth, there's really only one way to ensure both spouses are taking full advantage of their rightful recreational windows. And that's if each of you receives the evil eye from the other whenever you take off on your respective outings. If both spouses glare whenever the other is loading his or her bike on the car, you're each likely getting out as much as—or more than—you should.

Marking a far cry from our pre-kid days when we used to tell each other what we did each day, oftentimes I don't even tell my wife what I do anymore, sneaking in my fix as clandestinely as I can. I slip my ski gear into the car when she's not looking, and head to the office in unsuspecting civilian clothes only to change into my requisite recreation gear later—free from prying, parenting eyes.

And even careful planning doesn't eliminate curve balls. That flat tire mountain biking has added ramifications once kids enter the picture. Once just an inconvenience to you, now these delays are also an inconvenience to the spouse at home with the kids. Keep a backup plan handy for when these delays surface. Call your spouse to let him know you're running late, or enlist a friend or other family member to pick up young Paula from her piano lesson.

Before we wrap up this self-serving chapter on satisfying your own carnal desires, realize that there is strength in numbers. Pair up with other like-minded families to tag-team kid duty and plan your respective escapes. Whether it's at a condo, cabin, camping or the comfort of your own home, the guys can stand guard while the wives head out, and vice versa once their activity's complete. And the kids have the benefit of playmates the whole time. Then everyone can get together for well-earned beers and bratwurst afterward.

Also, don't overlook the power of babysitters. While there's a cost involved, it's better than the opportunity cost of not doing something. Besides, it lets you and your spouse—gasp!—actually get outside and do something together, a concept hitherto impossible without such a third party.

While many reserve such a luxury for dinner, drinks or a movie, bringing Mary Poppins into the picture can do wonders for your recreation and relationship. Use the time to go hiking, biking, skiing or whatever, and then top it off with a more conventional pastime afterward. The fee is a small price to pay for shooing the cobwebs off your gear.

Okay, so this whole chapter might sound a trite egocentric. "My God," you're thinking. "Doesn't this guy cherish time with his family?"

I certainly do. And that's the whole purpose of this book. I love my kids and wife more than anything, seconded only by doing things with them. But if you live right and take home anything from the following pages, you'll be doing plenty with your kids your whole life. So get out by yourself or with your spouse before kids enter the picture, and continue to do so after they come into this world. Throughout your child-rearing years, toilets and noses are likely to be running far more than you are. So don't feel guilty about taking a little Me Time while practicing whatever else this book preaches.

Chapter 2

BICYCLING WITH KIDS

"Nothing compares to the simple pleasure of a bike ride."
—John F. Kennedy

I SEE HIM EVERY WINTER MORNING while driving to work—a man on a bike, pulling a Little Troopers burley behind him. The burley, a chariot that attaches behind a grown-up's bike, is two-toned and obviously well-used. It has a blue bottom topped by a faded yellow canopy.

The man, wearing a brown wool hat, gloves, and a ski jacket with patches from different resorts, always has two kids with him. He stuffs them side-by-side in the burley for the ride to Soda Creek elementary school, drops the older one off and then returns home with the youngest happily tagging along for the round-trip ride. Sometimes the younger rider is standing up and holding on (we won't tell social services), and other times he's bundled up warm and cozy inside.

It doesn't matter if it's zero degrees outside and the rest of us commuters are peering through tiny slots etched out by our defrosters. He sticks to the ritual like ice to a mud flap, and it's instilling the principle of pedaling at an early age.

Even if you don't take it to these extremes, biking with your kids is one of the most natural outdoor pursuits you can do. It's an inevitable part of parenting—as much as wiping drool, changing diapers and picking up dropped forks from under the table.

At some point, however, you'll have to abandon the burley technique of Mr. Winter Wheels and teach your kids how.

When that magic time comes, don't approach it with tre-pedal-dation. It's a bike, not the birds and the bees. Yet it does represent a coming of age, for both you as a parent and your kid as a boundaries-be-gone explorer. Just realize that there's a progression to follow before your kids will be dropping the peloton. This development follows the same, well, cycle, for everyone, from tricycles, Big Wheels and burleys to training wheels and finally the Real McCoy—an honest-to-goodness bike, representing that giant leap forward for kid-kind everywhere.

GETTING THEM STARTED

Unlike many other activities, getting your kid interested in biking is a no-brainer. What kid doesn't want to learn how to extend his leash to escape mom and dad? But every kid's, shall we say, learning curb is different. Some take to it right away, as if gravity has always been a close friend. Others are petrified of all things pedal—especially after they hit said learning curb.

Take my friend Bill's kid, Bennett. Granted, he's a bit of an anomaly, a tiny fireplug whose fear genes disappeared from the DNA strand somewhere along the line. He schussed down Steamboat's toughest ski run, a double black diamond named Chute 1, at age three, and learned to bike without training wheels at age two. Brooke didn't pick it up until age six, and that was with constant bribes of trips to the FuzzyWigs candy shop.

Perhaps it's the gender. Boys, who are made from worms, snails and puppy dog tails, have less fear of the inevitable skinned knees that come with the territory (due, perhaps, to the worm's malleability and familiarity with dirt, and the snail's protective shell). Girls, at least ours, are made of sugar, spice and everything nice. Put spice on a bike abrasion and it hurts. Girls seem to approach it at a snail's pace, one grain of sugar at a time. Which is fine. They hit fewer said learning curbs than boys do.

Whatever your child's gender, treat the process like a grinding gear: if it's not there, don't force it. They'll figure it out in their own sweet time.

Regardless of how quickly your kids learn, you still have to teach them the basics. You can't spin your own wheels about getting your kids to spin theirs. Rare is the Biking Bennett who hops on the first time and John Waynes it into the sunset. Riding a bike is only like riding a bike once you know how. And teaching someone to ride a bike isn't like riding a bike at all. It varies every time.

How do you explain something as esoteric as balance to someone who barely has a vocabulary? How do you describe how to slow down so your pedaling progeny doesn't hit a bush, George of the Jungle it into a tree or Wile E. Coyote off a ledge? None of us really remember how we learned, and now we find ourselves yelling instructions from a grown-up's perspective to that of a child.

"Just balance!" we command.

"I am!" they'll yell back, instigating a round of inevitable bicycle bickering.

But you can't be quiet about it, either. How can you be, when you're running next to your kid and he's teetering above disaster? Of course you're going to yell. You're going to ward off danger and fend off evil, protecting your brood just like countless generations before you have. You're going to yell, "Pedal, pedal, pedal.... balance, balance, balance, brake, brake, BRAKE!" at the top of your lungs while your gene pool wobbles precariously above a cheese grater.

A quick pointer to avoid Jungle George's proverbial tree and other obstacles: Don't start your child atop Doomsday Knoll. No matter what phase you're in—Big Wheel, tricycle, training wheels or two-wheeler—pick a flat area, ideally one that's not bordered by barbed wire, precipices, boulders or those annoying Mack trucks. A good spot: sidewalks with adjacent lawns, which cushion the inevitable bail-outs. Another good spot: flat sections on the local bike path, which often meander through parks. The best spot: a parking lot of an outdoor mattress sale.

STARTIN' 'EM YOUNG

You're never too young to start riding, even if you're stuck inside. That's the premise behind Fisher-Price's new Smart Cycle, which is giving the fitness industry a helping hand by teaching exercise habits early to kids. Designed for three- to six-year-olds, the Smart Cycle is described as a "Physical Learning Arcade System" — a stationary bike, learning center and arcade game system all rolled into one, for just $100 retail.

The Smart Cycle (www.fisher-price. com) plugs into your TV, ready to take kids on what the company calls "learning adventures" while they pedal at the same time. As they pedal, characters guide them through learning discoveries, games and races, with multiple levels of play for different ages and stages. Kids can pedal, steer and learn at their own pace, visiting stops like Math Mountain, Shape Lake, Number Fields, and Letter Creek. They can also race with cars on-screen, against the clock or with another player. When they want to stop and rest, a joystick on the console lets them pursue other activities. It's not the same as being outside, but the Smart Cycle is certainly a smart start.

A SHORT HISTORY

You're not alone in teaching your kid how to ride a bike. Parents have been suffering through the plight almost as long as wheels have been going around. In the early days, even adults had problems adjusting to this new method of locomotion.

Not that you should launch into a historical diatribe when teaching — though it might impart a sense of expertise — but the first "steerable" bicycle of record was invented in 1817 by Germany's Baron von Drais. Accordingly, it was called the *Draisienne*. The key word, of course, is steerable. You'll quickly learn the importance of this trait when teaching your own kids how to ride. Balancing is fine, but doing so into a thorn bush will deflate tires and pride.

The *Draisienne* was made of wood, which is what your kids' heads will seem to be made of when you try to teach them. In what could be an advantage for teaching kids, it also didn't have any pedals. Riders propelled it by simply pushing their feet against the ground, kind of like those walkers toddlers use. In fact, the straddle-and-walk tactic it requires is still used by most kids learning today. The *Draisienne* was upgraded in 1842 to include "real rubber tires," but by then, just like the shelf life of a Transformer, it was already eclipsed by another model.

Designed by Scottish blacksmith Kirkpatrick MacMillan in 1839, the MacMillan velocipede was the first bicycle ridden with legs off the ground—an invention that would become the bane of children throughout the world. While the velocipede mauled its early riders like *Jurassic Park* velociraptors, it ushered in the two-wheeled world we know today.

The world's first mass-produced bicycle came into being in 1860. A harbinger of the sport's eventual allure to kids, it was designed by France's Pierre Michaux, an inventor who also built baby carriages and tricycles. Michaux was also one of the first documented parents to struggle with teaching his child how to ride a bike. When a customer brought a *Draisienne* in for repairs, his son climbed on board and tried to ride it, but couldn't. So Michaux made it easier by connecting the crank arms and pedals to the front wheel and the Bayliss-Thomas bicycle was born. It came complete with hollow tubing, axle bearings, radial spokes and rubber pedals—everything, it seems, except the Barbie bells and handle doilies kids use today.

Learning to ride the Bayliss-Thomas was as hard as getting kids to eat cauliflower. These are the bikes you sometimes still see in the circus, the front wheel markedly bigger than the rear, meaning a topple from the Eiffel Tower should you fall. Thankfully, the giant pedaling perch changed forever in 1879 when England's Harry Lawson invented the first bicycle driven by a chain connected to the rear wheel, with the pedals positioned in the middle. The design was perfected in 1884, including the equal-sized wheels still in use today. A later design by John Kemp Starley called the Rover improved upon this design with better saddle and handlebar placement, and adults and kids have been riding happily ever since.

Now you can lecture on the history of the bicycle during living room chalk talks. But words can only get you so far. Eventually, you'll have to pony up and get out in the teetering trenches. And that's when you'll wish your kids were practicing on a well-balanced pony instead.

BIG WHEELS, TRIKES AND TYKES

Your child's first foray into the world of human-powered, wheeled locomotion will likely be from a stroller. Though your child relies on you for movement and can sit there like a blob without having to balance, don't underestimate the stroller's value in the greater bi-circle of life. Like a toy truck on Christmas, it introduces them to the wonderful world of wheels and movement, and the fact that curbs and stairs are to be avoided like the plague.

When it comes time to pedal on their own, it will likely come in an age-old apparatus that loses a wheel up front, keeps two in the rear, and turns every kid who tries it into Easy Rider. It's...Big Wheel time!

There's a reason this simple hunk of plastic hasn't changed one iota over the past thirty years and is the same brakeless, out-of-control ticket to the emergency room it's always been. It works. Like a tricycle and the Bayliss-Thomas, its crank is attached to the front wheel for primitive-but-effective locomotion. Most importantly, the Big Wheel represents the first big step forward toward a lifetime of happy bicycling. No longer at the mercy of mom's whims in a stroller or grocery cart, your kid's eyes will open Big Wheel wide to the wonders of self-propelled wheeled transport. Now they're the ones calling the shots, free to roam the world and its staircases at will. It's also the time they'll get better acquainted with that demon known as gravity.

Still, out of all pedaling apparatus, Big Wheels are the most harmless for the sole reason that their diminutive riders are closer to the ground. There's less distance to fall. But they're still subject to Newton's laws and can easily careen out of control down a driveway.

The main drawback is that there aren't any brakes on the thing (details, details). Once the rigs careen out of control, kids' feet fly off the pedals as the front wheel spins faster than a roulette wheel. And the odds are better than they are in Vegas that your kid will crash before processing all this information and adjusting his spread-eagled ways.

Consider my daughter Casey's first experience on one. She borrowed a friend's and promptly took it to the top of our neighborhood version of the Hannenkahm before I could stop her. There she sat down and almost careened into the police blotter with no regard for the ninety-degree turn she'd have to negotiate at the bottom, or any clue that we had just changed her health insurance's co-pay program. Fortunately, just after her pedals started spinning with enough energy to power New York, but before she bought a one-way ticket into the ditch, I caught her and impending doom was narrowly averted.

Another downside to not having brakes involves your kids' shoes. Your footwear budget will rocket Imelda Marcos high as your kids burn through their soles by dragging their feet to slow down. This is especially true when they're wearing their why-didn't-I-think-of-those Crocs. While the sandals' soft plastic might make for cozy footwear, they're a complete crock when it comes to doubling as brake pads.

Regardless, Big Wheels are an invaluable stepping stone, so don't shun the gift of one at Christmastime or a birthday. While they offer the stability of three wheels, and hence little in the way of balance practice, that's still one less support than a stroller or even crawling. And as your child gets bigger, he can move the seat back, providing more reach to the tiny pedals before it's time to take the next big jump in revolution evolution: the tricycle.

The main difference between Big Wheels and tricycles is that tricycles put your kid higher off the ground, meaning that, like riding the Bayliss-Thomas, the rider has a greater, Himalayan-like distance to fall. While balance isn't an issue yet, except on tight-radius turns, toppling off certainly is. But it's bicycling Darwinism at work. Biff once and that memory will be called upon later, come two-wheel time.

Tricycles are a crucial component toward getting your kid on the path to pedaling. Like Big Wheels, braking can be a problem, solved by the same thrust-your-feet-aside-and-watch-the-wheel-spin trick. Shoes still become brake pads and the lawn a cushioning friend. And gravity lessons apply going uphill as well as down. With such a small-diameter wheel up front, pedaling makes a mountain out of every molehill.

A bonus over Big Wheels is that tricycles have a convenient step-up platform on back, which your kids can use to climb aboard. Eventually, they'll learn that they can just stand on the back platform rather than using the seat, and careen out of control just as easily as riding it conventionally. Not that you should encourage this, but this does offer the option of bailing out before they hit a curb—much like the Road Runner stepping out of a house before it plummets into the ground. Beep! Beep!

TRAINING WHEELS

Tricycle mastered, it's time for the next big step: training wheels.

Unless they're born with personal outriggers or an impeccable sense of balance, not too many kids skip the ever-important training wheel phase. Doing so would be like bypassing T-ball and going straight to the Minors. The beauty of training wheels is that they can be used on a real bike and then discarded like a worn-out Barney doll (or better yet, a new one) once the magical balancing milestone is reached.

But that won't be overnight. Your child, like ours, will probably use this rolling outrigger for a year or two. It allows them to experiment with brakes, balance and biking in one relatively safe-from-abrasions package. This is also the phase where they'll need to start wearing a helmet.

Sure, your kids will still come precariously close to tipping, the inside wheel lifting as they lean the wrong way, to the outside, during a turn. You'll cringe. You'll grimace. You'll brace yourself for the impending impact. But you just have to suck it up that they're going to biff a time or two. Though they have farther to fall than from a tricycle, it's all part of the natural progression. Spokes evoke scrapes. Say it loud and say it proud. But your kids will learn from every skinned knee. Perhaps next time they'll lean into the turn like they're supposed to.

Unfortunately, training wheels also offer a false sense of security, a pedaling version of a pacifier. They're a crutch. Much as I hate to admit it, at times Casey would even ride her training wheels while sucking on her pacifier, creating a double crutch crutch.

Training wheels aren't foolproof, either. Your kid hasn't mastered the basics of balancing or braking, yet is being turned loose on an apparatus that, even on the slightest hill, could well maim her. Worse, she'll be placing all of her leaning-the-wrong-way weight on a skinny little plastic wheel that wouldn't even work on a wagon. While it helps kids get the hang of riding, it's almost worse. It's like a canoe outrigger that you rely on too much, only instead of refreshing water below it's knee-scraping pavement.

Fortunately, you can make adjustments to hone the art of balancing. The key is turning the training wheels into a placebo. When your child is comfortable with them on the lowest setting, raise them a hair, which raises the ante for balancing. Now the training wheels don't kick into gear until the rider leans the wrong way a bit more. They can't just rely on them indiscriminately, even if they knew what that word was.

During this process you'll also discover the training wheel treadmill, which occurs if the training wheels are set too low and your child hits a pothole or other depression with her rear wheel. Suspended by the training wheels, the rear wheel will spin in the air no matter how hard your child is pedaling. Casey's gotten stuck this way at the bottom of our driveway time and time again, yelling for help while literally on the road to nowhere.

The best attribute of training wheels is that they come on your kid's first real bike, a milestone in itself. Not a tricycle, not a Big Wheel, but a real bike that they can still use upon graduation. Your kids will treat it like a favorite toy, turning the handlebars into a customized dashboard complete with multi-colored doilies, turtle-shaped squeeze horns and princess bells.

Training wheels offer a couple of less obvious benefits as well. When your kids leave their bike in the driveway like a pair of discarded pants, they enable it to stand up by itself, meaning no stooping over when it comes time to wheel it inside. Kids can also use the training wheels like a stirrup, stepping on them to climb onto the seat. They also represent yet another a pedal crank forward to another cog in the cycling chain: the trail-a-bike.

MAKING STRIDES

Leave it to technology, in this case a small company in Rapid City, South Dakota, to do away with something as venerable as training wheels. That's what purchasers of the new Strider have found about a new contraption that takes pedaling, and the accompanying height-off-the-ground it requires, out of the learning curve picture forever.

Billed as a "running bike," the Strider teaches kids age 1-5 years old how to safely balance and steer a two-wheeler, building up their confidence for the real wheeled McCoy. It eliminates the dreaded "trike tip-overs" and "training-wheel wobbles" that create fear and scars for life, and gets kids started younger than they ever would atop an Empire State Building with training wheels. The baby bike's inventor, Ryan McFarland, has tested it out thoroughly on his own two sons, Bode and Jesse, and maintains that it's so revolutionary that kids will never need a tricycle or training wheels again. "It makes training wheels obsolete," gushes parent and Strider aficionado Corey Crowder.

The key lies in its design. First off comes its weight. At less than 7 pounds (about a third of the weight of a typical 12-inch pedal bike with training wheels), kids can pick it up and propel it with ease. The propelling owes itself to a unique design that puts the seat just 11 inches off the ground, allowing even the most pint-sized user to straddle it easily. While they might look like penguins waddling it uphill, your kids will look like hawks on the descent, thanks to the ability to rest legs behind them on footrests integrated into the frame (they can also use these for bunnyhopping and other tricks).

The Strider comes with 3 inches of handlebar height and 5 inches of seat height adjustment to fit for several years before being hand-me-downed to the next sibling in line, an optional foot brake for advanced riders, and parent-friendly (read "airless") EVA polymer tires. Available in six colors (red, blue, yellow, green, orange and pink), its only constraint is a rider weight limit of 50 pounds. Info: www.stridersports.com, $98 MSRP.

TODDLERS AND TRAIL-A-BIKES

The trail-a-bike is a simple, one-wheeled contraption that attaches to the seat post of a grown-up bike and allows your child to pedal, or at least ride, happily behind you. Unattached, it resembles a bent unicycle with an uncomfortable-looking metal pole for a seat. Attach the clasp behind a bike, however, and suddenly, miracle of miracles, you can actually go somewhere with your child in tow.

While training wheels open your kid's eyes to a bike's possibilities, trail-a-bikes open their doors as to where bikes can take you. Suddenly, your kids realize they've taken a huge step toward becoming a grown-up, going where you go to Buzz Lightyear's infinity and beyond.

Best of all, they let you both leave home on a bike without having to load the car. And you can actually make miles, unlike chaperoning a toddler on training wheels. You won't be able to see your kid behind you, but rest assured she's back there, smiling in her helmet while taking part in this important step of cycledom.

I never had the luxury of riding a trail-a-bike as a kid. They likely weren't invented yet, and even if they had been, parenting was different back then. Juggling six of us, I don't think my parents had the time or desire to single one of us out for a ride. But that doesn't mean I'm not a late-blooming convert.

The whole concept, of course, relies on the fact that the child in back is actually helping you pedal and isn't just dead weight along for the ride. You'll notice this at your first hill. About the only way to tell if your rider is pedaling is to glance to the side in hopes of catching the crank of a pedal in a shadow. I do this with Casey whenever we're chugging up Pitkin Street on our way home. Sometimes she's pedaling; more often, not. And she has the uncanny ability to look like she's pedaling whenever I muster a glance. When my eyes turn forward again, it's back to coasting without a care.

Occasionally, I'll ask her if she's pedaling, invariably evoking a positive response. Other times I'll have Brooke, riding alongside us, spy on her for me. Only then is Casey likely to kick into gear. Passersby are also a big help in such clandestine surveillance, offering information with little prodding. "She's not being much help back there," most elderly couples offer, going to bat for grown-ups everywhere.

When she is pedaling, I can usually feel it. When you're carrying an extra thirty pounds (aren't we all these days?), every bit of locomotion helps. Her chain ring is smaller, so it's all relative, but every tooth of the cog she engages keeps me from gritting my own teeth when heading uphill.

If your child is pulling her own weight, you're almost out of the woods in getting her to learn on her own. Even if she's only helping you on the flats, it's the thought that counts. And it gets the point across that pedaling is integral to moving, moving is integral to balancing, and balancing is integral to riding. It's also what it takes to actually get somewhere like the ice cream store.

Like a joey riding in a kangaroo pouch, trail-a-bikes also provide an introduction into reading terrain. Your child can see where you take short cuts, how you bypass curbs, how you slow down and signal to turn, how you pass joggers, and how you lean.

She's likely to also point out every short-cut and trail in the neighborhood. Casey

points out a "secret" grass-lined trail every time we ride from our house to the bike path. If I forget to take it, I'm in for a scolding, oftentimes having to circle back.

The trail-a-bike also educates her in the world of off-road exploration. She's able to discern the difference between pavement and trail, and likes the latter more. Sometimes the "trails" she points out are just patches of dirt that lead nowhere, but I get admonished just the same if I don't take them.

She especially likes new trails and has a photographic memory for them. She could hardly contain her excitement on one new path we found, cooing and making other excited girl sounds from her perch in the rear. She yelled "Wahoo," giggled about the tall grass tickling her legs and grasshoppers jumping about, and belted out "I'm a mountain bike girl!" to no tune in particular. Thank god we were on a trail where no one could hear us.

We have a ritual before every trail-a-bike ride we take. Without a rearview mirror, I have to wait for her to signal me that she's on board and ready to go. The sign: she rings her bell and then squeezes her green turtle until it squeaks. Ring, squeak. Ring, squeak. Time to go. It's almost Pavlovian. As soon as she climbs on, she reaches left and then right, ring and squeak, never the other way around. I have to hear both signals before I can leave. If not, I'm in for another scolding.

Though I can't see her behind me, I know she's learning the basics of biking, from leaning to drafting Dad. She also learns when to lift her butt off the seat to avoid bumps.

"Ow!" she exclaims when we hit the slightest bump and she forgets to raise her rear. "That hurt."

But you do have to be careful. When riding with his daughter over pipe drains on trails near his home in Evergreen, Colorado, a friend once launched his daughter into orbit over such a bump. On one trail Casey demanded we take, I heard her yelp behind me after going over such a bump. I figured we had hit it a little too hard, her butt taking the brunt of the blow, but then realized it was just her little stuffed puppy with the blue canvas hat that had fallen out of my pack. A quick stop, bell ring and turtle squeak, and we were off on our way.

Godsend of godsends, trail-a-bikes also let you (brace yourself) actually accomplish things. I'll trail-a-bike Casey to the store and even day care or school. If she knows about the day care commute beforehand, she gets up, gets dressed, makes her bed and brushes her hair in record time. And you can see the smug look of importance on her face whenever we arrive.

To my chagrin, on one of these rides she figured out that she could take her hands off the handlebars and clap while we rode through tunnels. I couldn't see her, but I could hear the clapping, knowing it could only be one thing. Then it was my turn to admonish her. Call me a fuddy-duddy, but trail-a-bikes aren't designed for teaching kids how to ride without their hands.

As well as her little ritual of clapping through tunnels, she also had one of making me not pedal whenever we rode over bridges on the bike path. We'd build up our speed (the only time I really knew she was pedaling) until our front tire hit the wood, and then we'd sail up and over, barely making it to the other side.

Not that you'd get them for the bridge-cross-without-pedaling trick, but expect comments from passersby whenever you're trail-a-biking—whether your kid is on it with you or not. If you're riding solo, en route to pick your child up somewhere, you'll invariably hear, "Hey, it looks like you lost someone" as if the bystander was the first person to ever think of it. When that happens, I'll feign surprise, look back, and utter something like, "Hmmm...she was there when we set off. Guess I hit that bump too hard."

Which, of course, brings up the only real thing that can go wrong with a trail-a-bike: if it becomes unattached for some reason, it will send your kid off on her own rollercoaster ride. Actually, the good news is that since trail-a-bikes only have one wheel, that won't happen. If it detaches, it would just piton into the ground in a huge crash, sending your kid pitch-poling head over heels. But in all my years of trail-a-biking, I've never seen it happen. If it's fastened securely, it's not going anywhere.

Still, this fear arose when I was watching David Letterman and guest *Get Smart* actor Steve Carrell who went off on a diatribe about riding a trail-a-bike with his kid. He went on and on about having to make sure it was bolted on correctly, and how one time he looked back to see his child wavering back and forth all over the place like one of those Weebles Wobble But They Don't Fall Down. Chaos, in other words, just like he faced in the movie. Apparently, Mr. Smart could get a little smarter himself; he had forgotten to tighten the bolt onto his seat post.

Just like double agents, there are also double trail-a-bikes, which garner even more stares. These push-me-pull-you's feature two sets of seats and pedals behind the gear-grinding grown-up, and, of course, two sets of obligatory doilies, Barbie bells and turtle squeaks on the handlebars. They work pretty much the same, except that like driving a semi, they force you to take wider turns and wear out your brake pads faster. The only drawbacks are car-topping the behemoth, parking it on a bike rack without it extending out into the road, and the occasional cat-fight about who gets to sit where.

Speaking of sitting, there's an alternative to the trail-a-bike as well. Another contraption that lets you carry your kid behind you is the rear seat. This simple invention fastens above the rear wheel by attaching to your seat post and rear axle, letting your child ride in Pharaoh-like comfort behind you. Simply strap your kid inside it, much like you do in a car seat, and pedal away.

Since all they're doing is sitting there, and they're strapped in, you can use it at an earlier age than you can a trail-a-bike, and it lets you haul one of your kids with you wherever you go. There's no extra gear to lug around, you can still cartop your bike easily, and your child can still experience the fun of wind-blown hair and bugs in her teeth. Like the trail-a-bike, it also exposes your child to the wonder of watching countryside roll by, banking into turns and feeling mud splatter off the rear wheel through puddles.

Therein lies their only real drawback. Unless you have a mud flap on your bike, expect your washer and dryer to get as much of a work-out as you do from cleaning the rooster tails up your child's back. On the bright side, now you won't need a mud flap for your own back. Your kid doubles as one quite nicely.

THE PLACES YOU CAN GO

Perhaps it's the crowd I ride with, but living in Steamboat we get exposed to all sorts of zany kid-cycling stories. People bike with their kids everywhere, and not just to the store or to get their hair done.

No matter what cycling phase your kids are at, there are a variety of ways to involve them in biking. Don't feel like you have to wait until they can ride on their own before planning a trip. Whether they're on training wheels, a trail-a-bike, in a burley or riding by themselves, you can take them on everything from day trips to longer, more committing excursions.

That's what my friend Rob did when he came up with the over-zealous idea of taking his seven-year-old daughter on a leg-burning (for him, anyways), hundred-mile, three-day mountain bike trip from Steamboat to Dillon, Colorado. Rather than use a conventional trail-a-bike, he ad-libbed, cutting the aft seat post down from an adult tandem mountain bike so it would fit his daughter. Then he pulled a trailer behind that, laden with camping gear. "The plan, hare-brained as it was, was to go one hundred miles all on dirt between Steamboat and Silverthorne," he admits sheepishly. "But it didn't exactly go as we expected."

He pulled out maps and planned his route over Lynx and Gore passes, through the tiny town of Radium on the Colorado River, and finally via more dirt roads to Silverthorne. Somehow his wife thought it was a good idea and gave her blessing.

Though he could have banged out the route quickly by himself, the reality of riding with his daughter didn't quite match the plan. It took them seven hours just to get to Lynx Pass, with Rob playing Huff the Magic Dragon the whole way. So they camped in the rain and changed their itinerary to only cover half the distance. They rolled into Kremmling the next day, where Rob's wife picked them up at the ice cream store. "The first day took a little longer than I thought," he says. "But it was great—we read *Jonathon Livingstone Seagull* in the tent."

This brings up a cardinal rule of bicycling with kids. As with anything you do with them, change your itinerary if things don't work out as planned. And with kids in tow, they likely won't. You'll stop for bathroom breaks, dandelion-blowing breaks, snacks and more bathroom breaks. You'll fuss with helmets, tires, horns and those little flowery things that fell off your daughter's Croc. Even without such pit stops, you'll still make worse time than scheduled. You'll be either pulling them or pedaling at their pace, both of which will slow you down.

Perhaps no one has carried biking with kids to a higher, more painful level than Joe Kurmaskie, whose book, *Momentum is Your Friend* (www.breakawaybooks.com), details a trans-continental bike trip he took pulling his two sons, Quinn, 7, and Enzo, 5, one on a trail-a-bike and one in a trailer, four thousand miles across the country. The two-month-long trip took him over twelve mountain passes and through seventeen states, from Portland, Oregon, to Washington, D.C. It was so unprecedented that *USA Today* called him, "Mark Twain on Two Wheels."

Granted, Kurmaskie has an affinity for logging miles, one that no doubt has passed on to his kids. He admits he "misspent the better part of my youth on a bicycle, with a career total of 100,000 miles and counting…including six coast-to-coast marathons, a 2,000-mile epic across Australia's Nullarbor Plain, and up-and-down rollers on both of New Zealand's islands. I've chased ice cream trucks around Baja and pedaled a surfboard to the breakwaters of Jaco, Costa Rica. If a 12-step program for addicts of open-road adventure existed, friends would have tackled me to the ground years ago."

As for why he decided to make such a pedaling pilgrimage with his sons, he answers, "Here's the real reason. I've just hit 40, and there's no denying every man's desire to give the middle finger to the approach of midlife."

So he crisscrossed the Continental Divide, befriending everyone from Lynyrd Skynyrd soundmen to truckers and Kansas grasshoppers, all with kids in tow every pedal of the way.

BURLEY BABIES

A burley is a chariot of sorts that attaches to the rear of your bike and lets you tow your kids around while they happily sip sippy cups, eat gummy bears, cuddle with blankets and invariably fall asleep.

Though the word is actually the name of both a company and a product, it has become synonymous for any bike trailer for kids, which is somewhat odd because when you look at its spelling, its real definition is a thin-leaved tobacco from Kentucky.

Use one to pull your kids around, however, and you'll become more like its intended namesake: burly. Discovering that that extra "e" in the name stands for exercise, you'll smoke other riders, not tobacco, whenever you detach it and ride free of its extra weight.

Its name owes itself to a simple misspelling. Thirty years ago, a bicyclist named Alan Scholz started a business called Burley Bike Bags named for his wife "Burly Bev," a strong local bike racer. Alan and Bev sold their bike bags at the Saturday Market in Eugene, Oregon, a thirty-mile bike ride from their home. The first bicycle trailer he designed was made to transport these bags, and was fashioned from old swing-set pieces. He hitched up for a test run, only to see it fall to pieces at the end of the driveway. After revisiting the drawing board, he made a trailer strong enough to transport his daughter and get his bags to market. Soon, people wanted the trailer instead of the bags, and bike shops began carrying the Burley trailers. Ever since, the name "Burley" has become synonymous with "bicycle trailer."

The "burly" name without the "e" fits for a couple of reasons, one of which is that, believe it or not, the word "burly" also refers to a stunt-bike performer who puts a great deal of effort into performing a trick. You'll put a great deal of effort into pulling your kids around with it. And the trick it lets you pull off as a parent is being able to take a bike ride with your kids in tow.

Webster's more common definition of "burly" is "strong and with a broad, sturdy frame," which fits the bike trailer perfectly. No matter who makes them, today's kid trailers are a world apart from the old swing-set version, wide enough to be stable on everything from trails to washboard roads, and sturdy enough to withstand years of abuse.

They come in all shapes and sizes, from tiny, single bubbles that belong on *The Jetsons* to larger two-person models out of *Ben Hur*. Head to a bike path in any recreation-minded town and you'll see parents happily pedaling with these craft zipping around behind them.

Most come with seat belts and chest harnesses so your kids don't flop around like fish whenever you hit a depression, as well as a mesh screen and see-through plastic window that you can unfurl when it's cold or rainy (you'll want the screen to protect your kids from errant pebbles kicked up by your tire). With screens for air flow, plastic sunroofs and even pockets inside to hold drinks, hair bands and fake cell phones, most burleys have more amenities than our Subaru.

Size-wise, they come in one and two-kid versions. The doubles let you carry up to two kids in the main compartment, as well as gear and even small pets in the rear. Load it to the gills and you'll live up to its Burly Bev namesake whenever you encounter a hill.

But that loadability is their best attribute. The burley is a veritable backpack on wheels. As well as hauling kids, you can use it to carry everything from diaper bags and dogs to groceries and goulashes. We even use ours to haul inner tubes down to the river, strapping them like halos on top, even if the riders inside are anything but little angels. They also have side pockets for things like binkies, sippy cups, teddy bears and special blankies. If you're ever searching the house for that favorite stuffed animal—or are missing something important like your wallet, purse or car keys—check the burley. There's a good chance it's still there from the last time.

The single models are more streamlined. The good news is that their smaller size also limits the weight you can carry—a good feature if you live near hills. But it also can't carry the additional items a double can, making it less utilitarian (you'll likely use your burley for gear and groceries as much as for your kids).

Whichever size you choose, it attaches as easily as a diaper. Simply slide it into the appropriate notch on the rear part of a bike frame, twist the knob tight, latch the safety strap (which will keep it from becoming a solo sled in the rare event the system fails) and you're off with your own Chariot of Tire. About the only upkeep it takes is checking the air pressure in the tires, and cleaning it as you would your car. It even keeps your car cleaner by becoming the new catch-all for things like goldfish and gummy bears.

Not to get carried away like your little rider inside, but you can also attach a burley behind a trail-a-bike to create a giant, triple-rigged Dr. Seuss-mobile that terrorizes the bike path. Odd and cumbersome as it looks, this snake-like contraption lets you pull your eldest behind you on the trail-a-bike, with the youngest riding behind that in the burley. You'll get some strange looks, and possibly hernias when heading up hills, but it's an efficient system for when one kid wants to pedal and the other wants to be a passenger.

I did this quite often with my two daughters, snaking our way along streets, sidewalks and bike paths to go fishing, play at the park or swim at the river. Once I even stuffed the whole contraption to the hilt, with Brooke behind me, Casey behind her in the burley, our dog Bailey, towels, diaper bags, snacks and a pack-n'-play crib squished into the back, and an inner-tube lashed to the top. When I got to the beach at the river, I set up the pack-n-play crib on shore and plopped Casey safely inside it while Brooke and I swam and tubed.

There are a few things to watch out for when going with this super-sized contraption. One: don't take corners too tight. Do so and you risk a crack-the-whip effect that could send the burley and its passenger sailing. Realize also that you're now driving a

semi. Plan your bike path passes and parking spots accordingly, lest you commandeer the entire sidewalk. Park it in a conventional bike rack and it will stick out so far that the city will have to install detour signs.

Also think about your itinerary. One time I triple-rigged my kids to dinner at a friend's, only to be served Raclette, a fancy and filling French dish laden with meat and cheese. I burped it all the way up the hill home, cursing the triple-rig the entire way.

BIKE TIME

Soon it was time—the inevitable removal of the training wheels. The moment had come for Brooke to take the plunge into becoming a full-fledged pedaler.

It's a big step for a kid, akin to receiving a diploma. But instead of being filed away in a chest somewhere, it's a certificate that can be seen daily, proving to the world that you've come of age and have joined the big kid world of two-wheeled riders.

IMBA'S TAKE A KID MOUNTAIN BIKING DAY

Want a kick in the gear getting your kids started mountain biking? Join in on the International Mountain Biking Association's (IMBA) Take a Kid Mountain Biking Day, which celebrated its fifth anniversary in 2008. The program is designed to help young riders get outdoors on bikes by encouraging groups across the world to register on the IMBA website (www.imba.com) for prizes and to tally their numbers and miles. In a typical year, more than 100 groups register their rides, from across the U.S. and Canada to Japan, Australia and Mexico. Helping matters is longtime IMBA sponsor Schwinn, which donates kids' bikes to clubs and riders every year. "It's a great way for parents to pass along their passion for pedaling to their kids," says IMBA's Mark Eller, adding that close to 1,000 riders took part in its anniversary ride.

The event also benefits from its association with Trips for Kids (www.tripsforkids.org), an organization helping disadvantaged kids discover mountain biking. By organizing group rides and offering Earn-A-Bike programs, the nonprofit provides the materials, support and inspiration that individuals and groups need to help take disadvantaged kids mountain biking. Started in Marin County, California, in 1988 by mountain biker and environmentalist Marilyn Price, the organization has now grown to include more than 60 chapters that combine lessons in personal responsibility, achievement and environmental awareness through biking skills. "Some kids come from the inner city, some live on reservations, and some come from homes where there's just not enough money to buy a bicycle," says Price. "Despite their differences, all the kids have one thing in common – they're kids, and kids love bikes."

Reaching this milestone, however, often feels as distant as a Doctorate, for both parent and teetering toddler.

Finding balance in life is a life-long skill that doesn't come easily. My wife and I are still trying to find it in our own lives and checkbook, juggling kids with our increasingly busy work and recreational lives. Even our meals aren't always balanced, a slam-dunk mix of mac and cheese and mini-carrots. With all these imbalances in our lives, how could I expect Brooke to master the physical act of it?

Luckily, most humans have a genetic predisposition to it. Newborns practice balancing from the moment they're born. They balance on their backs as babies, eventually roll over onto their stomachs, and then graduate to the ever-stable four-wheel-drive crawl. When it comes time to walk, they teeter willingly, hedging their bets with errant grabs onto coffee tables, drapes and chairs. They topple and inevitably tumble down a stairway or two, but they learn from the experience and move on toward a well-balanced life.

Bicycles, however, create a whole new hurdle. While babies have been crawling and toddling since time immemorial, balancing on a bicycle didn't enter the gene pool until Baron von Drais's whack-o invention in 1817. That's less than 200 years of cause and effect abrasions to draw upon.

The art requires a basic understanding of gyroscopes and tops, toys your kids might be playing with at the same age they're learning to ride. Try this experiment off your basement ceiling. Hang a bike wheel from a rope tied to one side of the wheel's axle. It will fall flat. But spin it and it will balance on end, and then move around in a circle. Physics calls this precession, and it's why a bike balances when moving. As Karen Lingel, a staffer for the website Straight Dope, puts it, "Bicycles are equipped with a pair of gyroscopic stabilization devices that require the motion of the bike in order to operate—these devices are known as 'wheels.'"

Here's more on the dissertation. A gyroscope creates angular momentum, whose magnitude depends on everything from the speed of rotation to the object's mass. Not that you'll have any luck explaining any of this to your kids still learning their lefts from their rights, but the Right Hand Rule says that if the fingers of your right hand point in the direction a tire is spinning, your thumb will point the direction of the angular momentum vector, Hector.

In short, if you lean left, you turn left. A wheel's spin turns a tipping-over motion into a turning motion. Other physicists with too much time on their hands (i.e. no kids) point to the fork design as a factor in balance, citing both its bend and the angle it makes with the road. That's why it's nearly impossible to ride a bike with the handlebars turned backwards, and why children's bikes often have a greater bend in the fork so they're easier to keep upright.

Whatever, science nerds. And forgive me if your head is now spinning faster than a bicycle wheel. Physicists can argue precession, angular momentum, fork and head-tube angles, frame trails and contact patch orientations all they want. None of that is going to help your kid balance on a bike. The school of hard knocks will impart the lesson more than any thesis.

Unfortunately for balance-challenged Brooke, she had one more genetic hurdle to overcome: my own sense of balance as a youngster was relatively skewed. Instead of crawling on hands and knees like most kids, I skipped that phase and motored around the house on hands and feet, butt Himalaya high in the air. Baby movies show me with rear end mooning the ceiling and diaper sagging below. My parents thought my bastardized crawl cute, and laughed whenever they rolled out the 8-mm baby films. But it underscored a defective balance gene I passed on to Brooke.

Thankfully, she crawled fine. But it took every trick I could think of to get her biking on her own. I don't want to label her a spaz, because that reflects on me. But she certainly seemed balancing-challenged. I ran behind her on the flat pavement of the cul-de-sac near our house on Manitou Avenue. I brought her up to our yard and had her coast down on the grass, which offered a softer landing. I brought her to the school's soft, spongy running track to lessen the biff's impact. None of it worked.

Taking the training wheels off is as risky a venture as potty training. It's like swapping a diaper for underwear. It's a game of trust, but also Russian Roulette. Make the switch too soon and you'll lose ground rather than gain it, and have to deal with the mess afterwards.

While cheerleading never comes into play with shedding Pampers, it does when teaching your child how to ride a bike. But it's difficult to assess its merit. No matter where I took Brooke—grass, bike path or parking lot—my feeble-minded instructions were always the same. "Pedal, pedal, pedal!" I'd yell in vain. "Just balance!"

The balance rebuke was just plain worthless. I'd yell advice; she'd career out of control and fall. Then I'd repeat the cycle, she'd fall off the cycle, and we'd both end up worn out.

Gravity, I learned, is a stronger teacher than any grey-haired father or professor. And it's guaranteed you'll get more grey hairs yourself during the process. Your child will remember an abrasion far more than an admonishment. Bottom line: expect some bumps and bruises along the way—on both your kid and ego.

If the learning curve was tough on Brooke, it was tough on me as well. There's something just not quite natural about enticing your kid to go hurtling down a hill without balance or brakes, teetering a split second away from falling. It goes against everything Darwin ever touted, and everything you ever thought you knew about parenting.

It would seem that survival of the fittest would favor those who simply stayed put rather than subjecting themselves to the trials of learning to ride a bike. But in the long run, it probably has survival ramifications of its own. Had cavemen been able to bike, they might have better been able to escape erupting volcanos or charging mammoths.

But even they would have had to conquer that thing called balance. Newton's first law of motion states that a body in motion continues to move at a constant speed along a straight line unless acted upon by an unbalanced force. On a bike, that unbalanced force is your wobbly kid. It can also be the curb or ditch at the end of the line.

Keeping Newton's laws closely at hand, I re-doubled my balancing efforts with Brooke.

Everyone has different techniques for teaching kids to ride: the old raise the training wheels so they're off the ground trick; the old run, push and cringe; the old let go while pretending to hold on; the old metal pole rammed behind the seat as a giant lever; and the old let them figure it out for themselves, I'm watching the game.

The trick, I learned, was tricking her.

"Don't let go! Don't let go!" she'd cry every time I jogged behind her, holding the seat.

"I won't, I won't," I'd reply.

But then I'd secretly let go, however briefly, keeping my hand just a brake pad's length away, to see how far she could ride on her own. She wouldn't make it far, and I'd have to re-grab quickly to prevent a topple and loss of trust, but it reaffirmed to me, at least, that the dormant balance gene was perhaps surfacing.

It was like playing poker. She didn't trust me, while I was trying to bluff her. She'd glance back to make sure I wasn't lying about holding on, and sometimes even catch me in the act.

"I've got you, I've got you," I'd lie, further dismantling her trust.

When she did bust me, I lost whatever progress I had made up to that point and had to go back to running and holding, my back paying the stooped-over price.

Balancing just isn't one of those intuitive things you can easily explain. It's easy to teach that fire is hot and ice is cold. Balance is a bit more esoteric.

"Just lean a little more equally on each side," I'd proffer feebly.

Wham! She'd go down.

The only solution was to continue briefly letting go whenever I felt she got going good enough. Sometimes I'd let go and grab a hold again before she knew it, so when she looked back there I'd be, holding on diligently. "Don't let go, don't let go," she'd admonish again. "I won't," I'd lie.

And so it went, day in and day out with no real progression. Perhaps I had a dysfunctional kid, one of those children who would never ride a bike, a fluky youngster missing the balance gene who would go through life as a non-biker, riding through her college bike path with training wheels.

When I explained my plight to my neighbor Rick, he offered his solution: a metal pole that he stuffed behind his daughter's seat, letting him walk alongside. While it didn't help Brooke's balancing act, it did stop me from having to bend over to grab the back of the seat. But while it saved my Advil and chiropractor bill, it did little to solve our problem.

Another friend told me to teach braking before balancing. That way when Brooke got going, the fear of impending doom would be lessened. I tried that, too, with a regression to a training wheel session, but it did little to ease her, or my, anxiety.

Just as we were both exasperated and reaching the end of our respective ropes, we had *The Breakthrough*. It came in two parts. The first followed the real estate slogan: location, location, location. To prevent errant crashes into the ditch and bushes, we went to a flat piece of pavement that was wider than our street down at the Strawberry Park Elementary School. The second ingredient was borrowing a much smaller bike from her four-year-old friend, Bridger.

Two years younger, Bridger had already mastered the balancing maneuver, so the bike had historical good-luck juju on its side. Brooke knew Bridger had balanced on it, so she figured she could, too. Best yet, it put Brooke that much closer to the pavement, lessening the fear factor of a fall. Get unbalanced and she could just put her foot down to right herself. Instead of falling into a perceived precipice, she could now touch her feet to the ground at the first hint of trouble.

It was all we needed to send her on her way to the Tour de France, despite her knee-in-the-belly riding position. Standing behind her as usual, I pushed her off, running alongside with my hand on the seat. Then I let go and...miracle of miracles, she kept going! She was wobbly, but she made it all the way to the fence on the other side, her grin as round as the tire's rim. It's the type of moment in fatherhood that makes you swell with pride. Your progeny, with your genes and prodding, pedaled a bike. I felt like I deserved a medal as much as she did, and it was I who boasted of her accomplishment to others even before she did. By the end of the session, she was starting by herself and turning like a boomerang back to the start, even leaning into turns.

Casey followed a similar curve, using Bridger's same good-luck bike. Whether proof of my pedaling professorship or not, she mastered it more quickly without any biffs at all.

Brooke quickly progressed into a full-bore rider. She got a bike with a front shock at age six, while I didn't get my first one until age thirty-five (and who needs it more, a man at thirty-five or a nimble kid who only needs a distraction to recover from an injury?). A year later I took her and her friend Madeline on their first "real" mountain bike ride, shuttling up Buffalo Pass and riding two thousand vertical feet and seven miles of single track back down into town. While it didn't go so well at the start—if that's what you call a complete breakdown into tears—once we got past the initial loose, gravelly part, she became herself again and had a blast, singing the entire time.

Later, when both Casey and Brooke were riding, we took them camping at the mountain biking Mecca of Moab, Utah, tents pitched just a short ride away from the Slickrock Trail, where a dotted line leads you across miles of baby-bottom-smooth bedrock. They walked when they needed to, rode when they wanted to, and generally loved every coasting, boasting moment of it. I got a few glances from the lycra-clad while pushing Casey's doily-handled Huffy through the desert, but it didn't matter. They had become mountain bikers.

The take-home from all this? Ignore the "You're pushing her too hard" glares from your spouse, don't dive into dissertations on balancing, and keep at it. You'll likely stumble upon your own tricks for getting the job done, and when you do, pass them on to others so they can learn from your mistakes and successes. For us it was simply a bike with good mojo that was sized for Tiny Tim.

PEDALING THE MICKELSON TRAIL

It was Kurmaskie's venture onto the Katy Trail, a rail line converted into a 225-mile crushed-limestone bike path, that we've emulated with our own multi-day family mountain bike rides (albeit ours have been a bit more tame). We've taken our kids on Utah's 100-mile-long White Rim Trail, letting them switch between riding their bikes and riding in the air conditioned comfort of the four-wheel-drive shuttle rigs, and tied another in with a visit to the in-laws.

Somewhere in the Black Hills of South Dakota there's a ride named Mickelson Trail. At my sister-in-law's wedding in Deadwood a few years ago, my friend Ben, with his wife, Lisa, and two sons, Cole, 9, and Max, 6, snuck away after the ceremony, convincing a member of the wedding party to shuttle their car down to Hill City. They then biked the Mickelson Trail, one similar to the Katy Trail tackled by Kurmaskie, along an old railroad grade with little more than a credit card and burley. Granted, Ben was a little more adventurous with his kids than we were. Just a year later, he took them on a multi-day bike tour of Sweden, with Cole riding his own bike and Max piloting a trail-a bike.

While my wife and I don't have quite the gumption, stamina or loose brain cells as Kurmaskie and his cross-country ride, we were jealous of Ben's Black Hills trip. That sounded more our style—a smooth bike trail meandering through the Black Hills, plopping the credit card on the counter for a cold beer and warm bed afterward. The next time we had to visit the in-laws in South Dakota, we vowed to tackle the Mickelson Trail as a family as well.

The opportunity arose a year later when family matters brought us back to Deadwood. This time, we loaded the car with bikes, trail-a-bikes and a burley and we soon found ourselves at the trailhead for our big adventure.

Our trip started in Mystic, South Dakota, an abandoned mining/sawmill town buried between forest-covered ridges in the Black Hills. A sign near the trailhead read: Rockford 4.7 miles, Hill City: 14.6. We were heading to the latter, over-nighting at the Comfort Inn along the trail and then continuing on to Custer.

The beauty of this type of family trip is that, unlike the White Rim, all you need to bring is a credit card—no tent, sleeping bags, stoves or major meals. All we needed was our day gear, clothes to change into at the hotel, and, of course, our means of locomotion.

In the olden days, this locomotion was locomotives. The George S. Mickelson Trail follows the historic Deadwood to Burlington Northern rail line. Originally built in 1868, the line was abandoned in 1983 and converted in 1998 to a 109-mile bike trail from Deadwood to Edgemont. We'd be riding a thirty-mile portion of it, using our legs as our pistons—while hoping our kids didn't become dead weight.

While our credit card would take care of food and lodging, we did have our kids along, meaning our gear list grew accordingly. This included a trail-a-bike for Casey, bike for Brooke, burley for one or both should they get tired, snacks, rain gear and mini-hydration systems. I also had to upgrade our patch kit, and buy spare tires that fit all the oddly shaped wheels.

Matching our assortment of gear at the trailhead was the variety of folks riding by. There were young couples, elderly couples, friends and families, some familiar with biking, some not. One elderly rider wore a t-shirt that read, "I may be old, but at least I don't have to work today." Every one of them turned to look at my centipede-like contraption while passing.

Mistake number one was not realizing that the burley wouldn't fit onto my wife's bike because of her disk brakes. That meant that it had to go on mine, behind the trail-a-bike Casey would be riding, which also only fit on my bike's seat post. While the caterpillar-like contraption wasn't new to us—I'd been pulling the triple-rig on the bike path back home for the past few years—it did look oddly out of place on a multi-day excursion. Without fail, it evoked subliminal comments from pedalersby of "You're not really going to be pulling that on this trail, are you?"

My wife didn't see any of these looks. She was shuttling the car down to our endpoint in Custer while I stayed at the trailhead with the kids. Bike and tow-behinds rigged, and errant comments answered, we swam in a Black Hills brook to beat the heat while we waited. For the kids, that, and subsequent dips, would be more of a highlight of the trip than the actual riding.

Another discouraging sign, aside from the rollercoaster-like rig behind me, was the rollercoaster-like trail ahead of us. Though the trail only reaches a maximum four percent grade thanks to its railroad heritage, every single person coming the opposite way marveled at the long downhill they had just ridden. I tried to distract my kids from hearing the news, but unfortunately that was the direction we were heading—up a four percent grade for the next seven miles to Red Fern. Our not-so-crack-of-dawn start also meant that, after shuttling, we'd be starting at a peak-of-Black-Hills-heat 1:30 p.m. on a searing June 24. I tried to forget the fact that the thermometer the day before crested ninety-four degrees in Deadwood.

A general rule of thumb when pulling a burley or otherwise biking with kids: stick to gradients that match your children's age. Four-percent is not overly grueling, but it is with a burley, trail-a-bike and two kids in tow. The heat got to both Casey and Brooke after the first two miles, and then they both came groveling to the burley behind Casey's trail-a-bike. We stopped, awkwardly tied Brooke's bike to the top with it overhanging like a mushroom cap, and continued along our merry, sweating way.

The problem was threefold. First was the heat. Second was the weight, including Casey, Brooke, Brooke's bike, and the duffels full of day gear. Third was the pulling apparatus. Since all the weight was in the burley at the tail end, the now-weightless trail-a-bike lifted into the air with each pump of the pedal. It wasn't the most efficient towing apparatus. I felt like my own version of the *Little Train Who Could* as I pulled them upward and onward, sweat pouring over my brows with every crank of the shaft.

We found respite from the heat in several old railroad tunnels that had been blasted through the granite. Trapped inside the mountain, the cool air was a welcome break. Brooke, perhaps feeling sorry for me, or tired of dodging the sweat flinging off my brow, kindly offered to pedal her own bike again after about two miles, which put us back on the track to making time. We followed the creek for a ways, and then biked over a series of restored railroad trestles. If they were strong enough for trains, I reasoned, they'd be strong enough for the train of wheels behind me.

The kids did great. The entire trail was composed of chipped limestone, making for a smooth ride for both Casey on the trail-a-bike (she, too, got out of the burley after a while) and Brooke's front-shocked special. We passed a sign for "Wade's Gold Panning" and stopped to give it a go, earning a few speckled flakes of Black Hills gold for the fifty-cent fee, and then continued on our way. At every abandoned cabin we passed, Casey would ask "Who lived there?"

Despite our hot, mid-day start, our timing at day's end couldn't have been better. The trail's last turn took us into Hill City just in time to hear an 1880s steam train sound its whistle and pull up from the town of Keystone. More importantly, we arrived just as poltergeist-type clouds circled ominously overhead, foreshadowing an impending storm. At our family reunion in Deadwood, we learned that my wife's cousins had just lost their barn to a tornado three days earlier. These clouds looked capable of the same fury, creating winds that could spin faster than our wheels. Playing Brave Sir Robin on Bikes, we quickly made tracks to the Comfort Inn.

"It's too bad Dorothy from the *Wizard of Oz* didn't have a hotel to go to," said Brooke as we parked our bikes off the trail in the back and scampered inside.

The hotel is located right on the trail. As I wheeled our steeds inside a storage room in the basement, I saw four other bikes from other trail-riders taking shelter from the storm.

Once checked in, it took the kids a whole seven seconds to find the swimming pool and cannonball in to wash away the day's grime. After that, it was time for buffalo burgers at Buffalo Bob's (not to be confused with his more famous brother, Bill). The kids devoured them, and we topped it off with ice cream before retiring to rest up for the next day. The kids were asleep before their heads hit their pillows.

The night's rainstorm dampened the trail into a tacky texture for the next day's seventeen-mile ride to Custer. But it didn't dampen our spirits.

"It smells good," said Brooke as she helped me wheel the bikes out of the basement under bluebird skies.

Before heading out, we gorged ourselves at the hotel's continental breakfast, and picked up Subway sandwiches next door for the day's lunch. Then we filled our water bottles, threw the duffel back into the burley and prepared for Day Two.

"My butt's sore," whined Casey as she climbed on her trail-a-bike. "The seat's giving me a wedgy."

She learned the wedgy word a few months earlier, about the same time she learned how to cannonball into swimming pools. The only help I could offer her now was to tell her to pull her shorts down and climb aboard.

Next, she scrunched her face up while waiting for her helmet to be snapped. She could do it herself, but it always added fifteen minutes to our departure time. Helmet fastened and wedgy fixed, I waited for the bell to ring and turtle to squeak and then we were off, the steam train whistle blowing as we headed out of town.

We made it a whole half mile before our first swim stop under a bridge in a small creek. A mile later we followed that with belly flops into a beaver pond, and shortly later we explored a creek passing through a culvert near the Rafters Guest Ranch, complete with the deepest swimming hole of the trip. Inside the culvert, someone had used a muddy finger to paint a picture of a hunter and a bison. "I don't think those drawings are from real Indians," said Brooke.

"Why not?" I asked.

"It looks like mud," she replied.

She was right. But though the drawings weren't authentic, they sparked a conversation about Indians and animals that lasted the next few miles.

We rode over several more wooden bridges, prompting Casey and Brooke to yell and sing just so they could hear their vocal chords vibrate on the planks. The planks were likely harvested from row after row of identical-looking ponderosa pines lining each side of the trail.

"They look like dominoes," said Brooke. "I hope they don't tip over."

Six miles later, at Mile 54, we took a Skittles break. In another three miles we crested a pass, marking the end of the uphill. In the distance, the Crazy Horse Memorial sculpture, carved into a giant, granite outcropping, beckoned us forward.

We passed a twosome pedaling recumbent bicycles, a Boy Scout troop from Colorado riding the trail the opposite direction, and several couples. When you're biking with kids as we were, everyone is noticeably friendly, perhaps reflecting back to their own days spent with offspring. A couple on a Harley even waved at us from the road, prompting Casey to give them the thumbs-up sign. At times we actually made it look enjoyable and easy. Thankfully, no one witnessed the tantrums, or the mopped-brow times I had to pull everyone.

The trip also helped Casey and Brooke learn about setting and achieving goals. They'd keep their eyes out for mile markers, and ask how long it took to go between each one. The times varied from six to twenty minutes, depending on how many potty breaks we took and how much uphill there was. Brooke also learned about gears. "What gear are you in?" she'd ask constantly, to make sure she was doing it right.

They'd also play games. "I'm playing a game with pine cones," Brooke once blurted out of the blue, dodging them with her front tire. Casey, meanwhile, rode happily behind me, singing such songs as "The Ants Go Marching One by One, Hurrah, Hurrah," "The Prettiest Girl," and "Miss Mary Mac, Mac, Mac."

We finally cooled off at a water pump at Mile 49, taking turns sticking our heads under the faucet. From there we followed a lodge-pole fence that paralleled the trail through the Black Hills and into Custer. We ended the trip at the Custer Chamber of Commerce, again timing it perfectly. We arrived to a church celebration with free inflatable jumping booths, arts and crafts projects and, most importantly, snow cones. While the kids busied themselves, happy to be off their bikes, and covered their cheeks with sugary, blue goo, we grabbed the car, broke down the burley and trail-a-bike, and began packing. They were out cold before the first stoplight in town.

Chapter 3

SNOWSPORTS WITH KIDS

"Snow and adolescence are the only problems that disappear if you ignore them long enough."
—Earl Wilson

HOUDINI HIMSELF COULDN'T have gotten out of this mess. It happened on Why Not, the most beginner of beginner runs at our hometown resort of Steamboat Springs, when my daughter, Casey, 3, and I passed a man and his son tangled up in a children's ski harness. The webbing leash had mummied itself around his legs, trapping his kid beside him as if they were both rolled up in a carpet. Unless they could get untangled, they'd be forced to ski a three-legged race the rest of the run.

Casey and I passed the man and his pinned-to-his-side progeny and continued on our merry way. I'm sure they both eventually made it down, but not without further extrications from the leash.

I felt for him because I've been there. I'd used a similar harness-and-leash system teaching my daughters to ski. But as we skied by on the catwalk that day, Casey looking for jumps and secret passages and my twenty-seven vertebrae along for the jostling ride, I realized there's a better way. While items like harnesses and handwarmers can certainly help, there's more to teaching your kids to ski than gadgets out of a box.

In a recent story entitled "Schooling Buster" for *Ski* magazine, political satirist P.J. O'Rourke admittedly gave up on teaching his two-year-old, Buster, to ski. And this was after consulting such marquee books on the topic as *The Teaching Guide for Children's Instructors* and *Technical Skills for Alpine Skiing*. To his way of thinking, the main purpose of the ordeal was that strapping on skis would help his progeny meet girls as a strapping young lad. In fact, his story ended while après skiing when a barmaid sized up two-year-old Buster and said, "Oh, you are soooo cute." Hearing the remark, O'Rourke ended his essay thusly, "My job is done."

With apologies to Mr. O'Rourke, there's more to the end result of teaching your kids to ski than meeting members of the opposite sex. Granted, that's important. But skiing with your kids, and being with them every glide of the way as they get better, is one of the best recreational pastimes you can do as a family.

Depending on your age, you might remember the Cheerios TV commercial showing a Ward Cleaver-type family happily skiing down a sunny mountainside. I sure remember it, and ate my fair share of Cheerios as a kid because of it.

Much like Cheerios themselves, there will likely be holes in any ski outing you take with your kids. You'll forget gloves, deal with cold toes and tantrums, retrieve dropped gear, and often throw your arms up in exasperation. But family ski memories are some of the most cherished that you and your kids can have.

Of course, they won't all be perfect. A friend, whose three daughters ski with ours regularly, once told me about her two-year-old daughter, Amelia, who threw a world-class tantrum on her back in the wet, puddly aisle of the shuttle bus after she'd been kept out for "one run too many." While other passengers tried to step over her, the mom turned to anyone within earshot and moaned, "Does anyone know what I can do?"

Well, here's one thing. You can learn from my successes and mistakes (mistake: sunscreen in the eye), and from those of our friends who have been through the plight and emerged at the other end as one of those families who actually has fun on the slopes.

I was lucky. My mom and dad went out of their way to pile all six Buchanan kids into the family station wagon for regular forays to the slopes. Though I don't remember my parents actually teaching me how to ski—they were more the type to stick us in conventional lessons, turn us loose on our own or have the older siblings "watch" us—they saw the lifelong benefits of such strap-them-to-their-skis-and-let-them-go excursions.

I remember the multi-day trips best. We'd pile into the car with the ski rack stuffed for pre-Eisenhower-tunnel road trips up Interstate 70 to Vail and Aspen. Invariably, one of us would throw-up, forcing a quick roadside clean-up. It happened to all of us who squirmed into the rear-facing "Exorcist" seat in the very back. At first it was cool to sit back there, like being in a fort. But the nausea made the novelty wear off as quickly as Mom could scrub the results off the upholstery.

If Cheerios-filled throw-up didn't slow things down, forgotten items did. Depending how far along we were when said item was remembered—be it a parka, ski boots or glove—we either turned around to the glares of Dad or made do without.

A thousand bathroom breaks later we arrived, hopefully, on the right day. Once we accidentally showed up at Aspen's Continental Lodge the night before our reservation. Showing the resourcefulness the head of any skiing family needs, my mom placed us under couches and behind drapes in the hotel lobby until morning. I still remember the look on the janitor's face when he hit me under the couch with his vacuum cleaner during his 5 a.m. cleaning. Built-in wake-up call taken care of, we piled out of our respective hiding bunks, depleted the continental breakfast—which, you guessed it, had little boxes of Cheerios—and hit the slopes, returning later that afternoon to check in properly.

My parents seemed to be in it for the après as much as the actual skiing—especially since social services wasn't yet an issue. I remember one time being left in a bar at Snowmass and some guy asked me how long I'd been skiing. I was six at the time, and proud of my answer. I told him four years (I'm pretty sure that's correct, too). Then he stood up and announced the fact to everyone at the bar, and bought me a Shirley Temple.

Other times, especially at Aspen and Vail, we'd end the day at The Slope, a bar that played nonstop ski movies and served

JUMP INTO SNOWSPORTS IN JANUARY

Wondering when to try your hand (and legs) at skiing with your kids? You might as well start the year off right and take the plunge in January. SnowSports Industries America (SIA), a nonprofit trade association for snow sports suppliers, has officially declared January as "Learn a Snow Sport" Month. As part of the promotion, the association has designated one day during the month as Winter Trails Day (www.wintertrails.org), which offers free learning opportunities for cross country skiing and snowshoeing at more than 100 locations in 24 states (and it's perfect timing for any get-in-shape resolutions you might have: the association cites statistics saying these two sports can burn 45% more calories per hour than walking or running at the same speed). Winter Trails is part of Winter Feels Good (www.winterfeelsgood. com), a national initiative to explain the health and fitness benefits of snow sports, with events at Nordic Centers, alpine resorts, national and state parks and on U.S. Forest Service lands. The consumer-oriented program helps prepare children and adults for a snow sports experience by offering instruction in the basics of alpine skiing, cross country skiing, snowboarding and snowshoeing.

free popcorn, allowing our parents to gravitate toward the back in kid-free comfort while we sat on rug-covered terraces staring at the screen. That's where I saw Ed Lincoln throw his first Lincoln Loop, Wayne Wong and his red bandana gyrating through bumps, and someone nicknamed Squirrel start a freestyle contest on Aspen's Ridge of Bell by jumping out of a tree.

The point is that family ski trips can create memories that last a lifetime. As a parent, you'll forget about the puking and bus-puddle tantrums and remember the highlights, and so will your kids.

What other sport lets you stand there, as if on an escalator, and watch the world's classroom pass by, from trees and snow banks to clouds and other skiers? It's like starring in your own race car video game, or watching the world unfold on an IMAX screen, only it's all in the Great Outdoors.

Just like your day on the slopes, skiing with kids will always have its ups and downs. But it doesn't have to be as hair-raising as it was for the gentleman tangled up with his son on the catwalk. The following hints should make the process easier.

DOWNHILL SKIING

Step One: Getting Out the Door

If you live near a ski resort, consider yourself lucky if for no other reason than you're saved the car-ride commute. But you can't escape the quandary of packing the car, dressing the kids, and hopefully getting out the door.

The number one rule: don't forget anything. If possible, put everything—underlayers, socks, bibs, parkas, gloves, helmets, goggles, boots—all in a pile in your mud room beforehand. While your kids are wrestling on their gear, deal with your own needs (there's nothing worse than remembering your kid's goggles but forgetting yours), and then load up their skis in the car. Then go back to help them, which often means having to start all over again.

The dressing debacle is often an All Star Wrestling match, with tantrums the inevitable winner. Heads and arms will be stuck in the wrong holes, boots will wind up on the wrong feet, and pants will go on backwards. "In this corner, wearing ski pants passed down from his sister and a sweater hiding his head...Fiiiiidgeting Franklin. In the next corner, wearing an exhausted look and disheveled hair, Maaaaad Mom! Now wrestle!"

A word of advice before the bell rings: make sure everyone has gone to the bathroom before the layer tussling begins. More ski time has been lost to kids saying "I have

to pee," after the final glove has been pulled on than any other single delay.

Bathroom mission accomplished, it's time to begin grappling with the layers. Long underwear, socks, shirts, ski pants...oops, forgot the normal underwear, so off everything comes, and start all over again. Remember to get the toe seam right on the socks, and to pull them over the long underwear so they don't slide down. And avoid the itchy kind, if there is such a thing.

Don't think it's over when the bibs and parka are on. Most kids want their gloves tucked into their parka sleeves, even for the car ride. The final melee is cramming their feet into the ski boots, one of the most awkward of all dressing steps. Children's feet don't naturally slide into plastic cinder-blocks. They bend and wriggle in all the wrong ways, and you'll often have to switch them from sitting to standing to gain better entry. Then ~ after re-adjusting the boot's tongue, and hearing painful protests from your kid's tongue ~ once you miraculously get a foot in and buckled, she'll say it's itchy or the sock's not right.

Eventually you'll get to the point where your kids want to put their boots on themselves. Before you sing Hallelujah, brace yourself for them to be on the wrong feet when you return from buttering their toast. How they can do this and still be comfortable is one of life's great mysteries. Shoe-horn a grown-up's foot in to the wrong boot and it won't last a second. But a kid will wear them all day that way if you don't intervene.

Hint: wait on the helmets until you're actually at the resort—put them on too early and your kids will raise the itchy issue again, and tear them off as if they're harboring an ant colony. But don't forget them, or the goggles.

Though it sometimes results in errant lens scratches, we keep our kids' goggles fastened to their helmets, so both travel in tandem. That way we can't forget one without the other. Remember the helmet and the goggles hitch a free ride, and vice versa. The only problem with this technique is the dangling lens effect when not in use; it puts the goggle in plastic-scratching contact with every item in sight from car trunk to garage and back. One or two grazes and you can play tic-tac-toe on the lens, and chaching-chaching goes the nearest retailer's cash register.

When the tantrums come about leaving home—it being too cold or someone missing blankie and Camel—persevere with promises of sleep-overs and any other bribes you can think of to get everyone out the door. We use an end-of-the-day visit to Dippin' Dots as our final *pièce de résistance*.

Eventually, you'll get everything ready (don't forget the snacks) and make the pilgrimage to the car. Yup—all that work and you're not even at the car yet. That's when you have to watch your Young Frankenstein walk down icy steps in his ski boots, making you cringe with each gait. If kids have a hard time negotiating steps in tennis shoes, put both ankles in a plastic cast and add ice and it's a sure recipe for a tumble. But at least they're padded with their ski clothes.

Once you make it to the car, you're nearly home-free—at least from the packing part of the equation. Try to convince your kids that they don't need their parkas on in the car. Save their sauna for after the slopes.

You'll get better at the process as time progresses—especially since every ski day means at least five complete dresses and undresses: one at home, a couple for the bathroom, one at the lodge, and a final one again back at home. It's the lodge ones that are stupefying—kids simply explode out of their ski gear as soon as they set foot in a cafeteria. It's almost Pavlovian. Lodge, strip. Look the other way and your kid will be down to his underwear, pants scattered over the floor alongside errant pickles. Don't fight it. Sweep the mound of discarded gear under the table and start the All Star Wrestling process all over again after the hot chocolate and pizza.

If you're heading out for a multi-day vacation and have multiple children in tow, there's more work to do. You have to pack regular clothes, toys, blankets and books as well as the full complement of ski gear. Take the following advice from *Ski Press* writer Moira McCarthy. She suggests buying a different colored duffel bag for each kid so you can easily pull the bags out of the car and shuffle them to the right rooms. Another suggestion: splurge on your accommodations so you're not forced into lights out at 9 p.m.

Carrying Gear

Unfortunately, the process only gets worse before it gets better. The real work begins as soon as you step out of the car. Now you have to carry not only your own equipment to the lift, but also your kids' gear (and often even the kids).

It's a lot like over-zealously grabbing too many items while away from the cart in the supermarket. Only with skiing, all the items are big and awkward, a mix of brooms, pans, cantaloupes and eggs. It's the Achilles heel of any kid ski outing, and there's no good way around it. In fact, it's probably led to more parents giving up the sport than any other single aspect of family skiing. Wily veterans might make it look easy, but don't be fooled. Beneath that perfect form and calm demeanor is the gear-carrying grimace every other grown-up is wearing.

Rubik would delight at the problem. The quandary: you have at least twice the usual amount of gear, but only half the arm power with which to carry it. That's right. If your kid is age four or younger, you need to keep one arm free to hold her hand. One less arm, twice the gear.

With practice, it's not so bad with just one kid. But single-parent it with two or three kids' gear and you'll envy the multi-armed octopus.

Eight arms would be nice, because that's how many items you'll have to carry; and that's if you're only schlepping for you and one child (four poles, four skis). Look around any resort and you'll see a variety of techniques for getting the task done, from the ever-awkward Chest Clutch to the Gunslinger, where the poor, hapless parent corrals everything at the hip.

While none of these techniques are perfect, a few are better than others. Here's one I've found to work. Carry your skis over your shoulder as usual, and then grab your kid's skis with the same hand. The trick: counterweight the tip of your skis with pressure from your forearm, leaving your hand free to carry your kid's skis. Do it right and you can also clutch two sets of poles in the same rapidly shrinking hand. All this frees up your left hand to hold your child's hand when lumbering from the parking lot to the bus or lift.

Another fatherly favorite is the grovel approach. Cup your right arm and hold everything between it and your torso in an awkward, jumbled-up pile. It won't win you any style points, but if it's a short walk it'll get the job done.

Both of these techniques are even harder when you're dealing with telemark skis, which, without ski brakes to keep them together, slide away from each other like you and your kids do on the slopes. They also grow tougher when the ambling meltdown occurs and your child becomes a piece of equipment as well. Then you're carrying a jumbled-up pile of kids and gear, treating them all as one in the same.

The whole ordeal is an art form, with an infinite variety of partial solutions. I once saw a mom sling her own snowboard bandolier-style across her back, and then carry her kid's skis horizontally in front of her with both hands. Junior then sat on the skis facing her, straddling her stomach. Voila! A moveable ski bench that you could

carry straight to the chiropractor. The more Yuppie type might even employ a backpack that can carry both Junior and his gear. But while this turns the heads of the grown-ups groveling next to you, it also adds another piece of gear to the equation.

The best solution: a pre-emptive strike by minimizing gear. For starters, discourage poles as long as possible—even when your youngest sees everyone else using them. Your kids will drop them, struggle with the straps, and change their mind about using them halfway down, leaving you to pick up the pieces. They mean two more awkward pieces of gear to carry before you even get to the slopes, upping your cargo load by twenty-five percent. Now you have eight long, skinny items for just two hands—and only one if you're still in the hand-holding stage. Poles' only silver lining comes when your kids master them and can move themselves on the flats.

Throw another kid into the gear-carrying mix and you're in a realm that stumps even Pythagoras. Now you have to improvise. When skiing with Brooke and Casey, I sling my skis across my shoulder, and use that same hand to carry my poles and another pair of skis (see Technique #1, outlined above). Then I use my free hand for another pair of skis and poles. If I have to hold Casey's hand, I have her grab onto the end of these. It's awkward and thankless and has me grimacing all the way to the gondola.

The best solution follows that of skiing in avalanche terrain: limit your exposure. Drive as close to the resort or bus stop as you can, open the back hatch and let everything fall out. Then go park and walk back to the mound hands-free.

Also, use buses whenever possible. But realize that they, too, aren't a walk in the park. You have to set all the gear down to put your skis into the rack, and then pick it all up again to board. And woe is the parent who has to fight for a place in line. You stand a better chance of making front row at a Hannah Montana concert. Be prepared for everything to explode into the aisle once you're inside, and to repeat the whole process in reverse when you disembark. But it beats the supermarket-aisle walk across the parking lot.

A final piece of gear-carrying advice: make your budding skier wear his helmet across the parking lot. If his head's itchy, take it off and give him a good scratching, but put it back on for the stroll. Otherwise, like that roast in Aisle 4, it adds another awkward item to the already-hard-to-carry mix. If keeping the helmet on evokes a tantrum, your only choice is to spear the chin strap with your pole or drape it over your shoulder-slung skis Huck Finn-style. But know that eight items have now become nine, enough to push even an octopus to the brink of ink-fleeing despair.

Hitting the Slopes

So you actually made it to the slopes! Congratulations! If you have any energy left, you might actually be able to ski.

Barring day care and ski school, both viable options for your sanity if not your pocketbook, it's time to hit the hill with your children (which, by this point, may make you want to hit your children as well). Before digressing into what that entails, realize that doing so can provide some of the most rewarding family memories you'll ever have—more than that summer road trip to Aunt Ethel's or puppy-in-a-box at Christmas.

Consider my friend Pete, who recently adopted two rambunctious sons, Otis and Oliver. He's the owner of a ski shop in town and can't espouse enough the virtues of skiing with his brood. "It's the only thing Otis does in life that he really has to concentrate and focus on," he maintains of the hellion on skis. "It forces him to focus on something and teaches him the consequences of his actions."

"Plus, it's also the only time he listens to me," he adds. "When I say stop, he stops. When I say go straight, he goes straight. He certainly doesn't do that at the supermarket. When skiing, he realizes that Mom and Dad are actually right about something, that there's a reason to their rhymes. It's the one physical activity we can do together and actually both have fun."

Of course, it will also lead to some of your most trying moments on skis. You'll hike up for dropped gear, bend over to fasten bindings, follow your kids into jarring "secret passages," and draft your brood as if in the Tour de France to protect them from steam-rolling passersby. You'll snowplow until your quads scream, pole-tow kids until your shoulder pops out, follow them off flat-landing jumps that rattle the spine, and clean more spilt hot chocolate than you ever thought possible. You'll also enter a new realm of meltdowns, when Junior sits down like a llama, spittle and all, and refuses to budge.

But throughout this, you won't remember the bad times as much as the good. Those "Race ya', Dad's!" and "Lemme go under your legs!" will punt the meltdown memories into the next mountain range over.

Here are a few pointers to make the ordeal easier. First and foremost, don't take them on runs they shouldn't be on. Save the double-blacks for checkers back in the condo and stick to the mucus-colored greens. If it's cold, make sure they're wearing the appropriate gear, from hand warmers to helmets. Save the frosting for Frosted Flakes. Finally, respect their boundaries like you do the resort's ropes. If your kids are tired and cold, head inside. Remember, it should be fun.

In Steamboat, which is home to some sixty-nine Olympians, people have as many ways to get their kids started skiing and snowboarding as there are snowflakes on the mountain. Some ways are better than others, and everyone—including tangled-up Houdini above—has their own preference. Following are a few that have withstood the test of both time and tantrums.

BRING 'EM ALONG FOR THE RIDE: BACKPACKS

Just like Trix are for kids, backpacks are for hiking, right? Nope. While they're indeed great for family strolls and hiking, backpacks are also an invaluable tool for skiing.

When your toddler is wobbling simply trying to walk, putting him on a pair of slippery skis and pushing him down a hill doesn't seem particularly suitable. In the early years, before your child can walk or is stable enough to ski on his own, your best bet is putting him in a pack. Not all ski areas allow this, so check beforehand. Of those that do, they'll likely restrict the activity to surface lifts (pomas, rope-tows and T-bars) or gondolas, where a Quasimodo-size hump on your back won't be quite the liability it is on a chair.

Find an area that allows it and you'll be that much more ahead of the game when Junior skis himself. He'll see people skiing around him, feel the rush of wind on his face, and discover the sensation of scenery passing by. If you can't find a resort that allows it, take him on easy backcountry or cross-country forays, which will instill the same sense of motion.

Fortunately, Steamboat allows it on the gondola and poma. Not many other resorts do. We learned this when we tried to load the Lion's Head gondola in Vail with Casey in our pack, only to be confronted by the ski patrol in the lift line.

"You can't ski here with her in a backpack," they said.

"Oh," we replied, adhering to the motto that it's easier to ask forgiveness than permission. Still, we saw our family day on the slopes disappear in the blink of a goggle-covered eye. One of us was now relegated to watching Casey at the town library while the other skied with Brooke.

If you plan on going this route, make sure you're a proficient skier before subjecting your gene pool to your tumbling miscues. If you regularly face plant instead of pole plant, think about face painting with your toddler instead. If you're not sure of your abilities, err on the side of caution and leave the backpack for later (or practice with a sack of potatoes first—when you can end the day without turning them into mashers, you're ready to strap in Junior).

If you—and more importantly, your spouse—are comfortable with this approach, it's suitable any time after your child can hold his head up by himself. It also provides the perfect napping spot when après skiing afterward.

The first time we used ours came when we took Brooke on a road trip to Jackson Hole, Wyoming, and Sun Valley, Idaho. She was still nursing, which offered another advantage on the drive. Whenever it was time to feed, my wife would pull over and take care of matters, leaving me with a half-hour window in which to entertain myself. I could either stay in the car and listen to the slurping, or rally outside. So invariably, I'd put on my skins and skis and explore the nearest snow-covered hill for turns. I didn't have the least idea where I was, but it didn't matter. Nursing on the road led to exploring new terrain. I'd climb up, schuss down and arrive to a fed daughter.

We learned a lot on that inaugural trip, aside from skiing with a kid in a backpack. We learned how to change diapers in a crowded lodge ("Um, excuse me, would you mind moving your fries?"), that the Jackson youth hostel's walls are surprisingly thin, and that throw-up is easier to clean off a car seat when it's frozen. But it was the back-

pack that truly opened our eyes to winter recreation with our newborn.

While the practice isn't likely condoned by knee surgeons, it's actually not that hard. Backcountry skiers who can ski with a backpack will find it similar, other than the occasional drool in the ear and horse kick in the ribs. The key lies in the straps and positioning. Snug the shoulder and chest straps on both you and your rider, and position Junior low in the seat to avoid being as top heavy as a snow-loaded tree.

One of the first rules: buckle your boots and fasten your bindings before you put your child on your back. Otherwise he'll dangle upside-down with Santa-red cheeks while you're fiddling with your footwear. Forget to strap him in while doing so and little Kevin will become a crater.

Get your boots snug and skis fastened and then pick up the pack. This, of course, brings up the importance of a free-standing pack. Get one that stands erect on its own. That way you can load up Junior and set him upright while you're tinkering with other things. Then, once you're all ready, simply reach over and hoist him up onto your back.

If you're heading to a resort, you'll notice the addition of a pack in your first lift line. Your back now extends beyond its normal profile. A quick turn can make dominos out of everyone next to you in line.

When you're finally ready to shove off, stick to the groomers and easier runs. Having a k-k-k-kid on your b-b-b-back is not the time to hit w-w-w-washboards, moguls or the halfpipe. Above all, be careful. It's also not a time to be wiping out.

It's also important to stay attuned to their needs. Once, when Casey started whining halfway down a slope, I ignored her and kept going, thinking it was just the cold. It wasn't until I got to the bottom and saw people looking at me strangely that I took the pack off and saw that her left boot and sock had disappeared. Poof! Vanished without a trace. In their place were five dangling piggies, all of whom were warding off the cold rather than going to the market to get roast beef. Apparently, the shoe and sock fell off somewhere en route, probably on one of those back-jarring whoop-de-doo's. Regardless, I had a hard time explaining the situation to my wife back home.

Thankfully, save for my parenting esteem, all was not lost. While the sock went to the Great Lost Clothes Mound in the sky, the next day a friend—Paige, mother of Brooke's best friend, Madeline—was visiting the resort's lost and found and noticed a lone boot with Brooke's name crossed out on the back and Casey's stenciled in below it. Putting two plus two together, she knew it had to be ours, and returned it the next day.

And all's well that ends well. That weekend, I went back to the drawing board and emerged with two elastic bands sewn onto the bottom of Casey's ski pant legs. Voila!

Instant boot holders that kept her boots on her feet no matter how many bumps we hit on the way down.

A backpack is also a great transitional tool and safety net for when kids get tired skiing on their own. When she was first learning how to ski, Casey would often melt halfway down notorious Giggle Gulch, leaving me with no option but to awkwardly carry her on my hip while attempting to ski on my own. If orthopedic surgeons don't recommend skiing with a child in a pack, then they certainly don't this. A couple of times having Casey straddle my leg as I did a stem-christie was all it took to bring the backpack as a back-up. With this insurance policy, I'd simply pull over, plop her in, and continue along my merry way. Hint: tie your kid's skis onto the pack behind you, or put them back on Junior after she's in the pack, which will make her feel like a Nordic jumper. Then you, too, can enjoy the ride.

PERFECTING THE HANDOFF

Before you're actually skiing with your kids, you'll perfect the art of the kid hand-off, taking turns watching Junior in the lodge while your spouse takes a few sanity-recharging laps of her own. Unfortunately, there aren't too may options when you're lodge-bound with your brood. You'll either carry your kids around in your arms or in a backpack, chase them between cafeteria tables, or play games like tic-tac-toe with French fries. You'll feed them snacks, take them to the bathroom, and otherwise kill time in your glorified cell while waiting for your spouse to return.

Above all, you'll make sure that when your spouse comes back (assuming he or she does) to trade off, you'll be ready. Your hand-offs will become second nature, like that of a baton in a relay. Your spouse will show up with a smile and—Boom! -- the kids will be in her hands while you're out the door, yelling the lunch report as you leave.

Not all hand-offs will go smoothly. There'll be diapers to change, messes to clean, and even kids to find. And some will be worse than others, even away from the lodge. Once, while trading off at a friend's house, my friend Mike fastened his infant son, Jack, in the car seat and accidentally locked him inside the house while he was stuck outside. While Mike frantically tried to figure out a way inside and what he was going to tell his wife, Jack stared up at him through the living room window from his perch in the seat. And that's right when his cell phone rang. It was his wife, Alicia, checking up on how things were going.

Graduation Time: Free Riding

So it's time for Junior to graduate from the pack to the actual slopes. Buen suerte!

While kids take to skiing at all ages, we started ours at age two, and didn't get very far. We spent far more time in the lodge changing their clothes and cleaning up hot chocolate than we did out on actual snow. When we did make it outside, we pulled our kids around by our ski poles, and occasionally made it as far as the magic carpet (see "lifts" below). While this might not seem worth the effort, it at least got the snowball rolling—which is what our kids became as soon as they tried the sport on their own.

Even if you put your kids in ski school, they won't be there forever. There'll be times when you're teaching them yourself. Familiarize yourself with two food items from the cafeteria beforehand: Pizza Pie and French Fries. Only you'll never mention them as casually as you do at the lunch table. You'll be yelling "Pizza Pie! Pizza Pie! Pizza Pie!"—childspeak for snowplow—at the top of your lungs as if your child's life depended on it, which it does. Then, once your kids heed your elderly advice and start to get the hang of the momentum-slowing snowplow, like a concessionaire at a football game you'll yell "French Fries! French Fries!" so they don't pizza pie themselves to a standstill on the flats, requiring you, the raw vocal-chorded parent, to pull them.

Some trendsetters forsake these handy little metaphors and don't teach the wedge, or Pizza Pie, at all. Instead, they tell their kids to put their hands on the outside of their knees and to "push the magic button" to turn and slow down. Push the right magic button to turn left and push the left magic button to turn right. Push both to slow down. Then you're simply yelling "Magic Buttons! Magic Buttons! Magic Buttons!" to get them to slow down rather than "Pizza Pie!"

Use whatever works and whatever they'll listen to. A friend employed the Magic Button technique with his second child, Bennett, and maintains that he learned much faster than his first son, Max. "We didn't even bother with the snowplow," he says. "It was all magic buttons." He might be onto something. At age 3, peanut-sized Bennett became the youngest person in history to ski down Steamboat's double-black Chute 1.

Without using such teaching crutches (poor word choice when talking about skiing), you're likely to become one of those parents who grab their child's jacket by the shoulders in a desperate attempt to slow them down and keep them upright when things go awry. That's not a technique you want to rely on.

Just as it does for adults, equipment also makes a big difference. Halfway through her breakthrough season at age 3, we upgraded Casey to skis that had more of an hour-glass shape to them and her learning curve eased like the bottom of a ski slope. It gave her a solid platform to stand on, and she could actually arc a turn when setting an edge. Most importantly, however, the skis had ladybugs.

THE EDGY-WEDGY

To prevent the dreaded spread-eagle splat—a syndrome that occurs when both tips veer outward until little Billy belly flops—consider the catchy-phrased Edgy-Wedgy. While you might feel silly asking for one a retail counter ("Uh, excuse me, do you have an Edgy-Wedgy?"), and cause the clerk to check the back of his drawers, the concept is simple: two clamps attach to the tip of each ski, and are attached with a few inches of bungee material so the tips can't shoot apart like strands of morning hair. Though the manacles dampen your kid's ability to get out of a snowplow, these magical clips force your child into a permanent, gravity-thwarting Pizza Pie, putting your mind at ease whenever Newton's Law rears its head.

Alas, like all things too good to be true, it also has a downside. It makes it hard to perform a proper French Fry to build up speed, meaning you're often pulling your child on the flats. Like its underwear namesake, it also doesn't allow for much freedom of movement. Shackle your child in an Edgy-Wedgy and he'll have less mobility than in a three-legged race.

The device is also not without its hassles. Invariably, one of the clips will pop off, leaving your previously training-wheeled child all alone to face skiing's school of hard knocks. In those cases, your only hope is to Eric Heiden your way forward to catch up, grab your kid's jacket like the do-it-yourself parents above, and re-fasten the clip once the situation is under control.

When using the Edgy-Wedgy, you'll often ski backward in front of your child, coaxing him along with cries of "Attaboy!" and "C'mon, you can do it!" while the other spouse chastises you for being too far away and making your child ski too fast. This means becoming adept yourself at skiing switch (or backwards), like those new-schoolers who do it on purpose. Pull it off correctly—try a lip curl while pointing your index finger at other skiersby—and you might even look legitimate.

HARNESSING THE HARNESS

Perhaps the most common device for teaching children to ski is the ski harness. The concept is simple. You fasten a belt around your kid's waist and then hold onto two straps trailing behind to keep him under control. Most straps are adjustable, allowing you to start with them short to keep Junior close at hand and then lengthen them as he progresses down the slope and the learning curve. But don't be fooled; no matter the strap length, it's as much of a pain as carrying your kid's gear. Just ask Houdini, above.

When you put the straps on their shortest setting, so you're skiing right behind your protégé, you act much like a puppeteer, keeping young Pinocchio upright. When he starts to list, you simply lift him back up. But this means staying uncomfortably close—you're literally breathing down his neck gaiter. And when he actually starts careening downhill with you so near, you're so close behind that you barely have time or room to react and execute a snowplow to slow the whole train down.

Hopefully, for your back's sake, you'll graduate from the puppeteer short leash phase quickly. Then it's time to raise the training wheels by letting the straps out. Like letting him have the car thirteen years later, you're extending his leash, letting him test his own boundaries and better roam the countryside at will. With the leash lengthened, your kid will be in more control—or lack thereof—of his own destiny. But you're still there in case that destiny careens him toward a tree. The downside is that with you now five or ten feet behind, there's more strap for you both to get tangled up in (again, just ask Houdini).

Another downside to the harness is that, eventually, once you both reach the flats, you'll want to let go and let Junior ski on his own. This means you either have to stop and un-fasten the whole confounded contraption (at which point you either unclip the straps and stuff them in your jacket, or wrap them around your child's waist a few times) or have him drag the straps behind him, tangling everything in his wake.

While unfastening everything seems a better alternative, it's a hassle. The gradient frequently picks up again a short while later, leaving you rigging and de-rigging the entire run.

Controlling the whole gizmo is also an art, much like controlling the slack in a water ski rope. Run ahead of the leash's slack and you're not much use as a brake. Be overly protective and you'll pull Junior backward and affect his ability to turn. You also need to beware the train wreck syndrome. When your kid falls you only have a split second to react before steamrolling him over. With practice, you'll learn to sense potential biffs beforehand through body language—arms flailing and teetering on one ski means likely crash ahead — and then either play Giuseppe or make your own Pizza Pie to prevent the fall.

The whole business is a bit of a Catch-22. Sure, you can catch your kid with a harness, and therein lies its beauty. But after untangling lines all day, you can also catch a serious case of never wanting to do it again. Look around at any ski resort and you'll invariably see a proud mom or dad holding the leash of a harnessed youngster. But none of them make it look easy, and you rarely see the same parent at the controls twice in a row.

None of this is to say you shouldn't give it a tangled whirl. In the early stages, it's one of the best techniques you can employ. And you don't have to get the most expensive, yuppified harness from the Sky Mall catalog (try www.luckybums.com). There are also plenty of improvisations that work. I've seen people jerry-rig kid harnesses out of Hula Hoops, putting one end around a kid's waist with the parent holding the other, and even bicycle inner tubes, which provide a high degree of shock absorption, but leave black streaks on jackets.

Whatever you use, the harness serves a vital role. It's a safety net, for both your child and spouse waiting on the sidelines, and a surefire way to get your kid skiing on his own. Like brushing your daughter's hair, just put up with the tangles.

THE OL' POLE EXTENSION

With Kid #2 (Casey, for those keeping track) I made it through the tangled-up-in-blue harness era much more quickly. The reason is that a friend, former kids' ski instructor Julie Maus, showed me a technique involving only a ski pole. No extra gear to carry, no ropes to get mummified in, and no hassle. Plus, her own two-year-old was light years ahead of three-year-old Casey in skiing ability, so I figured there had to be some merit to this new-fangled, untangled technique. "We didn't even use a harness for her," she says of her daughter, Lily's, skiing curve. "She went to the pole technique right away."

Actually, the pole-extension technique isn't new-fangled at all. It simply involves holding your ski poles out horizontally across the slope and letting Junior grab onto them whenever the pull of gravity is too strong. Its beauty is in its simplicity. When you encounter a hill that your child can't handle, simply hold your poles out for him to grab onto. This slows him down—the desired outcome for mom or dad watching in horror—and keeps his weight and hands forward, where they should be.

The harness works great for the initial foray onto the slopes and when you don't trust your kid to provide brakes. But once you start letting him go on his own, a harness' limitations show themselves like Punxsutawney Phil poking his head out of a groundhog hole. The pole technique provides instamatic brakes. Hold it out for the short steep section, and let him ski on his own once things mellow out.

It didn't take Casey long to develop a Pavlovian response to the steeps, including the drool. At the first sign of increasing gravitational pull, she'd put her hands out front, ready to grasp at the oncoming poles as salvation. Once she knew she was safe, she'd let go and schuss away on her own. It also builds trust between you and your child. They need help, you're there to provide it...hopefully.

The technique's only drawback is that you have to be on your game. It's not the time to be day-dreaming about the eggs you forgot at the store, or staring at the passing beautiful, snow-covered trees. Stay close at hand and don't let your child stray too far from your side. Like Clint Eastwood, be quick on the draw should things go awry. Always be within a quick pole plant or ski skate to catch up and extend a helping hand.

It almost got to the point where I'd hear *The Good, The Bad and The Ugly* theme every time Casey started careening out of control. Reacting like a gunslinger, I'd then flick my poles up from my side to save her. Blondie, The Good, the pole-bearing savior.

I will admit—to you, not my wife—that a couple of times I did let Casey stray a bit too far, like Eastwood missing the shot to break the rope hanging his partner. When that happened, I'd skate frantically behind to catch up and render the offering. On steeper sections, you can even use your poles like the harness above, extending them under your kid's armpits and letting him hold onto the grips while you hold onto baskets, with arms fully extended.

Whether it's little sister syndrome or better genetic make-up, I will say this: Casey did progress more quickly than Brooke. And we both got in more ski time without having to untangle ourselves from the harness.

Once your child is skiing on his own, poles also serve another purpose. Whenever you get to the flats, you can execute the old pole pull by extending your basket (which makes a good grip) to your child and letting him latch on for additional momentum. If it's just a short way, wind up and sling-shot him forward, your shoulder socket determining the degree of propulsion. Your kids will get remarkably good at it, and start looking for your help whenever they fizzle out on the flats. Casey did this constantly, looking over her shoulder whenever her momentum slowed for that ever-present pull from pops. Somehow, kids also always intrinsically know just when to let go to maximize the slingshot-like momentum.

If you're pulling them for a long way, try skating and pulling at the same time, using your other pole to help you skate while extending your remaining pole to your child. It won't win you any Nordic medals, but this human poma will have your kids quickly learning how to tow. If you're skiing with more than one child, you can also try the train, pulling more than one at a time. Just be careful it doesn't pull your shoulder out of its socket at the same time.

THE T-BAR

Not to be confused with its lift counterpart, the T-bar, as its name implies, is a specialized T-shaped contraption made specifically for teaching kids to ski. Basically, it's a long, plastic T-shaped pole that you put under your armpit while extending the giant "T" end for your kid. Your child then stands in front of the crossbar, sitting on it when necessary and grabbing the shaft with his hands.

It's kind of like training wheels for a bike; your kid can stand on his own, and when the going gets rough he can grab onto the pole more tightly and switch some weight to his derrière.

The only drawback is its size and awkwardness compared to a harness, and the fact that you have to lug it around the mountain Christ-like if venturing anywhere other

than the bottom lift. If you thought simply carrying your kids' ski gear around was harrowing, throw this awkward item into the mix. It's like you're bearing a giant crucifix.

Making up for this is the fact that, should Junior drop his glove, you can use it as a rake to scoop dropped gear down toward you instead of climbing back up the hill. And since there aren't too many of them out there in circulation, it's easy to find when you head back outside from the lodge.

Lifts

The first few times out with a kid under the age of three, you'll be lucky to simply get their gear on, let alone glide anywhere. To get uphill, you'll likely carry your toddler rather than rely on technology. But believe it or not, all that will change. There will come a time when Junior will be interested enough in the sport for both of you to benefit from a mechanical advantage.

A variety of lifts service today's ski market, some more kid-friendly than others. Rickety two-person chair over jagged precipices without a safety bar? Not kid friendly.

High-speed quad that slows down at each ramp, with foot rest, bubble enclosure and Barney illustration? Kid-o-rama. As with the actual skiing, there's a natural progression to getting kids comfortable on lifts.

MAGIC CARPET

Unfortunately, the magic carpets used by most ski areas aren't quite as fast and nimble as the ones employed by Aladdin, or even the moving carpet in *The Jetsons*. In the first place, they only go straight. Second, they're as slow as a kid getting ready for bedtime.

Still, whether in a lesson or home-schooled, this is where your child will likely ride his first lift. Actually, "lift" has little to do with it. You simply scooch forward onto the "carpet" and watch the scenery slooooowly pass by.

It's basically a conveyor belt, much like those moveable walkways at an airport, only without some womanly voice saying, "Moving walkway nearing the end. Please exit carefully." The only difference is that they're moving uphill and you don't have people hurrying past with Starbucks in their hands. And kids are wearing skis, not sneakers.

If you get on one and follow your kid, you'll feel like you're in a time warp. Everything is as slowed down and molasses-like as the trip down the hall to the principal's office. If the conveyors in *The Jetsons* moved this slowly, they would have invented another means of locomotion.

But be grateful it doesn't whisk you away. Otherwise, there'd be freeway-like pileups at the ride's end, kids and gear atop one another in a massive heap of carnage with you, the parent, left to pick up the pieces.

But it's worth it all for the expression on your child's face the first time he steps on. He'll take a few tentative shuffle steps, then a few more, and then—Whamo! He's on the carpet and moving upward—and on his way up to his first-ever lift-accessed ski slope.

Actually, it's not really up. Nor is it really a slope. Most terrain accessed by magic carpets resembles more of a bowling lane, with your tiny neophyte skiers being the pins that get knocked down But it's skiing, and your kid is now well on his way to mastering the sport.

Simple as these contraptions look, don't just stand back and ogle your kid's progress from the bottom. He'll likely require some help getting off at the top—a hand to pull him off the carpet, or encouraging words of "Keep walking, keep walking!" That's when he'll need to do the Frankenstein, heel-locked shuffle again to get from moving ramp to solid ground.

More than likely, your kid will ask you to hop on and join him. Put pride aside and climb aboard. You'll feel self-conscious when you stand upon it, especially when you realize you could walk backward blindfolded faster, but your kid will appreciate your being there with him, even though you checked your conceit back at the on-ramp.

You'll know you're ready to graduate onto bigger and better lifts once your kid starts employing freestyle moves on the ride up. He might try riding sideways or even backward during the ascent, or even try the old one-ski-on and one-ski-off trick, all of which are a sure sign that carrot lifts and pomas are just around the corner.

THE CARROT LIFT

At Howelsen Hill, Steamboat's city-owned ski area downtown, a glorified rope tow affectionately called the Carrot lift used to be located thirty yards away from the carpet. For kids, it was like making the jump from kindergarten to first grade.

The reason for the name owes itself to the orange handles coming by every twenty feet that your kid grabbed onto to be whisked upward. It was the first natural progression up from the magic carpet, while still a step down from the poma.

Casey took to it easily at age three. When the orange handle whipped around, she'd wind up both arms and throw her whole body at it, wrapping her entire torso around the handle in one giant gravity-defying embrace. Then off she'd go, jerked up-hill and holding on for all she was worth.

On her first attempt, she somehow managed to detour her back under the knee-high cable next to it, which pinned her down and forced her to hunch over at the waist for the entire ride. The lift operator had never seen it happen before. "I'm okay," Casey bravely croaked, pinned nearly prone by the cable. But she held on. By the top, she had learned to simply scootch over a bit to the main uptrack to ride erect.

Though stopping before the emergency shut-off cable strung across the top took some getting used to (at one point she tripped it, shutting off the lift), she quickly found a new sense of independence on the slopes. As loyal Dad, and with pride already sucked dry by the magic carpet, I followed on the carrot closest behind (behind my thighs to save my back), yelling words of encouragement the entire way.

Casey's carrot for the carrot ride, of course, was the ski down, a small slope she was perfectly capable of navigating herself. Unfortunately, the first time she veered to-ward the terrain park where the bigger kids were jumping and rail sliding. Wasting no

time, she headed toward the biggest box slide and launched slowly off the entry jump, schmack-dab into its leading face, which she splatted onto like a fly on a windshield. "I'm okay," she croaked again, reaffirming her newfound carrot-lift-inspired independence.

Then it was back to the bottom for a total of twenty self-sufficient laps on the lift, each one creating more confidence than the ride before. It helped having a friendly lift-op forcing every rider to say "Booga-booga" as a password before being allowed to ride. But the real incentive was the sense of empowerment it offered.

How much was it on her mind? That night for dinner we broke out a bag of mini-carrots as the nightly vegetable (don't tell me you've never done that as a time-starved parent). "Look, Dad," Casey said, holding one up and grabbing it. "It's just like the lift, only I can eat it. Chomp."

THE DREADED T-BAR

My psychologist would rue my bringing up this dark scar from my childhood.

Thankfully, the aptly named T-bar, whose letter I can only surmise stands for "torture," is more or less a thing of the past, which is a very good thing, considering the emotional scarring it's left me and countless other children of my generation.

But just as my god-awful memories are still there, so too are pockets of T-bars strewn throughout the country. So you might as well familiarize yourself with it for your kids' sake.

The majority of my ill will toward the apparatus is owed to the ski area where I grew up: Lake Eldora, outside of Boulder, Colorado. Other bad feelings stem from incidents at Winter Park, at one time home to the Meteor and Comet, the two fastest T-bars in the world. They could whip you uphill at a whopping 820 feet per minute, 300 feet per minute faster than any other chairlift at the time, and 400 feet per minute faster than the next closest surface lift. For kids, that spelled one word: Trouble, with a capital T, that rhymes with P, that stands for Pain. It also led to inevitable carnage, the type that dragged kids along kicking and screaming for the ride.

Fortunately, Eldora was closer to Boulder so we went there more often, escaping the rocket ship ego-destroyers of Winter Park. But Eldora's T-bar was no slouch, either, meaning the tiny resort in the foothills of the Rockies bears the brunt of my vengeance.

It might have to do with the ominous signs on subsequent lift towers as you approach the top: "If you should unload," read one; "And stand in the way," read another; "You might get hit," read the third; "By a T today!" How comforting, especially for a kid scared to death of them in the first place. They might as well have placed a picture of the Grim Reaper on the towers. And his guillotine of a scythe bears a striking resemblance to the contraption that carried us upwards.

Before the resort's Cannonball chair was installed, the T-bar was the only way up from the base lodge to the top, whisking featherweight and frightened-out-of-their gourd kids up 1,000 vertical feet in twelve minutes. The problem was that its springs out-powered the weight of the average kid. This meant a primitive parasail ride every time you went solo, which, in Eldora's notorious windy, icy conditions, happened more times than not. That's why lift attendants tried not to let kids ride alone. They didn't want children launching into orbit on the way up, impeding research at the nearby National Center for Atmospheric Research in Boulder ("Uh, Houston, we have a problem").

The solution was that they made you go with someone, which wasn't so bad if you were matched with someone of similar size. The extra weight was often just enough to keep the contraption grounded on the steep section and over awkward bumps and transitions. But, invariably, you'd get paired with Kareem Abdul Jabbar. While the T-bar clipped you in the crook of the neck, it was down around Kareem's ankles, forcing your partner into a back-breaking stoop the entire ride.

Once while suffering the height differential of riding with Lou Al Cinder, the T-bar stopped. It wasn't so bad, apart from trying to carry on a conversation with his shin and the fact that his back resented the prolonged torture. After the awkward pause, during which he looked at me as if I were responsible for the back injury causing him to miss the NBA playoffs, the lift started again and away we went, only to see it stop again twenty yards later. "Hello, Mr. Shin, nice weather, huh?" Then we were off again. When it stopped for the third time, the contortionist had enough and bailed for greener pastures, disembarking and skiing through the forest to the nearest slope.

This was all good and fine, save for the spring's-stronger-than-the-the-kid principle and the fact that we were positioned at the bottom of the ride's steepest pitch. When the T-bar started again, it lifted me off the ground and spun me a hundred and eighty degrees so that I was now facing downhill, my ski tips dangling helplessly in the air. This time Houston really did have a problem. There was nothing I could do except hold on. If you feel bad for me, feel worse for the two T-bar riders behind me, who witnessed the whole thing and realized I might come hurtling into them at any second. I could tell from the look of terror on their faces that I probably had the same expression.

I held on the whole way in what has to be a Guinness record for getting dragged uphill by a lift. I stared at the people behind me the entire time, save for when two errant bumps spun me in complete pirouettes, only to once again settle me in feebly facing backwards. When I rounded the knoll at the top, past those friendly Grim Reaper unloading signs, and the lift operator saw me, his college education at the University of Colorado kicked in and he stopped the lift just in time to deposit me plump in front of the lift shack. I never saw Kareem again.

Thankfully, not many resorts still persecute their pint-sized patrons with T-bars. With most of them going the way of the dodo, I won't needlessly bother to go into the ins and outs of riding them with kids. Suffice it to say that if you encounter one while skiing with your kids, be afraid...be very afraid. About the only thing you can do is pair like-sized kids with each other and tell them to hold on, or break out the Ben Gay for your back.

POMAS: THE MILDER COUSIN

Pomas, on the other hand, have withstood the test of time. Many areas still employ them for kid runs, as flat connector lifts and even as final assaults on wind-scoured summits.

The reason might lie in their singularity of purpose. They're designed for only one person at a time, so there's never a Kareem effect or need for a ballistic-strength spring. In short, there's no one else to mess up your ride. Any mistakes are purely your own; unless, of course, you're taking one—or both—of your kids up with you.

But just like T-bars, they can still cause consternation for kids.

When Steamboat's Skeeter Werner kids program comes to Howelsen Hill's poma lift twice a year, it's full red alert. Parents volunteer at stations along the way to pick up the pieces and shuttle human debris off the track before the next kid arrives. When riding through this gauntlet of protection as a grown-up, you hold two-second conversations with each of them. "How's it going?" "Nice grab back there." "Nice save." "Got any coffee?"

Kids biff left and right, are scooped up by volunteers standing on the sidelines, and are then sent through the woods to the slopes to try again. It's like the Foreign Legion for lifts, and probably one of the most experienced poma rescue squads in the world. But there's really no other way to learn. It's like riding a bike while being attached to a giant pogo stick. There just comes a time when your kid has to step up to the poma plate and literally swing away.

Not all pomas are as intimidating for youngsters as the steep one at Howelsen Hill. As with many other resorts, Steamboat's Rough Rider Basin has one that's perfect for kids. It's relatively flat and short, and for the kids it's often as much fun as skiing down. Once they learn to stand up rather than sit down, they're instant experts.

But as Howelsen attests, not all pomas are so amicable.

Before my kids were poma ready, but quite capable of skiing down Mile Run looping around the mountain's back side, I'd simply carry them up the poma in the backpack, tying their skis to the back of my pack with a cam strap. At top, I'd take them out, put on their skis, attach the harness if necessary, and away we'd go.

Despite the look it garnered from lift ops—kid in pack, skis tied behind her, Chamonix here I come—the process was rather involved, especially when Brooke needed help up the lift also. Then, while Casey was in the pack, I'd have Brooke straddle my thigh, and carry them both up, getting a three-for-one deal on one poma seat. Though the technique worked, it was awkward and garnered looks of empathy from lift ops. And it meant only three or four runs before my back screamed in protest.

If you don't have a pack, and your kid is too gun-shy and light to ride on her own, carrying is the only option. For this, you have a few options: you can lift them up and carry them on your hip, straddling your thigh en route; hold them between your legs in front of you, with their skis on the snow; or have them face you and straddle your stomach, resting their back against the poma pole. "I'm like a baby," laughed Casey the first time I tried this technique. "Goo-goo, gah-gah." Plus, it afforded her a view of her friend, Gabe, trying to ride the poma solo for his first time right behind her.

It was at this point that I learned a fine-tuned rescue trick. When Gabe invariably fell, his dad, Marko, riding the poma behind him, would reach down and grab him in a drive-by scoop, carrying him in whatever position presented itself to the top. It was like scooping up a lacrosse ball on the fly. Gabe was so conditioned to this technique that he'd lie where he fell and simply extend his arms up in the air like a referee indicating a touchdown, while waiting for salvation.

CHAIRS AND GONDOLAS

Fortunately, there will come a time when you get salvation from the dreaded surface rides in the form of airborne lifts.

At first, riding a chair with your kid will seem intimidating, what with a giant head-high hunk of metal whipping around a bullwheel about to clip Junior in the noggin. Then comes the dangling hundreds of feet in the air part, your kid's inseam so small that his legs are straight on the seat with skis pointed skyward.

Granted, it's not a ride at Disneyland. But it doesn't have to be intimidating. Today's high-speed quads and six-packs slow down for loading and unloading, and if you're on an older-school slow lift, there's usually still plenty of time to scamper up the loading ramp. Plus, since many lift ops in ski resorts have their Ph.D.s, they're more than qualified to punch the stop button should things go awry.

The first hurdle is the maze. With pole-less kids, your best bet is to pull them through the line by extending your ski pole. Once you get into tighter quarters, put your poles in one hand and pull your kid with your other hand, which keeps them closer to you. Note to the foresighted: try to have your kid's ticket out beforehand, so the checker isn't rooting through umpteen underlayers to the stares of impatient skiers behind you.

At the loading ramp, continue pulling your child's hand with your own and then, when the timing's right, shuffle forward to get to the loading zone before the next chair does. This is where most mishaps occur. The parent/child unit fails to arrive in time and one or both of them miss the proverbial boat.

Rule number one of chair loading: don't be afraid to have the attendant slow it down. Who are you trying to impress? The girl behind you? The repercussions aren't worth racking up any cool-guy points, and it's not really something worth bragging about at the bar afterward. "Yep," you could boast to your barmates over your Manhattan, "I got little Johnny to the ramp without the lift even slowing down."

The only other place for a potential miscue is in the lifting-of-said-kid onto the chair. There are two options. You can either have the attendant help (in which case you have to ask, and make sure your kid is on the attendant's side), or you can do it yourself. It's not that hard, especially on detachable quads that slow down the process. On fixed-chair lifts, the chair comes rather quickly, so you have to act fast. You'll develop a favorite side. I put my poles in my left hand and Casey to my right. When the chair comes, I reach my arm around her back, place my right hand under her right armpit

and my left pole-carrying hand under her other armpit, and then lift her onto the seat.

It's tougher with two kids. Your best bet is to sit in the middle and ask the attendant to help with one while you focus on the other. I tried to handle both Brooke and her friend once at the same time on Steamboat's Sunshine lift, and Brooke ended up dangling from my arm as the chair left the ground.

Once everyone is safely on, pull the safety bar down. It's not so much that they'll be able to reach the footrest, but your trepidation will be at rest knowing your kids are secure. If there isn't such a bar, make one by putting your poles across their laps and holding it with your hands. Not using a footrest isn't going to gain you accolades from your peers.

There are two options for the actual sitting. Since their leg spans barely equal the seat depth, either slide them forward enough so their knees bend at the chair's edge, which puts them precariously close to the abyss below, or move them all the way back against the backrest, which leaves their feet jutting skyward, with no knee bend at all. For the latter technique, make sure the edge of the chair doesn't unlatch their rear bindings. This happened to Casey once on Steamboat's Preview lift and we watched her ladybug ski flutter helplessly to the ground, leaving us with a peg-leg descent to retrieve it. Make sure their ski boots are on tight as well. I have another friend whose son once lost both boot and ski to the gravity gods.

Securely on, you'll whittle away the time singing songs, fielding questions, counting pole towers and chairs, giving them snacks, and wondering what the heck you'd ever do in case of an evacuation. When the top comes, tell your kids to lift their ski tips up (which they'll likely be doing anyway), and then help them off by giving them a gentle nudge on the back. A test of maturity comes when they ask to get off by themselves. You can let them, but keep a hand on their backs ready to help just in case.

Loading and unloading is far easier in gondolas. The only problem is that, unlike riding a chair or poma, everyone's skis aren't on their feet, but in your hands and arms. This means carrying everyone's gear again, just like you did from the parking lot. And you have to abandon the over-the-shoulder carrying technique in favor of the vertical-in-hand approach to lessen the chance of shish-kebobbing your neighbor. If it's a long line, you might have to walk a few steps and then put everything down again. Hint: stash everyone's skis and poles (including your own) near the ski school line up front and then pick them up after wading your way hassle-free through the line.

Once in the gondola, anticipate a "Five, four three, two, one... blast-off!" count-down, and your kids moving to the forward portion of the cabin. The beauty of gondo-las is that you can fuss with things you forgot en route. You can slather on sunscreen, tighten ski boots, fix goggles, zip zippers, and do anything else overlooked in the battle of getting them out the door. Details taken care of, your kids can now play patty-cake, tic-tac-toe on the window, sing, embarrass the other riders, and talk about the upcoming day as you rise skyward.

The only really hard part is untangling the mass of gear inside the cabin at ride's end and somehow getting back out the door with it. More than one parent's skis have continued around the bullwheel while the parent dutifully tracked down goggles, hel-mets, gloves, poles and skis from everyone else. I'd bet a kid or two has accidentally made the round-trip ride as well.

Family Skiing

It hit me when Brooke was six and Casey three while we were on a ski vacation to Winter Park and all four of us were actually making turns down an easy blue run, my wife and I telemarking behind our come-of-age offspring. We'd made it. We were in our own Cheerios commercial and were actually skiing as a family.

It's a big accomplishment, and ski hats off to you when and if you get to this point. To get there, you'll go through all the trials and tribulations above, and even more that I haven't listed. But it's worth every tantrum, dropped pole and sunburn.

I still remember times from when I was a kid—breaking my ski in half in the back bowls of Vail; not looking uphill in Aspen and careening into someone skiing with his leg in a cast; losing my ski, boot and sock all in one wipeout at Lake Eldora; my first pair of skis with "real" metal edges; and playing a young Al Capone by figuring out a way to get multiple Reese's Peanut Butter Cups from a vending machine and then selling them on the bus ride home—and I'm looking forward to creating these memories and more for my kids.

Luckily, Steamboat is conducive to it—the Daddy/Daughter Downhills, the Soda Pop Slaloms (which this year fielded more than 300 children), and the street events during the Winter Carnival, where kids on skis get pulled behind horses down Lincoln Avenue. With these, of course, come the more harrowing memories, like the time I took Casey into the skier cross course and she veered off track into a ragdoll tumble that brought the lift operator scurrying down. And this past year's Winter Carnival, when, at age six, she asked for the fastest horse and held on for dear life, not letting go until a block past the finish line and earning a third-place showing among all six- to nine-year-olds. "She's going all the way to Craig, ladies and gentleman!" the announcer blared, referencing the town forty-five minutes down the road. But all these fade in time, replaced by the better ones.

On a family trip to Snowmass, Casey once actually fell asleep on the chair lift, her head resting against my side when it was time to raise the footrest. I'm not saying you should ski your kids this hard, but it's the sign of a good day.

Games Skiers Play

So everything's hunky-dory. You've gotten the gear figured out, gotten everyone on and off the lift, your kids have been through the school of hard knocks, and you're actually skiing as a family. Now keep it fun. If they're bored, your kids will trade their boards for another sport faster than it takes their toes to get cold. Spice up your time on the slopes with some games.

Secret Passages: For some reason, kids have an affinity for finding and following each other through secret passages. These are little trails through the trees that often connect slopes, or simply zig-zag all over the place before returning to the same one. Unfortunately for the parent following along, the twistier, narrower and bumpier the better. They're usually riddled with more whoop-de-doo's than the average spine can tolerate. Another drawback for grown-ups: while kids can snowplow in them to slow down, our skis are usually too long to do the same, leaving us careening out of control with errant clumps of powder our only brake pad. But kids savor them to no end, polishing their skiing skills in the process. While skiing these corridors isn't a game per se, it is for the kids, so encourage exploring them as much as possible...or as long as your back can withstand it.

Human Slalom: To do this, you need a group of five or more people. Station everyone down the hill about ten yards apart as human slalom gates, and then have the top skier ski around each one. Once she's rounded the last person at the bottom, have her stop ten yards below, and then the new person at top begins slaloming through the same people. You can make your way down an entire slope this way, teaching your kids to make turns. Just be sure the course doesn't accidentally veer toward the trees or other obstacles, and that your kids stop far enough beyond the last person to keep the turns from getting too tight.

Ski Circles: Another favorite is the old tie-your-poles-together-and-whip-each-other around-in-circles trick. For this, wrap your pole strap around your other pole's basket: you grab one end and Junior the other. While one of you is facing uphill, the other is facing downhill. That person skis to the side while holding onto the end of the elongated pole and then does a quick 180-degree turn to pull the other person around like a skiing push-me-pull-you. It's a perfect way to have fun on long groomers, and you can actually garner momentum with each rotation. Just make sure the slopes aren't too crowded when you enact this human whirlpool.

Ski Under the Legs: One of the simpler games you can do is to have your kids ski under your legs. Keep your stance wide enough that they can get through, but not so wide as to lower your groin unnecessarily. More than once I've been facing uphill, knowing my clearance was suspect, only to have Brooke career toward my privates with her helmet. You can have them go under your legs while you're facing uphill or downhill. Though it means skiing backwards for a short while, facing uphill lets you see them coming. If you're facing downhill, you never quite know when they're going to come schussing through.

Tree Snowfall: So this one, admittedly, is a bit on the dorky side. But I once busied Casey with it for a solid half hour, with her in hysterics. Simply hit a tree trunk with your pole to have snow fall on your child's helmet. Then save the big avalanche for you. Casey liked it so much that we were late for our meeting with Mom.

Resort Features: Take advantage of any and all kid-specific areas ski resorts offer. Most have trails with Disney and other cartoon or animal characters (unfortunately, most in "secret passages"), and many also have kid-friendly terrain parks with mini-halfpipes, rail and box slides, jumps and mini skier cross courses. Just make sure your kids know the full ramifications of speed and getting airborne. Though she aced it the day before, Casey once hit a jump a bit too fast and promptly biffed derrière over Mrs. Pott's tea kettle. But she earned her stripes from this and other wipes, and it was nothing a cup of hot chocolate couldn't placate afterward.

Ski School

Of course, you can bypass all of this and take the route of most by sticking your kids in ski school and paying to let someone else wipe your kids' noses, feed them snacks, fetch dropped poles and gloves, and otherwise teach them to ski. If you can afford it, this is the best alternative and will give your kids proper instruction. It will also enable you to get more skiing in as a result.

Most parents go this route at some point or another, for good reason. You can only teach them so much yourself, and your kids will actually listen to an instructor. When you try to explain to them how to do a snowplow, they often ignore you. They'd rather career into a fence. When an instructor does, they're all hat-covered ears.

The hardest part, at least the first time, is the drop-off, where kids get funneled into various chutes and then herded into like-minded groups according to ability. When it comes time to part ways, some kids go happily while others cry and suffer separation anxiety. The instructors have seen it all so don't worry. Your kids are in capable hands.

If anything, you might feel for the instructors who are taking your kids under their charge (so don't be afraid to tip them afterward). But also remember that unlike you, it's their job. And rest assured that your kids will love it. They're paired with kids of similar ages and ability, and treat it as a giant outdoors Romper Room. Plus, they learn the finer nuances of skiing to boot.

Our parents used to put us on the bus to Winter Park every weekend as part of a program called Chalet Comets. It should have been called Chalet Vomits, because that's what I did every time, showing up at my class with stains hurriedly cleaned off my ski pants at the resort bathroom. It was enough to earn me the nickname "Puke Gene" from my endearing friends. But the classes were great, like babysitting with an additional purpose, and we did it as long as budgets and barfing allowed.

If you live in a metro area within an hour or two of a ski area, enroll your kids in a once-a-week, season-long program, and augment that with family ski trips. As with piano lessons, your kids will learn basic fundamentals from their instructor, and then practice them with you—all in the key of ski.

There is, of course, a critical mass of age involved. Much below three and your child will basically be in daycare, or at best, the magic carpet. Which is fine if you can afford it, and you want to ski with your spouse or older child. After age three, your kids will begin to pick up hints and technique and the fruits will follow quickly.

Ski schools also offer the type of encouragement and camaraderie your kids can never find from family. Consider the awards Casey and Brooke earned at the end of their respective programs just last year. They each came home with framed certificates touting their strengths. Casey's read "Most Likely to Be Heard on the Entire Mountain" and Brooke's heralded "Best Snack Sharer."

SNOWBOARDING

There used to be a stigma attached to snowboarding. Its followers were knuckle-dragging, boxer-short-showing rebels, spawning such jokes as "What's a snowboarder use for birth control?" and "What's the first thing a snowboarder says when he meets you?" (Answers: His personality, and "Sorry, dude .")

Not so anymore. Snowboarding is keeping the snowsports industry alive, and is drawing far more young participants than skiing. Heck, I'm even a snowboarder (and wear boxers, thank you), opting to take my board out half the times I hit the slopes—hit being the operant word. And if it's good enough for me and millions of other converts, it's good enough for my daughters.

The process now is a lot easier than it was back when we saw our first Snurfer under our Christmas tree. It was bright red, had metal staples hammered into the top for traction and a rope extending from the tip to your hand for a modicum of control. We'd take it to the hill in our yard and either careen into the juniper bush or face plant in the street. Today's boards are so user friendly that grandma can join in on the grinding action, and its image is Hannah Montana cool.

The main benefit, naturally, comes down to carrying your kids' gear. Instead of having to lug two skis and two poles around per child, you're down to one simple, easy-to-carry plank. And it even comes with a strap on it, meaning your kid can carry it bandolier-style over her shoulder. Going from four awkward items to carry to one is reason enough to jump on the snowboard bandwagon. But there's more. It's also three fewer items to inevitably forget or lose.

Add the boots to the equation and there's more reason to celebrate as a parent. Instead of locking your kid into slippery cinder blocks that make him walk like Frankenstein or bride thereof, snowboarding boots are slipper-soft and comfortable, allowing your kids to actually walk, and even run, by themselves. Since your kids don't need you as a human crutch, this frees your hands to more easily carry gear and grab your wallet.

Still, I'm of the persuasion that it's easier to get your kids solid on skis first so they can go into snowboarding with a better grasp of the whole gravity sport thing. They'll

know how to read the terrain, keep their momentum on the flats, get on a lift, and, yes, cut off skiers.

When a kid falls, or gets stuck on the flats on a pair of skis, he can get up with the help of independent leg motion and then skate or pole his way downward. Not so on a board. Since both feet are locked down, you have to keep your momentum going. The only way around it is to take one foot out and push off the snow as you would a skateboard on the pavement, which is a hard concept for kids to grasp.

If your child wants to learn, it's easier for you, the parent, to be on skis the first few go-arounds. That way, if your child falls and needs help you can skate or pole back up to her. If she drops a glove, you can retrieve it. If she sits down and cries, you can hike up to offer console. Once you're below them on a snowboard, it's game over unless you grovel.

Conversely, kids also like to see their parents in the same compromised position as they are. So they'll love it if you give snowboarding a whirl as well and biff alongside them. It humanizes you. If you do give it a go, try to stay above your kids so you can better help them. It's hard to crawl uphill with an anchor on your feet.

The same theory holds if you're a boarder and your kids are learning to ski. You might find it easier if you go out on skis as well for a while—at least until they stop dropping their gear all over the mountain and testing whines. Otherwise, be prepared for a few grovel sessions.

To spare you these problems, a lesson is the best bet. Instructors have time-proven ways of handling the above scenarios and more.

Already an accomplished skier, Brooke has taken two snowboard lessons, one per year for the past two years. And she's loved it, primarily because she, too, recognizes it as cool. And now Casey, at age 6, is asking about it also. Baggy pants can't be too far off.

But while snowboarding is technically easier to learn than skiing—someone of even PeeWee Herman coordination can be riding blues after a few days—it also has a school of harder knocks. The problem is that darn bottom edge. Catch it and you're flipped over faster than the blueberry pancake you cooked at breakfast. There's simply no recovery time. Catch that edge and you're going down hard. And you'll cringe every time it happens to your protégé.

Fortunately, kids are young and rubbery and absorb such hits far better than we brittle adults. And evolution teaches them to learn faster than the previous generation, resulting in fewer spills. Combine this with a slew of kid-sized products—including tiny, rad-graphic boards, boots and pants—and don't be surprised if it's your own kid saying "Sorry, dude," to you next time you're out together.

TELEMARK SKIING

Some people just plain like to make things harder. These are the folks who have four kids instead of two, three dogs instead of one, and make their own pasta instead of whipping out the Top Ramen. They're also the ones who telemark ski instead of regular alpine.

If snowboarding has a stigma, so does telemarking. But it's changing. It used to be associated with tree-hugging, raisin-eating, granola-making, knicker- and balaclava-wearing sorts who generally shun conventional norms. "What the...why don't you go back in the woods where you belong?" the alpine-lofted barbs would go.

While it's still considered earthier than snowboarding and alpine skiing, all that's changed. And it, too, is the perfect pastime to do with your family.

Telemarking is a sort of cross between cross-county skiing and alpine skiing. You're still employing gravity to make turns, but instead of having your heel locked down like a fixed mortgage, it lifts free, allowing you to perform telemark turns and face plants with equal aplomb.

As I found with our kids, the sport is also perfect for skiing with your kids – especially when they're in the early years. If you're an accomplished alpine skier, being stuck on greens and blues while your kids learn the ropes doesn't really test your mettle. Throw on a pair of teles, however, and now you're back to the knee-dropping drawing board. It handicaps you and lets you practice something aside from wiping runny noses. On the same wide open groomers where your kids are wreaking havoc, you can work on perfecting your own turns, weighting the back and forward skis just so and arcing the outside of the rear ski's edge into the inner edge of the front ski for one giant, Thanksgiving turkey-like carve.

Another benefit is the free heel when it comes to fetching gear or loved ones. Perform a mitten rescue on alpine skis and you're either side-stepping or herring-boning your way back uphill. Telemark bindings let you kick and glide—or at least scooch around more easily—whether you're pulling your child across the flats or hustling back to see why he's crying. They're also lighter than alpines, meaning you can carry them more easily in one hand, freeing up more carrying capacity for kids' gear. You'll also inevitably fall more, which makes your kids feel better about their own miscues.

Aside from the learning curve it involves, the main drawback concerns following your brood through those God-forsaken, bumpy secret passages. Where on alpine equipment you can avoid bone-jarring whoop-de-doo's fairly easily, on tele gear your heels aren't held fast, meaning that every once in a while you pitch overboard.

At first your kids won't know the difference between telemarking and alpining. It's all skiing, and they both lead to hot chocolate at the end. While they can discern the difference between snowboarding and skiing, the two skiing cousins are too closely related for them to notice that on one, the heel is free and the other, locked. But right around the time they start noticing differences in anatomy among genders, they'll be able to tell the difference between the two skiing disciplines.

While the thought of a child saying "I don't alpine, I tele," might seem a bit snooty, there are concrete advantages to kids taking up the sport. My friends Todd and Julie gave their kids telemark equipment once their kids started getting too out of control on regular alpine gear. It was a way to shackle or handicap them and slow them down, they reasoned. Better they fall slowly more often, than hit a tree once, fast. In a nod to Darwinism, it's also a way to keep them off runs they shouldn't be on. Of course, this didn't work for my friend Bill's kid Bennett. He was ripping on teles at age 4, and they didn't slow him down one bit.

Telemarking also appeals to kids' inevitable counter-culture embrace. If everyone else—especially parents—is on alpine gear, well by golly I'm going to try telemarking. To that I say, support whatever encourages them to get outside.

Brooke asked to try them when she was eight, so we rented her a pair. She flailed around all day with her friend, Madeline, and they had a blast. She also tried them on a three-day hut trip, adorning them with skins for the climb to the cabin and runs once there. She's not a convert yet and we're not pushing her to be. But we figure there are far worse things she could be experimenting with.

RESORTS CATERING TO KIDS

Snowmass, Colo.: As the second largest ski resort in Colorado (bigger than Aspen, Aspen Highlands and Buttermilk combined), you'd think Snowmass might be better at losing kids than wooing them. But with a special kids' area with reindeer, tree-threading secret passages lined with Disney characters, three terrain parks, and wide open groomers, it's about as perfect a family resort as you'll find. In addition, 95% of its lodging is ski-in/ski-out, meaning easy hand-offs and access to macaroni and hot chocolate. There are also campfire sing-a-longs with s'mores, a kids' crafts center, nature programs, Nordic trails, and fireworks and big air displays right outside your window. If your kids are sick of the slopes, they can try a hot air balloon, dogsled or snowmobile ride, take to the water slides at the rec center, or head to the only zipline in the country where you start off on skis. In 2008, the resort completed a new, interactive, 25,000-square-foot children's center at the base village. Info: www.aspensnowmass.com

Steamboat Springs, Colo: Try as you might, you'll have a hard time losing your kid anywhere at Steamboat Springs, Colorado. The resort's new Mountain Watch program provides all kids in lessons, as well as free-skiing families wanting to take advantage of the program, with radio-frequency collars so parents can track their location from kiosks the whole time they're on the mountain. Lose your kid at the lodge? Simply find where he is

by surfing a nearby kiosk. The resort also has a kid-friendly poma at Rough Rider Basin, acres of family-suitable terrain in aptly named Wally World, and both a kids' and more grown-up terrain park, featuring Mavericks, one of the biggest Superpipes in the country. Info: www.steamboat.com.

Waterville Valley, N.H.: Waterville Valley, N.H., offers special Kid's Venture Kamps, which are ski school programs that combine lessons, rentals, lunch and rewards. Rentals are provided in a special Kids Kamp rental facility to make things easy, and while enrolled, kids travel around to special kid-sized WV Zones where they can earn special pins that they can wear on a special Kamp bandana. Best yet, entry to the ski school building is through slides and chutes. Info: www.waterville.com.

Smugglers Notch, VT: There's a reason why Smuggler's Notch, Vt., has been ranked number one for family programs by *Ski* magazine for more than ten years. Its Treasures Child Care center has giant fish tanks in every room, and even one-way mirrors for parent viewing. Kids do homework in a room called The Sorcerer's Hall, with a magician teaching magic tricks while offering hints on doing better at school. When it comes to skiing, kids start off in the Little Rascals on Snow program before graduating to become a Discovery Dynamo and eventually a full-fledged student at the resort's Snow Sports University. Teens, meanwhile, can hang out in Teen Alley, boasting high-speed Internet, games, music and more. Info: www.smuggs.com.

CROSS-COUNTRY SKIING

Alpine skiing with your kids is all good and fine, but it's expensive. As a more affordable alternative, try cross-country skiing as a family. While it might not offer the adrenaline rush of alpine skiing, that can be a blessing to parents chasing their kids down the hill. Except at established Nordic centers, there are also no lift tickets, speed-crazed skiers and snowboarders to dodge, or crowded cafeterias to negotiate and further tap your kid-lightened wallet.

While they won't win you any downhill style awards, cross-country skis are infinitely lighter than their alpine brethren and come with bindings that attach to the toe of your boot, allowing your heel to lift to provide a "kick and glide" motion of propulsion. Of course, the free heel also provides for a kick and fall motion as well.

With the boots as flimsy as a pair of bunny slippers, expect your kids to be Bambi on ice their first time out. If they're anything like Casey and Brooke — who are at least halfway coordinated due to their, ahem, parents—they'll splat down face first the first time, and then turtle over backwards the next, with tips pointed skyward. Then you'll watch them grovel up and do it all again.

The skis are just plain hard to get a purchase on. When I took Casey out for the first time this year, she fell thirty-nine times in a mile-long loop (yes, she counted), landing in every position imaginable. The second time out she dropped the tally to a proud seventeen. But she still came back for more throughout the year, saying in her cute little voice, "I want to go crunch-crosstree skiing."

Hopefully your kids will be in a good mood about trying it—and will have had a good night's rest the evening before—because they're going to need every ounce of energy they can muster to clamber back up after each fall. They're going to fall backward, forward, sideways and sometimes every which way all at once. Once Casey fell flat on her stomach, only to immediately start eating snow with her tongue. If you're just starting out, you likely will too, which will make your kids feel better in commiseration.

Because of this, don't plan to set any distance records your first few ventures out. Try it at a park, local field or frozen lake—with no more of an itinerary than to make a complete circle, ending right back where you started.

One of the biggest impediments will likely be the cold. Make sure your kids are dressed appropriately, from boots and gloves to hat and pants, but that they're also wearing layers so they can discard extra clothing if they get too hot. It also helps to bring a thermos of hot chocolate to perk up spirits. Regardless of weather and whining, stick with it. Cross country skiing is a great family activity, once all the kinks are ironed out.

Speaking of ironing, at least that part of the equation is out of the picture now. In the olden days, people would pine tar their skis and iron on wax to create a kick pocket in the middle of the ski. Nowadays, all that's done for you at the factory.

There are two types of bases you can choose from: wax or fish scales. If you're just starting out, go with the fish scales—but don't tell your kids that's what they're called. It will only confuse them. I told Brooke that's what she had on her skis and received a resounding "Huh?" as a reply, followed by a comment about being mean to fish.

Fish scales are a series of tiny ridges along the ski's bottom that slide one way and grip the other. They're hassle-free and work in most snow conditions and temperature tantrums. The other option is go the wax route, meaning you have to decide what flavor of kick wax to rub on your skis—and your kids' skis—each outing. (Don't let them lick it—green isn't lime, and red isn't cherry.) In Steamboat, it's invariably Extra Blueberry. But it can range from green for cold days on up to red for warm days, and if you guess wrong, your kids will be the first ones to let you know by playing Bambi.

When it comes time to step onto the snow and get going, the first step is stooping over (why is it that all kid activities require the parent to stoop over?) and fiddling with their bindings. Kids won't be able to fasten them themselves, so you'll have to snap them in. There are two types of bindings: boots with a bar in front of the toe, which snaps into an appropriate binding; and a three-pin set-up, where tiny Polly Pocket-sized pins in the binding fit into receptacle holes in the boots.

Both are equally frustrating. You'll be down on your knee, lifting your kid's leg high into the air into a new yoga position to whack snow off the boot's bottom so it will fit. Then, just when you get it clean, your pride and joy will step into the snow again, forcing you to start all over. Hint: put your children's bindings on first, and then hope that they can stand up on them long enough for you to put your skis on.

Next come the poles. As with alpine skiing, your kids—and you by association—will have as much trouble getting their mittens through the tiny pole straps as they will with the actual skiing. It's like threading the eye of a fishing lure, except the line has five wiggling digits. Inventors made cross-country poles so the straps are adjustable, but for some reason they're always too tight. It's also hard for kids to figure out how to hold the grips. They'll try every variation but the correct one, where the hand goes through the loop and then over the strap, so they're holding onto strap and pole.

Once you get this far, you're nearly home free—except for the actual skiing part. Unlike alpine skiing, you don't need any special harnesses or other gadgets to get your kids going. If you can walk, you can cross-country ski. It's just walking with banana-peel-slick skis on your feet, with the benefit of poles to help with balance.

At first your kids will take small stutter steps without benefiting from any glide. Walking, they'll reason, would be much easier. But eventually they'll get the hang of it and you'll be crunch crosstree skiing as a family.

Doing so opens up a world of winter opportunities, not the least of which is exploring new terrain. While you can cross-country ski virtually anywhere there's snow, pick a location with a groomed trail or packed out road before playing Jeremiah Johnson and heading into the bush on your own. Also, check around for resorts catering to cross-country skiers. Most have groomed trails for traditional touring and skate skiing, the latter a great alternative for parents looking for a little more cardio. We'll often go to a Nordic center and take turns kick and gliding with the kids while the other parent skates on kid duty to go skate skiing.

You can also make an actual vacation out of it. Many resorts, like Devil's Thumb and Snow Mountain Ranch in Colorado, are destination-type resorts where you can rent cabins or lodge rooms right on the trail. Combine that with sledding, snowshoeing, igloo-building, snow angels and snowball fights, and you have a weekend as packed as your trails.

One of our best "expeditions" every year involves the *Great Cross-Country Ski Christmas Tree Hunt*. We go the same place every year, a trail up on Buffalo Pass outside Steamboat, and now everyone in our family can ski in under their own power. Granted, Casey still has a few falls; you can tell where she's been by following the crater marks in the trail. But they both love it – even if they look forward to the tree more than the actual cross-country skiing, as it means getting one step closer to getting presents. But the quest at least tricks them into skiing.

We bring the same sled that we used to haul Casey around in and Brooke before her, only now, we use it for hauling our tree instead of toddlers. The kids help with the selection process, often skiing away through the snow in search of better offerings, and then Dad gets to work with the saw. When Casey was four, I stomped out an area in the snow as a playpen of sorts, leaving her there with a cup of hot chocolate to fend off the wolves. The unpacked snow reached up to her shoulders, creating a natural barricade, corralling her inside.

A couple of times each winter we'll even cross-country ski to school, heading up the trail in Butcher Knife Creek to Strawberry Park Elementary. It's a semi-organized Ski to School Day, complete with a medal given to the kids at the end inscribed with the words, "I skied to school today!" On one of last year's excursions it was freezing out, about 5°, which didn't make matters any easier – though it did make them anxious to get to school. The kids all met at Stanley Park, geared up and ready to go. After much ado about bindings, we let the kick and gliding begin. The kids were veritable Chatty Cathies the whole way, blabbing about this and that while completely ignoring their white noses. With the parents behind carrying their books, they shuffled all the way to the school's front door, feeling pretty special when they skied past the traffic guard and finally arrived, medals in hand.

Crunch Crosstree: The Early Years

Before your kid is stable enough to cross-country ski on his own, you have a couple of options for still getting out. The first is using a kids' pack (see Bring 'em Along for the Ride: Backpacks in the Downhill Skiing segment). If you're stable on your skis, and have your kid bundled up, these can work great—though it's bit harder to get their boots through the tiny leg holes than it is tennis shoes in the summer. Just don't lose your footing on your skis and topple backward (believe me—I've done it), or inadvertently bend over to fix your binding, leaving little Billy dangling like a bat.

A better alternative is a sled, which serves much like a burley behind a bike. You can use them while skate skiing or cross-country skiing, letting you squeeze a work-out in while your brood is high and dry behind you. The only downfall is that, while your kids don't have a whip in hand, they might as well have. You'll notice the extra weight from the first step.

While you can find ultra-trick ski sleds these days that serve triple duty as burleys, joggers and ski sleds with the aid of a few attachments (I have one friend who jerry-rigged his burley into a ski sled himself), the best we've found are those that come with some sort of enclosure to keep Junior out of the elements. You can also use non-enclosed sleds, like those for hauling gear on Arctic expeditions, by wrapping your child in the canvas shell and having his goggle-covered head poke out the far end like a gopher, but it's forcing matters to do so often.

Complete with a backrest and waist and shoulder straps for the rider, as well as a clear plastic window to look through, our enclosed Kinder Shuttle (www.wildernessengineering.com) lets Casey nap out of the elements in her own little cocoon when not staring at my backside slogging up a hill. We unroll a sleeping bag and stuff it inside, creating snores before we're even out of the trailhead.

But it's not exactly cozyville for the parent pulling the load. If you're in shape and on the flats, it's not too bad. The first five minutes will feel like you're skating through molasses, but after a while you'll get used to it. Get to a hill, however, and be prepared to kick into turbo drive. Hint: if you're on cross-country skis, keep extra wax handy so you don't slip backwards more than necessary; if you're skate skiing, sorry, no hints to make it easier.

If you're kick-and-gliding in hilly terrain, put skins on to eliminate slippage. Then you can take them off for the downhill ride home, not even having to lift your ear flaps to hear the "Wheees" of your passenger in the back.

For all their virtues, sleds also have a few drawbacks. They tend to get bogged down in powder, so stick to the beaten path. Also, make sure that path is wider than two ski widths. If you're following a simple two-track trail, sleds tend to ride up the walls like a bobsled and tip over, leaving your kid dangling sideways and you with an awkward rescue.

When your kid graduates from the sled and is ready to venture out on skis of his own, bring the sled as back-up. You won't notice it behind you if it's empty, and it makes a nice Plan B so you can keep going after your child tires.

Your kid's first cross-country set-up likely won't be overly high-tech. It'll probably be a pair of plastic skis, with plastic bear-trap-type bindings that fasten around the toe of any winter boot. But though it looks good in the store and under the Christmas tree, and will give you a warm fuzzy about Junior's first skis, don't get too attached; these plastic jobbies are actually fairly worthless, offering little grip and even less support. Ours was a puke-green pair for Casey that she used exactly once, promptly falling on her butt. Then we got her a real pair, and saw her turn into Casey Jones.

HUT TRIPPING WITH TODDLERS

Call us psycho, but when our clan of friends first started procreating, we kept right on doing the things we were doing when we weren't blessed with child. One of these was going on hut trips once or twice a year, where you ski into a cabin for a few days and backcountry ski the surrounding mountains.

The beauty of this type of trip is that, unlike backpacking, you don't need to carry shelter, stoves, cooking gear or ground pads. All that's provided for you at the cabin. Just bring clothes, food and a sleeping bag.

If only it were that simple. Kids add a multitude of dimensions—like introducing a variable to a perfectly working math equation. First, you have to get them in there, which, in the early years, means loading them into sleds pulled by ever-weakening parents. Then you have to pack along mountains of additional gear, from kids' skis, poles and boots to their additional snacks, clothes, sleeping bags and blankies. It's a lot of work, and makes you reconsider the distance you need to ski, as well as your sanity. Unfortunately, we never really took distance into account, and kept going to the same huts we always did: the Taggart/Wilson cabins outside of Aspen, Colorado. They required a seven-mile ski in, and kids riding behind in sleds because we, and they, didn't know any better.

This is when we first started noticing the respective advantages and disadvantages of sleds vs. packs. While sleds let the ground shoulder the load and can carry more gear, you have to fuss with them more, especially when they list to the side. Packs put the weight on your back, which also isn't ideal. They also can't hold as much, meaning gear often gets strapped to the outside. The downfall of adding kids to the equation is that, at least until they can carry some of the load, you'll often be using both pack and sled at the same time. While mountaineers like Ed Viesturs might be able to handle this, it's not much fun for us mere mortals.

But all would be right with the world again once we arrived at the cabin. We'd unload, get settled in, and the kids would find cozy spots on the beds and play games by the fire. While other parents were skiing, the ones with the short straws would take the kids outside to play games and build forts, and then everyone would regroup for dinner, hot chocolate and more games before snuggling into bed.

The game changed considerably when everyone started having Kid Number Two. Then it just became too much work, both logistically and during the gear-laden ski in. So that's when we started targeting closer cabins. But even that's not foolproof.

I once took Brooke, solo-dad style, up to a friend's cabin for a simple overnight trip. It was only a half-hour drive from Steamboat, and, had we done it right, only about a half-mile ski in. No problem, I figured, to leave in the late afternoon and ski in the dark if we had to. The car got stuck in a snowbank while I was trying to park. After trying to wrestle it free, I decided to leave it there and deal with it the next day. By now it was dark and snowing. That's when I discovered that the batteries were out on one of the headlamps. As we skied up the road, sometimes I'd let Brooke wear it, and sometimes I'd wear it, all the while keeping a lookout for a track to the left that led to the cabin.

Whether it was the darkness, billowing snowflakes or my own ineptitude, we then overshot the trailhead by a good half hour. So we backtracked, finally found the trail, and skied to the cabin. That's when we discovered that it hadn't been used in a while, and had to dig it free of snowdrifts. By the time we had a fire going inside and soup on the stove, any thoughts I had of father-daughter bonding time playing games were absorbed by my daughter's snores.

But even waiting around the next day for someone to pull our car out of the bank didn't scar Brooke on the hut trip concept. A year or so later, we banded together with a group of five other sanity-challenged families and headed for a mid-winter trip to Vance's Cabin, a 10th Mountain hut near Ski Cooper off Colorado's Tennessee Pass. The key was bringing other families—the kids had friends along, and so did the parents. Just as important, the ski in was only three miles, far less than our earlier trudges to Taggart/Wilson, with only 556 feet of elevation gain.

Even that, however, can be formidable for children and gear-saddled adults. Our mistake was one of hut trip hubris. Thinking it an easy ski in, we brought the

HUT TRIP HINTS

- Make sure you know your route and have all the necessary maps, compasses and navigation gear
- Arrive at the trailhead early and give yourself plenty of time to reach your destination
- If your kids are riding in a sled, make sure they have the right gear to stay warm
- Plan your trip for spring instead of mid-winter; it's warmer and stays light longer
- While weight is at a premium, bring along one little comfort item per child; it'll make the hut feel more like home
- Don't go overboard; pick a hut close to the trailhead. Your kids will have more fun skiing in two miles than they will if it's ten.

HUT TRIP GAMES FOR KIDS

Hanging in a cabin is what a hut trip is all about. So make it fun with the following hut trip games for adults and adolescents alike.

12-pack Pick-up: All you need for this is either an empty cardboard 12-pack container (from whomever was dumb enough to lug up its contents) or a freestanding paper bag, that, and a set of good teeth and the limberness of Nadia Comaneci. To start, have players take turns standing on one foot and bending over and picking up the box or bag with their teeth. Those who can do it advance to the next round. Once everyone's gone, the fun begins: peel off an inch or so of the box or bag's height and have everyone try again. As long as people can bite it, keep the cycle going until there's only an inch or two left. The last person to do it (without pulling a groin) is the winner. Hint: tell kids to get their hands out in front of their faces should they fall when the going gets tough; young Bridger, 7, once failed to do so, schmacking his schnoz.

Butt Darts: What, might you ask, are butt darts? And is it something you really want to be teaching your kids? Fear not, oh fanny-frightened ones. It's simple and relatively harmless. What you need: a handful of backgammon chips (or other similarly sized objects); and a small cup. What you do: put those well-honed glutes to work by cramming a chip between your cheeks (pants on, of course) and then waddling towards a cup placed on the floor, where you aim and fire. Those who make their deposits on target advance to the next round, where you add another chip to the arsenal. Then whoever tallies the most direct hits, wins. Like the bag-grabbing game above, it's a game where the kids are on equal footing with the adults. Just ask Lily Starkey, 7, who beat us all by kerplunking four chips into the cup.

kitchen sink, even though the cabin had a perfectly good one. It's hard to go minimalist on such a trip. For some of the kids, we brought cross-country gear as well as alpine gear so they could have more control on the ski out. We also brought sleds and inner-tubes to use at the cabin, sleeping bags and clothes for everyone, and didn't bother with lightweight, dehydrated food. Instead we brought fare we'd normally cook at home, and beer and wine for the evenings' libations. Three miles or not, all this had to fit on either our backs or in the sleds behind us, a few of which kids were riding in. It was Grapes of Wrath Gone Skiing, with several parents having to take multiple trips, like setting up high camps on Everest, just to shuttle in the gear.

Once at the cabin, the kids had a blast and soon forgot the effort it took to get there. And it instilled the lesson that oftentimes you have to work hard for life's rewards. They took rides on the sleds on a hill outside, made snow angels and igloos, and then put on their pajamas for cozy time inside. And the parents had a blast too, taking turns skiing and watching the kids.

Despite the fact that Paige accidentally put three cups of vodka in the cornbread instead of water, and that young Annika got sick and kept everyone up all night (from a bug, not the cornbread), it was one of our most memorable kids trips yet. But we also learned our limits. My wife and I have made a vow to lighten the load next time, including no doubling up on ski gear, no heavy foodstuffs, and only one stuffed animal apiece. We'll see how it goes this year when we head to Janet's Cabin—hopefully, we'll remember our vow.

KIDS SKI EQUIPMENT 101

Helmets: Many resorts are now part of a new children's helmet program called Lids on Kids developed by the National Ski Area Association (NSAA), aimed at increasing helmet use among kids. The initiative requires all children ages 12 and under enrolled in a lesson to wear a helmet (www.lidsonkids.org). When it comes to fitting your child's noggin, err on the side of snugness. Make sure it fits securely (a helmet isn't one of those things your child should "grow into"). Experts recommend that your kid's eyebrows should still be able to move up and down, but without pressure points or cutting into the back of their neck. If it's too low on the head they won't be able to see, too high and it won't protect. Most ski shops have tapes for sizing, measured in centimeters around the forehead. You should also be able to get two seasons out of a helmet; check with your local shop about trade-in programs. Also make sure your child's goggles fit the helmet opening without leaving a David Letterman-like gap, and always fasten the chinstrap. Most importantly, instill the need to always stay in control.

Skis: When it comes to kids' skis, graphics are as important as construction. If your kids like the design, they're that much more prone to wanting to use them more. That said, and knowing that most of today's models will work for your kids' foray onto the slopes, instructors advise that when the skis are placed upright, the tips should fall anywhere between your kids' chin and nose when they're standing with the ski boots on. And don't be afraid of a slight hour-glass shape to them (known as sidecut). It will help them initiate and carve turns. As with boots, most shops offer season rental packages. Hint: in the early years, try a pair with small fish scales on the bottoms for when they're messing around on the flats. Casey's favorite pair of skis to this date? The ones with ladybugs.

Boots: Your kids will outgrow their ski boots faster than they'll outgrow their tantrums, so the best bet is to rent them either for the duration of your trip, or for the entire season if you'll be using them often. Most shops offer season rental packages that include boots and skis. Leave the fitting up to the expert at the shop so you don't have to deal with it (or take the blame if they complain later). An even better bet for the pock-

TAIL WAGS HELMET COVERS

Want a surefire way to get your kids to wear their ski helmets? Add some spunk with a custom animal-themed helmet cover. Tail Wags is the creation of Karyn Climans, a Toronto mother of two who started the business in her basement. A former costume-designer for her sons' school productions, she started creating animal helmet covers for two reasons. The first is that she's passionate about helmet safety following a skiing accident in which a helmet saved her life. Statistics show that using a helmet could have prevented 53% of head injuries occurring in children under fifteen. Secondly, she always considered helmets an eyesore until she designed a way to turn her helmet into a fashion statement.

The result: a line of helmet covers that turns kids' heads into everything from dinosaurs, zebras and turtles to cats, teddy bears, lions and bunnies. It even earned Climans Canada's Savvy Mom Entrepreneur Award.

"Parents know the importance of children wearing helmets while pursuing snowsports, but they're often faced with the difficult task of getting their kids to actually wear them," she says. "This provides a fun solution that can be enjoyed by the entire family. If these covers can persuade more children to wear their helmets, then my company has been successful." Info: www.tail-wags.com.

etbook is hand-me-downs. I still remember the bright orange Lange Banshees, complete with jet sticks bolted to the back, that I got from my older brother. And Casey is using Brooke's old boots as we speak. Another option: the new Idea adjustable kids' ski boot from Roces (www.roces.com). The boots are available in three different sizes, each model adjusting in four increments along the sole, and two in height, for six-in-one sizing.

Packs: Several multi-purpose kids' packs exist that work perfectly for skiing with kids in tow, whether you're cross-country skiing or an expert on easy groomers with alpines. The best come with shoulder, chest and waist straps for both the adult and rider, as well as a large compartment underneath for gear. Try Kelty (www.kelty.com) for a full line of options.

Basic Comfort Kiwaski Stroller Ski:
Turn your stroller into a pushable sled with the Kiwaski Stroller Ski. A set of four skis attaches to a stroller's wheels, letting you push your kid through the snow (www.basiccomfort.com).

LABELING YOUR KIDS' GEAR

Face it. Between socks, long underwear tops and bottoms, pants, sweaters, jackets, gloves, helmets, goggles, sunglasses, skis, boots and poles (that's eighteen items alone), there's more gear for kids to lose skiing than there is in any other recreational pastime. Fear not. A company called Stuck On You (www.stuckonyou.biz), has come up with a line of colorful vinyl labeling products designed to help you identify your kids' gear. Personalized peel-and-stick labels come in a variety of sizes and shapes and affix to goggles, skis, poles and other gear that often gets misplaced on the mountain. They're also waterproof and UV-resistant. If you want a more permanent solution for clothing, try the iron-on transfers in white, blue or pink. For boots, try the company's Vinyl Shoe Labels, heel-shaped labels that attach to the rear of each boot.

SLEDDING WITH KIDS

Okay, so sledding isn't skiing or snowboarding. But more people probably sled with their kids than ski and snowboard with them combined, so add it to your list of family, wind-blown-hair activities.

In a way, it's even better for you and your brood than resort-based gliding pursuits as it offers one thing lift-served snowsports don't: the Apple Jacks-burning hike up the hill every time your kids want to do another lap. While many resorts now have rope tows and inner-tubes as yet another cash-generating activity, all you really need to join this burgeoning brigade is a hill, snow and something to slide down on. And, of course, ample health insurance.

While hills and snow have remained largely the same over the years (save for any global warming ramifications), the sleds themselves have changed. From the simple Flexible Flyer invented in 1880, today's sleds have morphed at hyper-drive into an array of high-tech snowtubes, runner sleds and more. Consider the names of some of today's craft: The Mad River Rocket, The Rotator, Uncle Bob's Blast Snowtube, The Race Rocket, the Snosorus, and even the Kaboom Snow Tube. From metal and wood runners to plastic tubs and inflatable race cars, they come in every configuration imaginable. There's even Mountain Boy Sledwork's Double Child Kicksled that looks like it belongs in your living room, not on a snow-covered slope.

Why, when I was young, we had black inner-tubes, the kind that goosed you with their long, protruding valves, age-old Flexible Flyers that wouldn't steer, and wooden to-boggans that looked like a Dutch clog. And we liked it. We'd take said maiming devices up to nearby Chautauqua Park, whose Hahnenkamm of a hill was notorious for causing biffs of biblical proportions. Whether we were riding single atop a tube, or piled four deep on a toboggan, the end result was always the same: a scream-filled, out-of-control, blinded-by-snow careening straight into a bump that sent everyone flying. Perhaps that's where they came up with that Flexible Flyer name in the first place.

In today's liability-plagued age, the city has since put up fences on the hill to pre-empt the activity, and probably for good reason. We were lucky no one got maimed. According to recent studies, between 23,000 and 45,000 sledding injuries require medi-cal treatment each year in the U.S. More disturbing is the fact that an estimated 300 children die each year in sledding accidents.

As our teeth-clenching wipe-outs attest, therein lies the one thing that snowboarding and skiing have over sledding: the ability to steer the confounded contraption that's underfoot, or in sledding's case, rear. The problem with most sleds and tubes is one of control. There's simply little you, or poor Junior riding shotgun, can do to maneuver the thing and slow it down, other than holding on and eventually bailing out for dear life.

Sure, it's nice to think that you can turn a toboggan by getting everyone to lean at the same time. But in reality it's a bump-seeking missile that follows the fall line. It's the same with most other sleds as well, from saucers to inner-tubes. You can drag a foot, but that usually only spins you so you're careening backwards. Big help that was.

The only ones that offer any real semblance of turning are runner sleds and those new plastic jobbies with handles on the side that you can either use as brakes (brakes, what a novel concept) or pull independently to turn. But these can only be used effectively on a super-packed-out slope like a street. And even then their success is suspect.

Runners are especially so. They're designed so that the rider's weight on the runners creates pressure that causes a microscopic layer of snow to melt, creating an invisible layer of fluid that reduces friction and sends rider careening. While you're supposed to be able to turn the thing by pulling and pushing on the front handles, it's rarely the case. Coming into the hairpin from Chautauqua onto Columbine Avenue, rare was the runner-rider who could make the turn without going into a barrel roll first. And hard-packed snow does little to soften the pavement that lurks below.

The best thing you can do? In the early years, go with your kid so you're both in the same proverbial boat. That way you can monitor your bullet's speed. You technically have better judgment, which should lead to a safer ride.

When it's time to cut your kids loose on their own, find a safe spot, not too long, and not too short, and not too steep, but not too flat. You want them to actually move downhill. If you're on a steeper slope, make sure it's not riddled with bumps that act as landmines and has a long, flat run-out to dissipate speed before gliding to a perfect stop. Then be prepared to carry your craft up so they can do it again.

Chapter 4

CAMPING WITH KIDS

"One touch of nature makes the whole world kin."
—William Shakespeare

PERHAPS NOTHING EXPOSES YOUR KIDS to the Great Outdoors better than camping with them. The owl hoots, mosquitos, campfire stories, smoke-dodging and stars all create memories they'll relish for a lifetime, especially when they're back home in the comfort of their own bed.

But not all camping trips are created equal. Since they involve more gear than other outdoor pursuits, and you have to get that gear to your final resting spot, you have several options, from paddling (see Paddling with Kids) to carrying it on your back and using the car.

CAR CAMPING WITH KIDS

If carrying your—and your kids—gear on your back sounds like too much work, you can add some training wheels to the outdoor endeavor by taking your car. In a way, car camping is a lot like setting your tent up in your living room—you're never too far away from the luxuries of home, be it a bathroom, bowl of Cheerios or Barney on the boob tube. Its real beauty, of course, is that it lets Volkswagens and Volvos carry the load instead of your vertebrae.

This means you don't have to rough it—you can bring along whatever luxuries will fit, including barbecue grills, lounge chairs, and yes, even the kitchen sink. Space providing, you can also bring more recreational toys than you can shake a pogo stick at, from bikes and boats to pogo sticks themselves. And you'll want to. Most campgrounds are ideally sculpted for these activities and more, and every toy you bring buys you that much more time with your kids out of your mountain-matted hair.

We were never the car camping type until we had kids. But now we're total converts, our kids bugging us to do so a few times every summer.

On the way home from a weekend car camping trip to Moab, Utah, last fall, Casey summed up her sentiments about it from the back seat by blurting "I love camping so much!" completely out of the blue. It was out of left field, not related to anything whatsoever we might have been talking about. So I pursued the matter.

"What did you like most?" I countered.

She thought for just a second. "Climbing on rocks, and friends," she replied. "Oh yeah, and the baked apples."

The combination of comfort and recreation—and SUVs shouldering the load instead of your shoulders—is largely why car camping is one of the most popular family outdoor activities under the sun (which your car awning shades you from). According to The Outdoor Foundation, nearly 30% of youth aged six to seventeen take part in some sort of camping excursion every year, putting it only behind biking, fishing and hiking in terms of overall participation. There's even a program the Foundation sponsors with the National Wildlife Federation called The Great American Backyard Campout, a national celebration encouraging youth and families to go camping. An estimated 150,000 people take part every year.

Like it or not, most of these outings involve car camping. Even though it involves motorized transportation, which butts heads with human-powered recreation, it's as much of a recreational pursuit as anything else, and one that's custom-made for the whole family. Depending on what you strap atop your gas-eating mule, it also lends itself to other activities mentioned in this book, from hiking and fishing to biking and paddling. Most importantly, however, it introduces your kids to camping as harmlessly as possible, teaching them the basics of everything from weather and shelter to making fires and the perfect s'more (hint: two marshmallows, four chocolate squares). And believe it or not, despite all the packing and preparation it entails, once at camp, parents can actually get a reprieve from their child-care duties. Sure, someone still has to keep half an eye on the instantly scattered children. But left to their own accord, kids easily find things to do, and mom and dad can trade off kid-watching effortlessly.

Camping with kids is certainly nothing new, and I hardly expect the Nobel Prize for championing it. Parents throughout the world have been doing it forever, from nomadic herdsmen to today's yuppie baby boomers. But with today's hectic schedules and urban environments, it's easy to see the activity slip by the wayside.

After his wife passed away, my friend Robbie's dad, Bruce, piled all three of his kids—ages seven, nine and eleven—into a VW camper and took them from Princeton, New Jersey, for a three-month trip all the way to Mexico, camping the entire way. He brought his new girlfriend, Ricca, who got an instant dose of what all's involved in camping with kids, and she may never camp another day in her life. But my friend still remembers it to this day, and your kids will, too.

MARSHMALLOWS

Ahh, marshmallows, those gooey, corner-of-the-mouth-sticking, sugary confections approved by four out of five dentists. Yet for all the cavities they cause and gooey messes they create, like it or not, they're an integral part of camping with kids. So pack a bag of Stay Puff.

It goes without saying that you need the big ones, not the minis you put in hot chocolate. Whoever thought of shrinking marshmallows, anyway? Some confection scientist who called his wife down one night and said, "Honey, I shrunk the marshmallows!"? It's a good invention for hot chocolate, sure, but put the big ones in hot cocoa and they block the spoon from stirring, leave a ring around your lips, and otherwise impede imbibing. But the minis aren't what you want for roasting; you'd never find a prong small enough. You'd have better luck skewering rice with a safety pin.

So, roast the Big Kahunas. But only do so when heeding the Universal Marshmallow Allotment Doctrine. The general consensus among parents is that three each is plenty. Otherwise, your kids will be bouncing off the tent walls. Picture a hyped-up humming bird trapped inside a glass cage.

Thankfully, kids inherently seem to know their limit. It's a self-preservation mechanism, as if they know just when their marshmallowometer is maxed out. On one camping trip, Otis, 4, confessed to me about his binge the night before. "You know those two marshmallows I took out of the bag?" he whispered to me the morning after a night when his mom said he could only have one. "I stuck those two together." He got away with one, and he knew it. Only guilt caused him to fess up—but only to a neutral third party.

The first step is the fire. Don't break out the puffballs right after you throw the Duraflame on. There are enough chemicals in marshmallows that you don't need to add more. Real wood is best, both for flavor and that perfect brown-all-over bed of coals. Let the fire burn down until there are pockets of coals reachable by every child. These are the nuggets that lead to nirvana.

The next step is finding the right stick. While companies make "perfect" marshmallow prongs out of steel and aluminum, show some Jeremiah Johnson fortitude and knife-brandishing ability by venturing into the wilds and slaying the beast yourself. Hopefully, I don't need to tell you how to make a marshmallow stick, even though my wife never seems to be able to. But her nudgings have given me insight. Not too long, not too short; not too strong, yet not too flimsy. A slight bend on the end will make it so, when weighted with marshmallow, the stick bends perfectly onto the coals.

A note to fathers: I did get in trouble once when I gave Casey a stick that was too long and came with too many weird bends, making it a veritable weapon. With kids her age swinging their upper bodies and arms wherever they look, she brandished it like an

uncontrollable sword, almost giving her perfectly roasting neighbor, Emily, a molten, gooey eye. In my defense, aside from flame balls hovering near other kids' faces, it did offer the angles and trajectory she needed to find the perfect cave of coals.

The actual roasting follows one of several philosophies. In one corner, you have the Perfect Tan Clan. In the other, the Charbroiled Crunchers. And the two rarely cross over to the other side. If you like it one way, you usually abhor the other. Sometimes, the Charbroileders might try a black-and-tan, and the Tan Clan a flirt or two with flame. But for the most part, you belong to one of the two camps.

Not that they both don't get along. Because each requires a different environment for their desired result, the two rarely fight over the perfect roasting location. For one, any old flame will do. For the other, nothing but the most perfect bed of coals.

It's easier for kids to join the charbroiled crowd. They just don't grasp the rotation concept that well. The most important thing is to appreciate how your child likes them, and ensure the morsels arrive that way. Adults have their preferences; so do kids.

Eating the gooey, cavity-causing concoctions is another matter. Most Tan Clan connoisseurs prefer a perfect caramelized outer skin a la *crème brulee*, with a slightly melted layer underneath. The confection can then be eaten whole, or the outside layer separately, which lets the inner layer be toasted again. Whatever the end result – rare, medium or well done—they all stick to fingers, cheeks, mouths, and teeth equally. Keep some wipes handy before bedtime, and don't tuck your kids in without brushing their teeth.

A Brief Marshmallow History

Want to impress your kids and friends next time you're sitting around the campfire? Hit them with this little ditty on the history behind those gooey little cavity creators.

Marshmallows can be traced back to ancient Egypt. The confection was originally honey, flavored with the extract from the root of the marsh mallow (Athaea officinalis), which, to no surprise, grows in marshes. Unlike today, where kids fight over sticks and reach their hands into the bag as soon as it's opened, the original marshmallows weren't for the masses, but were reserved for royalty.

The modern marshmallow was developed in the early 19th century in France and Germany. Using the "cast and mold" process, confectioners whipped, sweetened and molded the gummy sap of the mallow root into a light and fluffy taste treat. Starch moguls later speeded the process, leading toward mass production and gelatin replacing mallow root.

Marshmallow manufacturing was revolutionized in 1948 when Alex Doumak, the son of a Greek immigrant candy maker, invented the "extrusion process," allowing the fluffy mixture to be piped through long tubes and then cut into pieces. Voila! The roastable fluff ball as we know it today was born. While it underwent a Cold War-type renaissance of sorts, today only three companies produce marshmallows in the U.S., down from the more than 30 in the 1950s.

For those who cringe at today's ingredients of corn syrup or sugar, gelatin, gum-arabic and flavoring, you can also make them yourselves by using powdered marshmallow root (or gelatin), egg whites, cane sugar, and vanilla extract. But good luck getting them to stick to a stick, whipping up the concoction at camp, or convincing your kid it's better than good ol' Stay Puff.

Campers vs. Tents

You don't even have to camp on the dirt if you don't want to. Fifth-wheels and pop-up campers let you cart along your creatures, as well as the creature comforts of home.

While we're beginning to feel loserish and left out among our circle of car-camping friends, we've always used a tent instead of a camper. Not that they're any better or we have some aversion to sleeping off the ground, it's just that we've never gotten around to getting one. We don't have those perfect little cabinets holding popcorn and hot chocolate and pots and pans, we don't have perfect little silverware drawers, and we don't have bedding packed perfectly, ready to go at the drop of a trailer hitch.

So maybe we have a teensy bit of camper envy (I can think of a worse envy to have). I remember this sinking in like a camper tire in the mud when we were once setting up our tent at a campground for a soccer tournament, and in pulled Elizabeth, solo-momming it in her fancy-dancy pop-up, complete with couch area, table, kitchen and a whopping two bedrooms. While I was still pounding in bent tent stakes, she had everything set up by herself and was already propping her feet up with a cold one while her kids disappeared.

When we head out with other families for weekend get-aways, probably three-fourths of them are now in some sort of camper, with only a quarter in tents. And one of those is my friend Bill, who owns the tent company Big Agnes and wouldn't be caught dead in a camper.

Our own affair with tents is rather ironic since there was actually a brief two-month period in my career when I served as editor-in-chief of a magazine called *RV and Camping, the Voice of the Midwest RVer*. My boss had bought it with the intent of forming a group, and then selling it off, but that didn't stop boxes of stories from arriving at my office and stacking up like cordwood in the corner. Unfortunately, the magazine collapsed like said pile of wood before I could run a self-serving family-camper review.

For us, it's boiled down to budget and laziness. How can you justify a $4,000 camper—the used price—for something you only use three to four times a year? Still, there's the camper converse: if we had one, we'd likely camp more, and it wouldn't be such a pain in the derrière.

The bottom line is that, as lame as it sounds, we've just never gotten around to getting one. We've looked at a few, and once even borrowed a friend's VW camper for a weekend, which I drove while wearing a long-haired black wig out of our dress-up box, along with some oversized, yellow-tinted seventies shades. Our kids loved it, if not my adopted camper-van persona.

This brings up the pros and cons of the camper-van scenario. The main pro: your bed, kitchen and shelter are always waiting like a loyal dog. Simply pile the kids in, head to the hills, pull into camp, pop the top and settle into your hammock. The primary con: while it gives you a portable bed, the portability stops once you're at the campground. You can detach a pop-up or fifth wheel, giving you a stand-alone vehicle for shuttling elsewhere: once you set up a camper van, you're stuck. You can't drive anywhere until it's all packed up again. The other drawback is that unless you can afford it as a third family vehicle, you're stuck driving it around to soccer practice.

Camper jealousy also comes into play. Whether you're in a tow-behind, RV or fifth-wheel, the whole thing can get a little obscene. Now, not only do you have to keep up with the Joneses and their pink flamingos at home, but also when you escape to the Great Outdoors. Some people even adorn their campsites with flamingos.

Drive around any campground and you'll see it: row after row of perfect campers or RVs, each one better than the next. It's like the Grinch rattling off the Christmas décor of Whoville. They come with awnings, mats, indoor/outdoor stoves, perfect little tables, satellite dishes, hoses and more; more accoutrements than we have at home.

For many, it's an art form, seeing how luxurious they can make their camping excursion and how manicured they can make their site. Luckily, our group of friends hasn't been overly bitten by that bug. Aside from Elizabeth's pull-behind, and our lotto-winner friend's plush RV, our peers' best one, owned by Cam, comes complete with a hinged door at the rear for loading bikes, that Voila! turns into a screen-walled porch when not transporting gear.

Of course, the best thing about campers follows the Field of Dreams ideology: if you have one, you will camp. Fork out the dough for one and you'll be more prone to use it. My buddy Paul, blessed with three daughters, has a pop-up and goes with his wife and kids all the time, almost to the point of overkill. He's my car-camping hero. Every weekend he's seemingly rallying somewhere—weekend trips to lakes, and at least two longer, self-serving surf trips to California every year. I feel like Homer watching Ned Flanders from my window. We barely motivate to host a barbecue party on a Saturday night, and he rallies to go camping. And we always feel jealous of him come Monday morning.

But they have history on their side as well, lending more credence to the importance of getting your kids outside camping. He and his wife, Allison, both grew up in families that regularly camped in pop-ups, and the pastime has clearly stuck. Now they're doing the same with their kids, who I'm sure will pass the torch to their brood.

Okay, we can praise campers and all their vinyl-cabinet cousins until we're as blue as the lakes we're camping near. But now, a case for tents.

Those in the tent camp will maintain that they're more versatile than campers, as they can be used backpacking, paddle-camping, bike camping *and* car camping, and they never run out of oil or overheat. When's the last time you carried a pop-up on your back? Tents are like portable forts you can take with you anywhere. Instead of getting underfoot—and wheel—when you're setting up a camper, your kids can even help with a tent, threading poles through sleeves, putting poles into corner grommets, and snapping everything into place. It's a project that gives them a say in their own sleep.

Tents also store more easily when not in use. Rather than an eyesore of a camper taking up your only driveway or lawn space when not in use (which is most of the time), you can stash them away in your crawlspace, garage or closet with the rest of the gear you should use more often. They're also way more affordable, a rarity with anything having to do with kids, and don't turn the car into a gas-guzzling atrocity, saving you more money. You can also set them up in your living room or yard, which often creates just as much fanfare as heading to the hills.

Of course, they also have their drawbacks. They're more of a hassle to set up, and admittedly less comfortable. Just an inch below your tiny pad is dirt, which is no match for the cushions of campers, no matter how many pads and pillows you bring. You're also on the ground, meaning water can pool beneath you no matter how good your trench or ground cloth. Sand and dirt also have one less step to infiltrate the perimeter, and there's no door that automatically swings shut to keep out the bugs.

The worst part, however, is that every time we car camp we have to re-pack the sleeping bags, food boxes and kitchen gear at home, load it all into the car, and then unload it again and set it all up at the campground. Then we have to repeat the whole process heading home, and unload it all again into the garage. Then, if we had fun—which, thankfully, we usually do—we have to repeat the process all over again the next weekend. It's a packing version of Groundhog Day. Because of this, it takes a little more motivation for us to rally than the average car camper.

A case in point came this past summer when I packed our now-tiny, four-door Subaru Legacy for a camping trip to Colorado's Independence Pass. Our daughter had

a swim meet in Aspen, and a bunch of families were car camping for the weekend at an aptly named (for kid camping) campground called Difficult Creek.

With a three-mile bike-path ride down to town and great biking at camp, how could I not bring the bikes? Our car had a cargo box, which we needed for the sleeping bags, pads and tent, so I jigsaw-puzzled two kids' bikes, two grown-up bikes and a trail-a-bike onto the remaining half of the roof rack. Some were upside down and others right-side up, overlapping and fitting in between each other like sardines.

Of course, since it was June after one of the snowiest winters on record, we naturally brought the backcountry ski gear as well. By the same reasoning, since we'd be close to Salida and hadn't seen my cousin, Homer, for a year, and it was the same weekend as the town's river festival, I brought my kayak gear as well. Five bikes (including the trail-a-bike) on half of a Yakima rack, as well as ski and kayak gear, all in and on a Subaru, joining the four of us, our dog, Java, a cooler, food box, duffel bags and camping gear. It was around then that I realized maybe there is something to the pop-up craze after all. While I was busy loading, everyone else was already long gone.

Still, the drive there soothed all thoughts of jealousy. It was great to be getting out, no matter the camping arrangements.

"It looks like those mountains got sun-burned," said Casey as we passed the red bluffs between Glenwood Springs and Aspen. "They didn't remember their sunscreen!"

"Those rocks were born good at balancing," added Brooke as we drove past a series of boulders on a hillside.

Those are the types of comments you just won't hear staying at home. But you also won't have to deal with setting up camp by flashlight.

Thanks to our late start—and fact that we don't have a camper — we showed up at a well-past-sunset-and-s'mores 10 p.m., swinging our flashlights like swashbucklers at the other perfect campsites all perfectly set up by their perfect families with their perfect campers. Then I began the rigging debacle all over again, this time taking everything off so I could access the cargo box, so we could set the tent up, so the kids could go to sleep, so Brooke could wake up for her swim meet, and so I wouldn't be in trouble for the kids getting to bed so late. So off came the straps and bikes in the dark, up went the tent in the dark—ooops, it's the short tent pole that goes through the fly sleeve, not the long one—and out rolled the camp pads and sleeping bags. Accustomed to helping, Casey jumped in and made a bed for Java.

It was cozy, sure. It was just a far cry from turning off the engine, rotating a trailer crank and grabbing the potato chips.

The upside is that we finally got a decent four-man tent — a Big Agnes Pine Island, which has helped our bedding-down tremendously. In the past, we made do with a tall Taj Mahal-looking cheap-o, the kind with inch-thick poles that crown over the center and a manufacturer name like Acme. Now, two large vestibules on each end accommodate Crocs, duffels and dog dishes, with enough room inside for all of us side by side — even though I'm the one who always gets left with my face squished up against the wall. Like the way we sit around the dinner table every night, my wife likes to sleep in the same configuration every time, right to left as you're looking down from our feet: Denise, Casey, Brooke, and squish-faced me, with Java, our dog, at my feet.

Though you can't add quite the bells and whistles to a tent as you can a camper, you can make it home. We keep a weird light rolled up in ours so it's always there, and it's the first thing my daughters look for when they climb in. It has three little bendable arms that fold down to various levels and you can wind it up until the cord is knotted and then let it spin until whole thing looks like flying saucer. Unfortunately, the first time I did this it led to a conversation about aliens and no one could get to sleep for hours, but that's beside the point. We did it again that night as the kids crawled into their cocoons.

We also put a mat out front to catch sand and dirt, and strung clothes to dry over the rainfly lines until it looked like a scene from Sanford and Son.

We made the next morning's swim meet on time, and stayed at the campground long enough—three nights—that we used all our collective toys. The packing and unpacking was well worth any frustration it caused.

The moral is this: it doesn't matter what type of roof you have overhead as long as you're out there sleeping under it and exposing your kids to the wonders of camping. Debate the Roe vs. Wade merits of tents vs. campers all you want; just do it around a campfire.

The First Family Forays

In a way, I feel lucky to car camp as much as we do. We live in an area where it's easy to do—if you call doing anything with kids easy. A half-hour drive and we're at a lake with kids exploding from the car. And unlike our friends Paul and Allison, I didn't camp with my family too much as a kid.

Still, we did wheel into the wilds occasionally, which etched memories of it into my brain like pictographs on a canyon wall. Granted, it was a bit more difficult for a family of eight than it is for our two-child family today. Piling six kids into a station wagon was puzzle enough, let alone fitting all the necessary camping gear around them— all in an era before the advent of rocket boxes. But since there weren't airbags in those days, sleeping bags, pads and tents made a nice substitute.

By definition, there's an inherent flaw in car camping that can't go unmentioned, and one that surfaced quickly in our family. Car camping entails driving, which, for the weak of stomach (as you remember from the Skiing chapter), means tossing any cookies you might have packed for dessert.

She might hate me for revealing this, but my sister, Cathy, was the resident ralpher in our family. Not that I was immune to the malady, either; but odds were, when the six of us were crammed in the station wagon, it was Cathy who led things off. Then the rest of us would follow like dominoes.

It could take place anywhere, from the rear-facing backseat to the middle seat, sandwiched between three other kids. Without air bags, seat belts or even car seats, we'd clamber over camping gear everywhere, and every location yielded the same result. My mom remembers one particular three-week road trip we took to Canada's Banff National Park, when the throw-up stops outnumbered the gas stops two-to-one, making her throw up her arms in despair. She also remembers the certain power it gave my sister. She knew she had the drivers at her mercy, and could stop the car whenever she wanted to, whether feigning or for real.

Soon, we all used it as a tool to stop the car. "I don't feel well," we'd fake, using it solely as an excuse to get out, throw rocks and otherwise thwart our parents' plans.

A more conventional way to kill time en route to our campsites was playing such time-honored car games as Ghost, I Spy, Twenty Questions and others that are still around today. My dad also gave us a nickel for each new wild animal we'd see on the drive. Brooke and Casey hold me to it today, only the ante's now a quarter. The only time he didn't was when we were in Yellowstone and a bear stood on his hind legs and poked his nose into the station wagon's rear seat and began sniffing my sleeping sister, Helen, while the rest of us were all off picnicking.

Don't feel like you have to camp for camping's sake, either. Sometimes it can be a means as much as an end. One situation lending itself perfectly to camping is our kids' team activities. Swim meet like we had in Aspen? Pack the tent with the suits. Soccer tournament? Pull out a map and find the nearest state park. It saves money on sterile hotels, and lets us sleep with the sunset while playing Soccer Mom.

It helps that other families often do the same, providing playmates for the kids. The events turn into a family-fest, filled with bikes, hot chocolate, marshmallows and "This Land Is Your Land" around the fire. At our daughter's annual soccer tournament in Grand Junction, Colorado, as many as ten families camp at James M. Robb Park in nearby Fruita, shuttling kids into games each morning and returning for après activities in the evening. Most families even stay an extra day or two just for the camping and nearby biking.

Admittedly, it isn't the most pristine location. It's only a Frisbee's throw from Interstate 70, and pavement leads to each site. But that makes it perfect for Casey and her bike, and Tristan, who just got new wheels on his skateboard. While true wilderness advocates might disagree, to everyone's kids it's the best site imaginable.

"This is awesome!" chimed Casey the afternoon of our first trip there, clearly enjoying the new-found independence of riding her bike from camp to camp without any supervision.

Even we grown-ups got into the action, lapping the paved campground circle on skateboards behind dogs and bikes, with baseball mitts and lacrosse sticks further complicating matters. And even pavement can evoke conversations about nature. On one lap, Casey noticed a squished toad that looked like it was on the wrong end of a Road Runner truck. All four limbs were splayed out in the horizontal Macarena, with the tongue performing a green Gene Simmons. "Eww, gross," said Casey. "Poor froggy." Later that night, a boy named Cain led a brigade of kids out to catch toads by flashlight. The hunting party came back with three, Casey cradling the biggest.

Every afternoon, we tossed Frisbees, baseballs, lacrosse balls and footballs, atop skateboards, bikes and pogo sticks. Everything was thrown in, it seems, except soccer balls, which is why we were there in the first place. I got in more sports than I usually do in a year, all in one afternoon. Add to that the playground with swings, slides and climbing structures, and the site's access to the Colorado River, where both kids and dogs played fetch, and it's a miracle we got the kids to their soccer games at all.

This brings up one of the most important things to bring on any camping trip, other kids. Sure, it's great to bond, Walton-style, with your family ("Goodnight, John-boy"). But your kids will have far more fun if they have camping peers to hang out with.

And since not all camping sites are created equal, having multiple families lets you congregate at the best one—one lucky set of parents' soon-to-be-trashed quarters—as Grand Central Station during your stay. Combine this with pre-arranged pot-luck dinners and it's a win-win for everyone.

The best thing about having other parents along is the swappage factor. Not among spouses, but for spare time. The fellas can sneak off for a ride or hike while the gals man the fort, and the women can do so while the guys take a turn. Even couples can do things together by leaving their brood in the care of trusted friends.

We've had so much fun camping, in fact, that we've created a bit of a monster. I can't ride down the bike path at home any more without Casey pointing to a random flat area and saying in her cute, high-pitched voice, "That looks like a good camp spot." Once, at one of Brooke's figure-skating competitions in Fort Collins (note to self: avoid figure-skating competitions), I walked Casey around the park outside, only to have her point out "campsites" next to every tree. "There's a good campsite," she'd parrot, pointing to patch of dirt under a pine. She even laid sticks down in the perimeters of tents and fireplaces.

However you approach it—be it backpacking or basing out of your car, using a tent, camper, RV, or hippie van, or going *au naturale* under the stars—camping is one of the best things you can do as a family. It instills life's basic lessons of food, shelter and clothing, which are usually taken for granted at home, and opens kids' eyes to the wonders of wilderness. And it makes them appreciate their own beds at home that much more.

Chapter 5

HIKING AND BACKPACKING WITH KIDS

"Backpacking: an extended form of hiking in which people carry double the amount of gear they need for half the distance they planned to go in twice the time it should take."
—Unknown

HIKING IS WAY SIMPLER THAN jogging, biking or any other gear-laden, bring-the-kids-along activity. In fact, it's one of the most basic things you can do with your brood. If you ignore every other kid-friendly activity in this book, put hiking on the summit of your list.

That's not to say that you have to reach a summit every time you hit the trail with toddlers. Simply going out for a stroll in the woods offers fresh air and perspective on what you can do together as a family.

There's a reason it's so popular: it's fun, simple, and, if you're not venturing far, it doesn't require any other gear than a pair of shoes. That means there's not much equipment for your kids to lose, or for you to invest in.

That doesn't mean there won't be any fussing involved. Utter the word "hike" and you'll likely hear "yikes" in return. For some reason, it just doesn't sound fun to most kids.

To combat this, don't label it as an activity unto itself. Better to just take them somewhere. You're not going hiking, you're going to a lake or waterfall, or even an anthill or mud puddle. The hike should be the means, not the end. And this means that, until your kids are convinced they like it, it helps to have an actual destination. It can be anything...a boulder, flower field, river or even a tree. You can even decide once you're on the trail. Do anything to avoid giving the pastime the stigma of the four-letter word it is.

For better or worse, the term implies walking on dirt. Not pavement or a sidewalk, but good old soil. And maybe that's a selling point you can use on your kids. "Come on, guys! Let's go squish some dirt!"

Hit a bike path or sidewalk and you're going for a walk, not a hike. It's a subtle difference, as grey as the clouds that are often overhead. Venture onto mother earth, however, and you've entered the realm of hiking.

The dictionary defines hiking as "to go for a long walk in the countryside, usually for pleasure." Therein lie the two defining terms: countryside and pleasure. If you go out into the countryside without pleasure, it's not a hike. Similarly, gain pleasure strolling somewhere that's not the countryside and it's not a hike, either. It's semantics, sure, but you need every edge you can get with kids.

While it's certainly not the case in flatter locales, in Colorado the term also usually implies going uphill. Perhaps that's what gives our kids pause about it. While trails in the flatlands often leave your heart rate as level as your elevation, you rarely go for a hike in Colorado without your breathing hiking up as well.

Despite our proximity to rock-outcroppings called the Flatirons while growing up, hiking was never a huge priority for us as a family. That we lived with a politician raising six kids probably had something to do with it. My mom could barely get dinner on the table, let alone laces on our feet. It's not that my parents discouraged it; it's just that there were always more important things to do.

Still, we did venture out occasionally, and those outings are largely responsible for me instilling the same ethos in my own kids today. In following the golden rule, my mom would bait us with destinations as nebulous as gathering pine cones or viewing aspen leaves. Once we even went with her to pick "holly" for the mantle at Christmas, only to later find out that it was poison ivy.

Which brings up that three-leaved devil. If anything can ruin a good hike, it's poison ivy or poison oak. Physically, it won't ruin the outing on the spot. It usually takes a day or two to sink in. But if your kid gets into it, and realizes he's done so, psychologically the hike is over. And it can lead to a cause-and-effect association that can take years to wash off.

I used to get a bad case of it like clockwork every fall, right during junior high football season. It's probably because I took advantage of the last days of summer to run around the foothills of Boulder, invariably tangling with the demon vine. That's also right when football practice started.

It never failed. I had bubbles of it oozing down my legs at every practice and game. The lone upside is that everyone was afraid to tackle me, for fear I'd ooze it onto them. If they couldn't see the blisters, they could see the pink calamine on my skin. "He's at the 40, the 30, the 20, the 10, touchdown!" announcers would say, if we had announcers, as I'd run straight to the end zone without having to make a single move. Then I'd gingerly peel my football pants off in the locker room, often ripping the scabs with it, while everyone moved away from me on the Group W bench.

I like to think I developed immunity to it after so much exposure in my youth. I never really caught it that badly in my later years, but by then I had also wised up and learned to avoid it. I also probably wasn't rolling around in the woods as much. But take my advice from lessons learned in the itchy hills of Boulder: three leaves means leave it alone.

Despite all that, I still count hiking as one of the most impressionable outdoor pursuits I did as a kid, not because of the scars the poison ivy left, but because it's the one activity that truly lets kids explore. We lived a block away from the foothills, and my parents would let us go out on our own as much as we wanted, which we did regularly at Chautauqua Park, the Flatirons and Flagstaff Mountain. It's not so much that they let us, but that they had no idea where we were. And they figured we'd get in less trouble in the dirt than we would downtown.

I remember the giant boulder we'd scale on dares, which doesn't seem so giant anymore. There'd always be one of us who couldn't make it up, who would then pretend that he didn't want to and was having just as much fun down where he was. We'd believe him and come down, too, spending hours damming up the local creek.

Hiking also opens the doors to kid communication. Once, while on a family hiking trip to Moab, Utah, my friend Edge's daughter, Abbi, 7, opened the nightstand drawer at the hotel and asked, "What's the...Holly Bibbel?" That sparked a conversation on religion, which was driven home the next day on a family hike into Arches National Park. When Abbi and her older brother, Stu, saw interpretive signs labeling the rocks as millions of years old, they noticed the obvious contradiction. This prompted dad to explain how different people believe different things. "What do you believe, Stuey?" he asked his son, who then pointed to the sign.

Edge also used a hiking trip to explain the birds and the bees to Stuey. It went off without a hitch, he said, with the Great Outdoors serving as the perfect neutral medium in which to break the icky ice. "You know when you wake up sometimes and it's kind of different down there?" he began. "Well..."

The bottom line is that you never know what's going to arise on a hike, and therein lies its beauty. More so than almost anything else, hiking puts your kids in the heart of Nature's playground, where anything from tree to stream to a mound of dirt is fair game for experiential frolicking. And since there's not much to it skillwise, it also provides the perfect spark for family conversation.

As with every other form of recreation with kids, however, you have to take the right steps beforehand to progress down the path properly.

Piggy-backing—Kids' Backpacks

In the early years—before your children can walk, and even during the toddler era—you'll have as much luck convincing them to hike alongside you as you will convincing them to let you tag along on a date later in life. "Uh, I don't think so, Dad," comes the typical response.

Thankfully, technology has solved this problem with the kids' pack, which lets you give Junior a modern piggy-back ride when venturing into the wilds.

Perhaps no other invention has better opened the doors for parents to get outdoors than this simple contraption. While it's little more than a two-holed bag with shoulder straps, its uses are as vast as the countryside it lets you traipse. You can use

A TRIBUTE TO DAD

If one person's nailed the nuances and importance of hiking with family, it's Michael Hodgson, president of outdoor news magazine *Snews*. The following was taken from a eulogy he wrote after the passing of his father, Peter John Hodgson:

"...There'll be no more walks in the woods talking about life. While my mother gets credit for introducing me as a tot to the outdoors and laying the seeds that grew into a life full of adventure, it was my British father who nurtured and watered the garden as I grew into a teen. Beginning when I was six, and for one Sunday every month over a three-year span, right after the last note faded away from the church organ my father played, we'd head off together into the mountains above Boulder, Colorado. My father still in his suit, pockets stuffed with several sandwiches, a few candy bars, a soda for me and a bitter lemon drink for him, would park at a trailhead, point up a narrow track snaking up a ridge or across a field and say, "Lead on." From that moment until Dad would determine it was time to head home, he would follow wherever my adventurous spirit took us. I treasured this time with him. And our mutual romps up and over rocks, across streams, and even the occasional snow bank opened my eyes and mind to a world of excitement and opportunity.

My father, a gifted musician, writer and teacher, would patiently wait until my breathless scampering and youthful clamoring for dad to "look at this" or "come over here" slowed sufficiently that he could point out the symphony being played all around me. I learned to hear music in the sound of a burbling creek, the dancing of aspen leaves, and the buzz of a fly over a sun-warmed rock. I gradually learned to walk and listen, observe and think. In time, I learned that the sound of my own voice drowned out the quiet teachings of the world around me.

As I grew into a teen and then a young man, our walks became the starting points of deeper conversations, often begun after hours of walking in silence, listening, thinking. No topic was taboo. No question discouraged. No answer judged or criticized. No dream quashed. Looking back over the years I was blessed with my father's time, I can see clearly that my successes and chosen path in life are inextricably linked to those walks with Dad."

kid packs to take your brood shopping, to the park, on errands, or even to ease the shuffle at the airport. But their main purpose is for taking kids hiking.

Like their name implies, kids' packs are backpacks designed for carrying kids. Simply throw them in, fasten the chest harness and away you go. Naturally, you won't be "away you going" as fast as you would without the extra weight on your back. But you also aren't carrying around the extra psychological weight of going bonkers at home.

Kids' packs also differ from strollers, joggers and Burleys in that I've yet to see a double one. I'm not sure if it's a design impossibility or that the market for such a contraption is limited to the Jack Le-Lannes of the world. Regardless, the end result —whether the kids are stacked atop of one another or side by side—would likely belong in Dr. Seuss.

While the double version hasn't taken off like it has for other kid-transportation inventions, this doesn't diminish the kids' pack's singularity of purpose in helping parents recreate with their kids outside. You just need one parent per Pampers-clad child.

As far as what age you can get started at, here's some heads-up advice. The kids' pack works as long as your child can hold his head up. In the early months, you might be relegated to using a sling or front pack (often called a Snuggly). Once they get big enough that your lower back starts protesting, they're ripe to move behind you. And once they earn their kid's pack degree, they can stay there comfortably until age five or six, or whenever your back starts giving you more grief than your kids. Even after your kid can walk on his own, bring one along for when he tires. It might be all you need to actually get to that lake.

As with the jogger and Burley, a kid's pack's best attribute is that it lets you, the parent, escape to the outdoors while you're still watching your child. Well, you're not really watching him because he's on your back, but you know he can't get into too much trouble back there, leaving you free to roam the wilds at will. (Actually, that's not entirely true; once Casey spit her lolly-pop into my hair, and another time she got tree sap on my scalp. But she was never in danger to herself.)

Another nice aspect is that the rider is never bored. How could you be when you get to hang out like a pharaoh and watch the world pass by? While you're watching where you place your feet and concentrating on your breathing, little Miss Princess fully realizes that that's your problem and responsibility. As such, she can just sit there and pick her nose, burp-up lunch onto said lollypop- and sap-encrusted hair, or look side to side at whatever marvels Mother Nature offers—a fluttering butterfly, a stream, the clouds, or a birdy, birdy in a tree. About the only direction your passenger won't be able to see is straight forward, which is blocked by the back of your now drool-covered head.

Don't think they have it rough back there. As long as they have a clean diaper, they're riding high on the hog, with nary a care. And since their entire weight is riding on their crotch, they'll be the first to let you know about any soiled diaper problems while you're treading the soil below.

The only care they might have is when they realize they can't escape the thing without their parent's help. And this gives you the upper hand, which parents need any time we can get it.

Your kids usually don't notice that they're entrapped while they're being shuttled around, because then they're having fun. But it sinks in as soon as you hoist the pack off and set it on the ground. Then they're stuck there, feet wiggling tantalizingly close to the ground, and yet still so far away. It's like leaving your dog tied up on a leash. They can see you, but are unable to do a thing about it. Of course, you never actually get out of eyesight with your kids that way, but their puppy-dog eyes will infer that they want out.

If they're asleep, which happens easily from the metronomic cadence of walking, you can even leave them there for a while, with no long-lasting scars. We've propped Brooke and Casey by fences at concerts, against trees in parks, and against chairs in

A SAMPLE PACK UNPLUGGED

Like that old Armour Hot Dog commercial ("Hot dogs, Armour hot dogs, what kinds of kids eat Armour hot dogs? Big kids, little kids, kids who climb on rocks…"), there are as many types of kid carriers on the market as there are kids. Don't skimp. Get one with the bells and whistles you need.

Here's one in particular—an Honors Award winner at the National Parenting Publications Awards (NAPPA) -- to let you in on a few key features: The Kelty KIDS Transit Carrier 2.1. The TC 2-1 (for you acronymically inclined) comes with an ergo shape to contour your poor, tired back, and is offered in bright colors for easy visibility and the ability to hide Go-gurt stains. Other features include a five-point child harness so Junior doesn't fall out whenever you tie your shoe, an adjustable torso length for when you want to hand the weight off to someone else gullible enough to take it, padded shoulder straps and waist belt, a back panel for ventilation (don't think you won't sweat), and the crème de la crème, a zip-off diaper bag complete with shoulder straps (believe me, when it's full of saturated cargo you'll want to zip it off). When not in use, the child seat folds away, allowing the TC 2-1 to be used as a daypack. Info: www.kelty.com.

restaurants and bars. While this doesn't work if they're awake, it is fair game if they're napping. The key is making sure you find something solid to lean them against. Otherwise it's turtle time and the nap's abruptly over. We've done this to our kids also, their cries interrupting the concert. They list, list, list and finally keel over onto their side, wallowing like an upside-down lady bug.

But that's the occasional price these piggy-backed princesses pay for such luxurious travel. Today's pack designs are as pampered as a pair of Pampers. Most have a comfortably suspended seat that allows their legs to protrude through holes on each side, with walls extending around their sides at the perfect height to support their arms. The seat's height is adjustable, so smaller kids can ride high and bigger children can ride low. Some even come with tiny stirrups for the rider's feet, just like a saddle on a horse. And you're the palomino parent.

We never used the stirrups much with our kids. They seemed more trouble than they were worth (the stirrups, not the kids). It was hard to aim their feet in just so, and the stirrups flopped around when not in use. We did find, though, that you can put things in them as a sort of pocket—stuff like rocks and pinecones that the kids thought

so important at the time but completely forgot about as soon as they got home. I once even put a beer in one as a coozie, but it sent the wrong message to passersby and had a short upright shelf life.

You can also customize your pack, pimping it out like your low-rider kid. We attached Casey's pacifier to a little strap that clipped onto the pack's side, giving her free rein as to when to Maggie Simpson it or suffer without. It saved tons of time from having to stop every time she pursed it out, and saved us from back-aggravating stoops to pick it up. When she wanted it, she knew right where it was and could grab it. When her cheeks were sore from sucking, or she realized how stupid she looked with a pacifier in all the time, she could spit it out and let it air dry for later.

Further yuppifying our set-up, we also had a tiny mirror attached to a bungee cord fastened to the parent's shoulder strap. If we ever wanted to check on the rider in back, we'd simply pull the bungee out to full length and cast a glance in the rear-view. It let us assess how things were going while still making time. At first these glance-in-the-mirror check-ups didn't result in much. Worst case: her pacifier had fallen out (which is when we invented the pacifier string). Then it was just for little squeaks and squawks, the kind that are impossible to find what's truly at fault. We'd look back to see that her sun hat had fallen over her eyes, or some other earth-shattering emergency. As a bonus, we could also use it to check if we had spinach stuck in our teeth after lunch.

While the mirror might be overkill, if it saves you one pack-unshouldering on the trail it's worth its weight and the looks from other hikers who think you might just be a tad vain. Its only downfall is that you can't use it to see the real culprit behind most riders' consternation—dirty diapers. For those, only the nose knows.

The pimping doesn't stop with bungeed pacifiers and rear-view mirrors. Some packs have detachable rain canopies so both skies and cries don't open up at the same time. Four little rods extend up from each corner, with a sunroofed, waterproof awning shading the rider. When not in use, it rolls up into a tiny bag that stores on the side.

Personally, I've always felt a little awkward breaking out the awning, as if we were doting too much on our precious little cargo. It's about as materialistic as you can get, especially considering that many women the world over carry their kids against their chests with a simple wrap of fabric. But if you can put up with the stigma of having a two-story building on your back, it'll save you having to take your kid out to put on a rain jacket, and will help ward off skin cancer, if not looks from fellow hikers.

Perhaps the biggest accoutrement to a kids' pack is the storage compartment beneath the seat. If your current pack doesn't have one, consider an upgrade. Like your child's toy closet, it will be filled before you know it.

Most such compartments are located beneath where your child sits, so your gear rides next to your lower back. And in a way, that makes sense. Otherwise, your gear would be riding on top of your child. Regardless, you'll fill this compartment to the brim, just like the laundry basket back home.

In the early years, the space will be absorbed with such baby necessities as diapers, changing mats, bottles, wipes, spare clothes and snacks, a lot of which you can keep in there for next time. Just remember to check how fresh the wipes are from time to time. We suffered through more than one of Casey's diapers after the wipes had gone sandpaper dry, which doth not a sparkling bottom make.

Depending on the amount of space available and how long you're hiking, you can also use the storage space to carry extra clothing, rain gear, and snacks for you as well. But don't count on it. You're second fiddle when it comes to space for your own needs.

A word of advice: make sure your pack is freestanding. Otherwise, it's like a bike without a kickstand. You have to lean it everywhere.

We've used both, and those that stand on their own stand the best chance of getting used. We had one that shrunk into a normal backpack when not carrying kids, and then expanded into a kids' pack by unzipping a magical compartment. It had its uses, sure. But it wasn't free-standing. Every time we put Casey inside it, it was a two-parent wrestling operation and jigsaw puzzle to figure out.

The technique *du jour*: like filling a trash bag with leaves, have one parent hold the pack open while the other loads the cargo inside. If you're by yourself, it's tougher. You'll experiment with every trick in the kids' backpack book, none of which work that well. You'll lay the pack on its side and try to slide your child in on his side. You'll prop it limply against a picnic table and then try to aim legs into the holes before it tips over. All the wiser, the next time your child will know what you're up to and kick and fidget to make matters harder.

You might also try to put the pack on first and then flip your kid up over your head and into the leg slots. While that earns you circus-like style points, it, too, isn't foolproof. You have to make sure your child is facing forward beforehand, and then have him ride without having his belt fastened. Either that, or then take it off again to fasten the chest strap, which defeats the purpose of the grandiose entry.

None of these techniques—the sideways slither, back flip or prop and drop—will earn you any parenting awards. With a freestanding pack, you simply open it up, set it on the ground, and lower little Jimmy in as if you were a human crane. Sure, freestanding packs are a little heavier and bulkier due to the metal supports required to achieve a secure base. We know this because we've knocked people's drinks out of their hands with such packs at the free concert series downtown. Look one way and —whamo! you're a bull in a house of cards. But its loadability is well worth the apologies and replacement drinks you buy your concert mates.

Like parents' waists no longer fitting into certain pants, eventually there'll come a time when your children outgrow the pack phase, both mentally and physically. When that happens it's time they hit the trail with you, carrying their own weight.

Pack Graduation

Though they won't be carrying much else besides themselves at this point, growing out of the pack phase is a milestone worth celebrating. No more visits to the chiropractor, no more wrestling them inside, and no more drool down your neck. But it also means no more making as many miles as you'd like.

Before reaching this point, hopefully you'll have had your kids walking alongside you a time or two so they have a basic grasp of the hiking concept. And hopefully you, and they, will have gone through a probation period where you bring the pack as backup, but they hike most of the way themselves. While kids at this stage usually only last for short hiking spells at a time, encourage it as much as possible. Repeatedly taking off and putting on kids' packs is a tiresome transition. Oftentimes, we'd put Casey in the pack, only to have her say she wants out, only to have her walk a hundred yards and want back in again. But stay the course and eventually they'll hopefully enjoy hiking for a spell.

When that day arrives, sing a well-deserved Hallelujah to the Ibuprofen Gods who got you that far and watched over your back and aching knees all those long, kid-carrying years. And get ready to enter a new era of perhaps shorter hikes, but ones where everyone's standing—and more importantly, hiking—on their own two feet.

BACKPACKING WITH YOUR BROOD

Too often, backpacking with kids becomes back-schmacking. Your kids tire and get bored, while you try in vain to whisk them upward and onward toward camp. Take heart as you're taking rests. Backpacking with your kids is one of the purest ways to get your kids immersed in the Great Outdoors, poison ivy, blisters and all.

Note that I said "purest", not easiest or simplest.

While you can certainly backpack with your children when they're still spurring your ribs in kids' packs, it's easier on the vertebrae and sanity when their weight is off you. I only went on one such backpacking and kid-carrying trip with Casey, and that number alone says something. Sure, we cheated by striking out only a mile from our backyard. But with Casey's weight added to the stockpile of gear on my back, even that was far enough.

It's better to wait until your kids can at least walk on their own—and not melt down halfway and need to be carried—before backpacking as a family. At least, that way you're not carrying them as well as the gear. And even then it's not a walk in the park. Your packs will be laden with sleeping bags, pads, tents, clothes, food, cookware, fuel, water, and virtually everything else you and your kids need, leaving you arriving in camp a grouchy, sweaty mess.

But while it's still a heavy load, a huge weight will be lifted from your shoulders; you'll discover another great outdoor activity to do with your kids.

The biggest beauty of backpacking is its simplicity. While it certainly requires more preparation than a simple sleep-over or car camping, compared to paddling, hut skiing and other overnight endeavors, it's easy as pie. Throw your gear on your back (and hopefully some of your kids' backs), hike and camp. What can be so hard about that? The only gear you need besides camping equipment is backpacks to carry it all.

Of course, therein lies the pastime's pitfall, and the reason more parents don't do it. By definition, backpacking means back-packing. You actually have to carry things. And even if you give your kids packs of their own—which, like your dog, you certainly should—your kids aren't going to be setting any weight or distance records. If you're lucky, they might carry their rain jackets, water bottles and lightweight sleeping bags, saddling you and your spouse with everything else. And that's if you're lucky.

But recreating with kids is all about making sacrifices, right? So you have to sacrifice some sweat to reap the rewards.

If this sounds a bit like Richard Simmons, so be it. I doubt his little buttocks of steel ever carried his kids' camping gear anywhere, let alone up a steep mountainside (more like a latte over to the stair-master machine). But until everyone's carrying their own weight, expect to invest some sweat and blister equity backpacking with your brood.

It's the backpacks, of course, that are to blame. I'm convinced people would pursue the pastime more regularly if they could just do away with the having-to-carry-everything part. It's our slovenly nature to abhor excess weight on our backs.

You can hedge your bet in one of two ways, preferably both: plan shorter routes; and forego the kitchen sink. You don't have to trek ten miles into Lake Hardtoreach to give your kids the backpacking experience and your chiropractor more billable hours. Pick an easier, shorter, flatter destination. Even a half-mile hike in somewhere can offer the illusion of wilderness and instill the fun of backpacking. Also, play it safe by going light. Forego the jumbo can of Van Camp Pork and Beans in favor of dehydrated fare, and leave the pillows and playthings behind (but go ahead and splurge with the Pop Tarts).

Above all, instill the notion that the hike itself is the end every bit as much as the means. Get across that that's what backpacking is all about—the journey, getting somewhere with your own two feet while bringing along everything you need to survive (which sometimes can include Fluffy the Bunny).

As part of that survival package, pack some ear plugs. If they're like ours, your kids will launch into "The Ants Go Marching One by One" and "I'm Walking on Sunshine" the whole way. But let them have their fun. They're earning it with every step.

Another tip: no cracking the whip to make them step faster. Save the slave-driving for chores back home. If your kids are tired, stop and rest. Have them drink water and eat snacks to refuel. If you plan your route correctly, and don't overshoot your bounds, you shouldn't feel like you have to make time or arrive at camp at an appointed hour. Adapt to your new surroundings—backpacking with your kids instead of just by yourself—just as the animals and plants around you do to theirs.

Backpack Beginnings

Growing up in Boulder, Colorado, afforded me ample back-breaking backpacking opportunities as a youngster. Most of the memories are quite pleasant: going with my older brothers to places like Jasper and 4th of July Lakes a half-hour from town. Since the hikes were relatively short—only a few miles—weight wasn't much of an issue. We brought everything from cast-iron pans to sausage links, piling it all onto our backs. And since my eldest brother, David, was a weight lifter, he reveled in carrying the lion's share of the load.

You can never tell what a child will remember from such excursions. I remember out-fishing David in a tiny stream once, and another time watching our dog, Boots, nearly drown after following us across a log spanning a swollen creek. I also remember my brother telling me about a booger in my nose that was making weird whistle sounds when we were trying to fall asleep, and him giving me full authorization to pick it free.

Another memory stems from an outing program called BLAST at Baseline Junior High School (the acronym created in the teacher's lounge stands for something, I'm sure). We were given a variety of activities to participate in, and I chose a parent-chaperoned backpacking trip to a creek behind Gross Reservoir, in the mountains behind town. I remember crawling in bat guano-filled caves—never believing for an instant that the critters could poop that much—camping beside the creek, and waking up to a freak May snowstorm that dumped fifteen inches of snow on us, sagging our tents to smithereens. Then I remember hoofing it to someone's house for help, where they found a whopping seven ticks in my thick, grown-out-to-be-cool, 7th-grade hair.

But those early experiences, whether with siblings or schools, bred a lifelong familiarity and fondness of the pastime. In 8th grade, I even spent six weeks in a teepee with a friend near Oh-Be-Joyful Creek outside Crested Butte, Colorado, which we used as a base camp for further backpacking trips. We actually went backpacking from our backpacking trip.

We set it up ourselves, first the tripod, then the other poles leaning in just so, finally covering the log frame with a canvas shell. Only during the first rainstorm, when we were inside dodging drips, did we realize we had put the cover on inside-out.

But you learn things like that backpacking, mistakes you likely won't repeat. Once, on a backpacking side trip from our teepee on a particularly overcast day, we accidentally crawled inside our tent a few hours too early. We waited hours for it to get dark by telling every knock-knock joke under the cloud-covered sun. Another time, we backpacked from our teepee over to Aspen to visit my brother, where we re-supplied out of his fridge before returning home. We didn't bring any money or enough provisions. Left-over pizza never tasted so good.

Then came the month-long Outward Bound course in Colorado's South San Juan Mountains, in 10th grade. Right off the bus they made us cross a creek in our boots, just to get them wet, all in the name of team-building with misfits from across the country. I did well, I like to think, largely because of my backpacking background. Of course, this meant carrying extra stoves and sleeping bags when others in our patrol collapsed, but I'd have rather been on my end of the spectrum than theirs.

I was also wise enough to avoid traps. After learning that a universal treatment for hypothermia is to strip down and lie naked in a sleeping bag with the victim, I was happily next to my buddies under a tarp when a less-than-attractive, high-maintenance female member of our group started yelling, "I've got hypothermia! I've got hypothermia!" under her solo tarp the next spot over. None of us took the bait, served up like a worm on a hook.

The hardest part of the thirty-day ordeal, aside from running a twenty-mile marathon over scree fields at 12,000 feet, was "mandatory solo," during which we had to make it three days alone without food. Our only responsibility was to build a cairn of rocks once a day so our instructor knew we were still sane and alive. While my journal has etchings of the perfect cheeseburger, and I figured out that my tarp had 10,432 tiny sewn-in squares on it, I credit my survival with backpacking and boredom-fighting skills learned at an early age (though telling solo knock-knock jokes isn't all that fun).

Tips for the Trail

Backpacking should bring you and your family closer to nature, not wanting to get farther away from it. It shouldn't be sanity-depleting. You don't have to tuck your kids kicking under both arms to reach camp, and parents don't have to get hernias from humping the load. To get off on the right foot, and stay on it until you arrive safely back at home, consider the following:

Practice Makes Perfect: Don't set out for Denali on Day One. Ease into things. Start with a simple day hike close to home to get your kids acclimated to 1) carrying a pack; and 2) spending the night outdoors with all sorts of creepy-crawlies. If they're up for it, add some rocks to their packs to simulate carrying a load (just don't let social services see). Another hint: camp in the backyard to practice sleeping in the tent, with the comfort of a pillow (and bathroom) never too far away. Just remember if you have the sprinklers set to go off in the middle of the night.

Have Your Kids Help: You, as a parent regardless of gender, will have your hands full carrying group gear. Give your kids their own packs as early as possible and have them pitch in, even if they're only carrying their water bottles, rain jackets and Raggedy Anns. If you can throw in their sleeping bags, so much the better. It's one less bulky item in your pack, and empowers them more than any other piece of equipment. "I'm carrying my bed," they'll triumphantly march.

Pacing is Everything: If they're not carrying their own weight in gear, at least make sure your kids are carrying their own weight. Unless they're too young to walk or you've exhausted every bribe in the book, don't give in and carry them. Have them hike as much as possible, even if it means taking a rest break every other step. Just realize that they're slower and tire more quickly, and often have their own plans about the route—including detours for bugs and mud. Also, don't stress about making time. You're not frantically getting them ready for school; if your child stops to pick up a pinecone, let him.

Experts recommend making just two to four miles per day, perhaps more for school-age children and less for preschoolers. Above all, hold out as long as possible before succumbing to the old ride-on-top-of-dad's-shoulders-while-he's-carrying-a-backpack scenario. You'll need your vertebrae for the way back.

Encourage Gaming: Games take kids' minds off the trail. Encourage them as much as possible. A trick I used once while Casey was still gullible enough to fall for it was the old pretend-she's-a-dog trick, having her fetch a stick I repeatedly threw up the trail. Another favorite is hide-and-seek, with the kids charging up the trail ahead of you and then jumping out from behind trees with a loud "Boo!" You can cover miles this way, without them even knowing that they're making headway.

Don't Worry, Be Happy: Hey, if it works for reggae, it works while roughing it in the wilds. It happens to all parents. One or both of you might get a little stressed-out during the whole packing and preparation process. That's fine; it's all part of the rallying-anywhere package. Just don't let it rub off on your kids like a case of poison ivy. Instill the right attitude by having it yourself.

Consider Bringing Friends: There's a reason kids want to play with other kids at home: it's more fun. What works at home works on the trail. While it's great to get out with just your own family—a perfect bonding experience with flowery fields, bluebird skies and perfectly tanned marshmallows—include other families, or bring along a trustworthy playmate. You'll have someone other than your spouse to commiserate with, and your kids will, too. If they have enough fun, they might not even realize they're hiking, or bog you down with those incessant "When are we going to get there?" questions.

Know the Code: No, there's not a universal backpacking code to memorize and eat before it self-destructs. But there are regulations, depending on where you go. Whether they're for fishing, campfires or campsite permits, know them for the area you're traveling in. There's nothing worse than packing, driving, and arriving at a trailhead to discover you can't go because you don't have a permit. Consider the following anecdote from my friend Edge. One summer he headed up Green Mountain near Boulder, where it's illegal to camp, for a quick overnight trip with his daughter, Abbi. They had a great time, but on the way down they encountered a ranger patrolling the trail. With their backpacks raising the ranger's suspicions, Edge had to white lie about it in front of his daughter to escape the predicament (yes, Abbi asked him about his little fib afterwards).

Share the Love: As a parent, you might get cornered into this at home: setting the table, cooking dinner, cleaning up, making lunch, feeding the dog, taking out the trash. But try not to at camp. Having your kids pitch in will make them feel like they're truly a part of the team. Give them chores, just like you should do at home. Have them help set up the tent, organize sleeping bags, filter water, or collect firewood. Plus, it will help take their minds off their blisters and mosquito bites.

Watch Out for Wildlife: So your own wild life disappeared as soon as you had kids. It hasn't disappeared in the mountains. Inquire at the ranger station before heading out about animal activity in the area. Don't intentionally head into bear country — there are plenty of bear-free areas to take your kids. If you do find yourself in Yogiville, teach your kids how to use bear spray (i.e. make sure it's pointed in the right direction), what to do in an encounter (the old adage, "you don't have to be faster than the bear, just faster than the slowest person in your group" doesn't apply with kids), and keep your food and cooking area well away from camp. Know how to react in encounters with other animals as well, whether it's a moose or mountain lion (hint: no "Here kitty, kitty, kitty").

Avoid Equipment Errors: You don't squish the soccer team into a VW Bug, and you shouldn't mash your camping gear inside a daypack, either. Get a pack that can shoulder the load (and even then, you'll likely still have gear hanging off the back). Experts maintain you should shoot for a large-capacity pack that weighs around four pounds and can carry a forty- to fifty-pound load, plus a few favorite stuffed animals. If mom's coming with an infant or toddler, bring a kids' pack, which usually weighs around six to eight pounds. Kids can use everything from their school packs to special hydration packs, complete with storage. Rule of thumb: saddle older kids with about ten pounds. For shelter, go with a tent for mosquitoes' and weather's sake, but also for the sense of security it provides. Kids have a natural way of getting cozy inside them, and a good night's sleep does wonders. Inflatable pads are warmer and more comfortable than closed-cell foam pads, but take more time setting up and are often as slippery as a six-year-old caught in a cookie lie.

Pick the Right Spot: Just as you do when heading to the movies, involve your children in the planning process. Show them maps and photos to get them excited about leaving their cozy beds. Experts recommend letting them select between options — that you've previously screened — to give them ownership in the itinerary (and that way, if something goes wrong, you can blame them). As for selecting where to go, consider things like distance, how well the trail is developed, and the end destination (ideally that involves water of some sort). Water also puts the kibosh on boredom, from skipping rocks and hosting boat races to catching crawdads.

Route Finding: On the trail, involve your children in navigation decisions (or at least pretend to). If they're old enough, show them how to work a compass or GPS, orient the map, and point out forks on the map as you reach them on the trail. Some parents like to trace their route on the map with a highlighter beforehand, though I've never been that foresighted. This is also a great time to recite the tale of *Hansel and Gretel*, and teach them that you can't always rely on bread crumbs.

When Weather This Way Comes: Kick your kids off Disney for a moment and tune into the Weather Channel. Many parents' greatest fear is rain, but don't let a little drizzle get you down. If a deluge comes, throw on the proper apparel and make the most of it. Sing "Rain, Rain Go Away," or "Raindrops Keep Falling on My Head." Hiking in rain can actually be fun. It brings out worms and puddles, and oftentimes even wildlife. Just make sure you dress appropriately. Layer fleece, hats and mittens under rain gear, and leave the cotton at home (except for their favorite princess jammies). If a storm hits while you're on the trail, keep snacks and a tarp handy to wait it out. Don't expect kids to tough it out and stay happy.

Mr. Heat Miser and Mr. Freeze: I loved this Christmas show as a kid, and can still remember the little jingle ("I'm Mr. Heat Miser, I'm Mister..."). But you don't want to face those oafs in the mountains. The best way to deal with cold is proper clothing and a warm sleeping bag, combining the two for the warmest option. Make sure your kid bags are either synthetic or down with at least two inches of loft, not those Linus and Lucy monoliths of yesteryear. If temperatures drop, use your own sleeping bag as a quilt. Heat is another matter. A hot tot can be worse to deal with than a cold one. Have your kids hike with hydration systems, and add flavoring to encourage their use. I'll often have water-chugging contests with my kids, though I'm not sure that's a skill I want them to master come college. Other hints for the heat: make sure they're not overdressed when hiking; remember the sunscreen; let them cool off in creeks or lakes; and get their clothing and skin wet to stay cool.

Meal Time: Kids get cranky without them at home, so don't miss meals in the mountains. For anything shorter than week-long excursions (and who in their right mind would take kids out that long?), experts advise emphasizing calories more than nutrition and packing food your kids like. If they don't eat granola at home, don't bring it backpacking (though our daughter now loves it). Also, offer frequent snacks rather than relying on three rigidly served meals a day. Here's what the good folks at *Backpacking Light* magazine recommend: 12-16 oz. of food per day (dry weight) for toddlers 3-6; 20 oz./day for children age 7-10; and 24 oz./day for older kids (all bets are off for teenagers, but then good luck getting them to go with you anyway). For the younger set, they advise repackaging baby foods into small plastic containers or zip-closure bags, with the caveat that it compromises sterility (the food's, not the dad's). If going with an infant (brave you), breastfeeding moms have it best—a ready-made meal that doesn't have to be packed. For the bottle-fed, use either washable or those with disposable liners, which can be pre-filled with formula or dry milk at home. The best advice? Toss in some junk food for morale.

Hygiene: Are other families as dysfunctional as ours? Are we the only parents who kept our similar-looking diaper rash ointment tubes next to our toothpaste tubes on the bathroom counter? I nearly made that mistake more than once (on my teeth, not my toddler's bottom). Or kept the kids' toothbrushes atop the dresser near the changing table, so dirty diapers ended up right next to the only household item that goes in your mouth? While you can get away with those kinds of mistakes at home, it's a different tale on the trail. If you're backpacking with a diaper wearer, good luck. Depending on how long you're out, your disposables will take up as much room as your food on the way in, and more on the way out. Here's another trick from *Backpacking Light*: cat-hole what's inside, let the diaper dry out for a few hours, and then transport the time bomb in an odor-proof zip-closure bag. When your kids are older, you get the lucky task of teaching—and, of course, illustrating— how to poop in a hole. Also, as at home, make sure your kids wash and/or disinfect their hands before all meals (remember the wipes).

Dealing with the Doldrums: If kids can get bored at home, it can happen in the wilderness. But forego their favorite toys for nature (you won't have any spare room, and you'll look like a dork having Barbie dolls hanging off your pack), which is a far better playground than any family room. How many playrooms have frogs, snakes, sticks and dirt? Kids are creative enough to turn the outdoors into a romper room sans props. They'll make forts out of sticks and leaves for bugs and fairies, throw wood into creeks for raft races, and find ways to keep busy that only kids can. Other hints: bring a field guide to identify plants, and encourage them to record the trip in a journal and show friends later. Also pay attention to animal tracks. Encourage your young trackers' interest in finding and identifying them, and determining their direction.

Safety First: Prepare for inclement weather, and have a bailout plan. Whether you're camping in your backyard, out of the car, or at 10,000 feet in the Sierra, you're bound to encounter situations that wreak havoc on morale. If no one's having fun, go home and try again later. Family backpacking shouldn't be something to endure. A final tip: give each child a safety whistle to blow in an emergency.

Leave No Trace: Unlike a kid's bedroom after a slumber party, or your living room after a – heaven forbid – birthday party at home, have your children follow and learn the Leave No Trace (www.leavenotrace.org) principles of backpacking. Like no toys strewn about at home, have them patrol your campsite for trash by turning it into a game – whoever finds the most wins!

Chapter 6

JOGGING WITH JUNIOR

"The world is mud-luscious and puddle-wonderful."
—E.E. Cummings

JOGGING WITH A CHILD IS A BIT of an oxymoron. Not that you have to be a moron to do it, but the two don't exactly go hand-in-hand.

Usually, you're chasing after your kids—reeling them in at the grocery store, herding them like cats at the park, or stopping them from venturing off the curb—not jogging *with* them. Intentionally taking them jogging with you? Puh-lease.

Just the other day while driving Casey to a friend's house, I saw a mom and dad jogging alongside the road up a hill. A few hundred yards behind them strode Junior, not enjoying their company and not enjoying the gravity-defying gruel. They weren't jogging with him, they were jogging in front of him. There was no socializing, no high-fives and no shared camaraderie. The only thing missing was a rope dragging him along.

It's not that the kid was a slouch. Far from it...he was jogging, complete with hat, mittens and parka. The problem boils down to one of leg length. As a gazelle-legged grown-up, you'll out-stride your child five to one. One long jog step, five pitter-patters behind you. For the child, it's a game of catch, without the ball. Secondly, while kids certainly can't stand still, they rarely exercise as an end unto itself. It's usually a means for doing something more fun: a game of tag, hide-and-seek, catching frogs, or chasing a sibling. Exercise for the sake of exercising? Sheer redundancy.

Kids also aren't hardwired to systematically get from point A to point B and back, all within an allotted timeframe. There are too many worms, sticks, butterflies, mud puddles and other distractions along the way. Remember those *Family Circus* cartoons showing little Billy zipping all over the place, with a dotted line marking his path? That's your child out for a jog. It's like trying to track a dog. Unless you have your kid leashed like said canine, that's the path he'll take if you expect him to stay by your side on a recreational run.

But this section's not about that. It's not about jogging *with* your children, as in getting them happily panting dog-like by your side, but about *you* jogging with your children in tow. And therein lies the beauty of technology. A simple invention, no more than a cart on three wheels, has opened the floodgates to letting adults dart around and burn calories while babysitting their brood.

The revelation – insert Hallelujah chorus here—is the aptly named jogger. While certainly not new, a contraption like this was unheard of in the '60s. Back then, parents were more concerned about running from the draft and running with the devil than running with their kids. My, how times have changed. Now, with Richard Simmons, Oprah and other heart rate advocates putting fitness in the spotlight, jogging has become mainstream, munchkins or not. As if chasing kids around the house all day isn't enough, parents want to exercise. And if that means doing so with children, so be it. Until your children are at an age when they actually want to jog with you—a rarity, because by then they're teenagers—doing so requires the jogger.

THE EARLY YEARS

The jogger follows the natural progression of all other "er"-ending contraptions technology has bestowed upon parenting. Add an "er" to the end of anything and you end up with something that makes parenting easier.

First in this long line-up is the walker. As its name implies, you put your kid in it to help him walk. The concept is simple. A suspended seat attached to four wheels lets Junior Flintstone around the floor, the balls of his feet propelling him this way and that like a water bug. Many models let you adjust the height, from full-on toes-off-the-floor diaper wedgie to full foot propulsion. Vroom, vroom. Thankfully, Darwinism usually ensures that these easy riders flirt with the stairs only once.

Most walkers come complete with a tray for snacks like goldfish, which spill off and get crushed into the carpet as the contrivance bumper cars into walls, coffee tables and chairs. Dogs learn to get their tails out of the way of the wheels, but stay close enough to vacuum the crumbs. Also, expect little Stevie McQueen to adhere to the universal walker law: he'll get most underfoot whenever you're carrying an armload of groceries.

In the early days, everything's a walker...trashcans, boxes, chairs, stools, pretty much anything except the actual walker. Kids will pull themselves up onto anything that will let them, and push it around if possible, all in an effort to join the ranks of the standing and walking elite. But it's the walker that represents his first foray into wheeled locomotion.

Next on the "er"-ending list comes the stroller, which, as its name implies, lets you stroll with child in tow. As the predecessor to the jogger, it's the first of parentkind's wheeled inventions designed not to make life necessarily easier for the child, but for the parent. With the stroller, parents can now, miracles of miracles, actually get something accomplished while on kid duty. They can run errands, stop by the post office, even walk the dog without being subjected to hernias from carrying their kids. They can push their kids around the same way they do an Eggo's-filled grocery cart, whether they're going for a walk or shopping.

Around this time you'll also encounter the jumper, a sort of stationary walker but also a staunch member of the "er" clan. Hang the spring-loaded seat from the ceiling, plop Junior in, and go back to washing the dishes and clothes until he gets bored. He'll use it to develop airtime skills (be wary if he starts practicing mute-grabs), leg muscles and rotational prowess (hint: wind it up and watch him spin). Its only drawback, which can also be a benefit, is that while it dangles your kid like a mobile, it's not mobile at all. Your kid's stuck there until rescued, which is at the parent's sole discretion. Unlike the other "er" contraptions designed to help kids move, a jumper's like a pogo stick caught in a hole. It keeps parent and child at home (though you can bring it to a hotel.)

ENTER THE JOGGER

Last but not least of these turn-a-verb-into-a-noun kid gadgets is the jogger, which takes the stroller concept a step farther. And it marks the end of the line of all these "er" contraptions because by the time your kids are done with jogger, they're usually big enough to venture out into the world on their own.

The jogger's different than these others, however, because it's the first in the entire "er" series that's actually made to help the *parents* recreate, not to help them get things done or help kids walk, but pursue an actual activity. A walker helps a kid walk, a jumper helps him jump, and a stroller helps you stroll. But while the latter is useful, it's often more of a means than an end. And it's certainly not made to get your heart rate up, unless you get frazzled every time Junior drops his pacifier. The jogger lets you jog.

Think of it as a stroller on steroids. It's a three-wheeled chariot, complete with room for the diaper bag, blankie and teddy underneath. Though they don't always steer straight—ours always veered left whenever I'd let go during alignment tests—they will steer you toward getting exercise while you're on watch.

A jogger can also serve as a stroller—and walker, for that matter, if a toddler stands up and grabs onto it. And you don't even have to jog with it. We use ours for simply heading to the park or bringing casserole and kid to a friend's house. But jog or walk, it'll open your eyes—and arteries—to the fact that you can still get a mountain full of exercise while watching the munchkins. We should all be thankful it's not called the sprinter.

Actually, it's hard to sprint with a jogger. Aside from the normal exercise you'd usually get jogging, you're now pushing an extra load, making it a lot like wearing leg weights (do it *with* leg weights and you're a real rock star).

You won't notice the extra weight so much on the downhills or flats. Once it generates momentum, it takes on a life of its own, leaving you drafting behind it like Lance Armstrong to his Tour team. And that's exactly why they all have hand brakes, just like a bike. You want to be able to slow the thing down with something other than your calf muscles should it start careening out of control and galloping back to the barn. That's why they also have leashes that loop around your wrist. In the odd chance it gets away from you, that's the last umbilical cord saving Junior from riding a runaway train. Granted, I've never seen a parent being pulled uncontrollably behind a jogger, dragging behind it while tied to the leash. But stranger things have happened in the world of parenting.

While you'll notice its momentum on the flats and descents, you'll notice its weight as soon as you try to defy gravity and head uphill. For us, this happens every time we head home from the bike path and confront the two-block-long ascent leading to our house. Unfortunately, it's always at the end of our excursion.

Push a jogger up a hill and you might start wondering why you felt so compelled to exercise in the first place. While a hill makes your kid more relaxed by creating a more steeply angled recliner, it has the opposite effect on the engine behind it. The jogger-on-a-hill setting puts any thigh-master category to shame. Even though a jogger is streamlined and aerodynamic with its triangular configuration, that doesn't offset the fact that it's more weight, or that you're the sole motor behind it.

Inclines, flats or declines, one thing's for sure: you'll feel people's eyes on you whenever you head out with one. Granted, babies draw attention regardless, whether they're in your arms, the car or even on the floor. But put one in a jogger and heads will turn like the contraption's wheels.

You'll either feel superior because you're actually beating the system, getting exercise while watching your child, or nerdy because you're so obsessed with exercise that you have to subject your child to it also. Diva or dork, the turning-passersby's-head syndrome is largely because onlookers a) have either been there before, and can commiserate; b) think you're a psychotic whacko who is so fanatical about fitness that you're willing to punish yourself to get your fix; or c) think the whole thing, and/or parent pushing it, is just plain cute.

Don't believe me? Try this experiment: try not to turn your head next time you see a mom or dad jogging with a jogger. Then, when you do give in and steal a glance, try to remember the thought that goes through your head. Most likely it will be, "Wow, there goes one dedicated parent." Not dedicated to the child in tow, but to his or her own exercise regime.

But don't knock it. It's a way to get some valuable Me Time when you otherwise wouldn't be able to. And a little exercise—in any form other than picking up after your kids—does wonders when you're on the front lines of parentdom.

Operationally, there's not much to this whole jogging-with-your-baby thing. Simply put the baby in, fasten the waist and/or chest straps, and jog away. Most have a locking brake that you can set when you park it, and a wrist strap attached to the handle bar. Wear it. Without it, all it takes is one heart-rate-checking space-out, holding one hand to your neck and the other up with a watch as you count, and your prodigy has just entered the Le Mans. You'll even want the jogger's leash on when you're just walking, which you'll likely use it for more than actual runs.

I've even invented a dorky game with the wrist strap, letting the jogger roll free on the flats until it speeds up and takes up the slack. My daughter then realizes it's going faster than it should be right when the whole thing, jogger and juvenile, stops with a jerk, causing her to laugh in hysterics. So I'm trusting a little strap that technically could break and send the whole contraption careening. It hasn't failed yet, and hasn't failed to make my daughter giggle.

The locking brake is equally important. You won't use the brake itself much when you're jogging—unless you're on a steep decline or you're a sadist and want even more

REASON #104 TO USE A JOGGER WITH A BRAKE

resistance. It's primarily there for the lock. I remember one time when my friends, Terry and Irta, had their toddler in a jogger at a barbecue downtown. They took their eyes off it for a split second and it started rolling. It went all the way across the parking lot, and then down a hill into Soda Creek, where it stopped with the front wheel in the water and the baby screaming. Lock the brake and they wouldn't have lost their brood or their place in the bratwurst line.

Using it is simple. Simply squeeze the brake and then depress a button that locks it in place. It's like a parking brake on a car. Put it on not whenever you're so inclined, but whenever your vehicle is.

Another unsung attribute of the ever-versatile jogger is its carrying capacity. Use it to go to friends' pot-lucks, carrying your dish in the mesh-lined tray beneath the seat. Bring it to the park and store soccer balls, Frisbees, blankets, extra clothes and snack bags beneath. Most also have a pocket behind the rider for things like sunscreen, water bottles and now-where'd-it-go pacifiers. We've even used ours without any kids inside, solely as a cargo carrier.

Like a car, your kids will eventually take pride of ownership in it. They'll customize it with little dolls and sippy cups, adding everything but the fuzzy dice. Like your dog seeing you holding a leash, they'll also get excited whenever they see you pull it out from the garage.

You can't fault your kids for becoming attached. Many joggers are as decked out as a Maserati. Ours even has a plastic sunroof sewn into an easily deployed shade- and rain-ceiling. We can't use it to check on the rider because it only gives the pusher a visual trajectory toward her feet, but it's a nice touch. If nothing else, it lets in light for the Queen of Sheba inside.

Other features include a slope for the legs leading to a plastic ledge where the rider can rest her feet, and two recline modes, more than our sofa lounger at home. It has everything, it seems, save for shocks making it go up and down low-rider-style at a crossroads. In fact, many of today's joggers do have shocks, some of which are better than those on my mountain bike. Other joggers are even more high-tech, converting into Burleys you can tow behind your bike and sleds you can take cross-country skiing. They're the type of thing Inspector Gadget might use if he had kids. There are three-, four- and even five-in-one kid contraptions that serve each purpose well, and take the pressure off your garage space when not in use.

It's when in use, however, that joggers shine. Though rare is the jogger that goes straight rolling on its own (often because one tire has less air than the other), it doesn't matter. You're always behind the handlebars steering. They're perfect for sidewalks, streets, bike paths and even wide, smooth trails. You'll learn to pop a quick wheelie to get over curbs, and to ease the rear wheels forward to get down them. About their only drawback is that they sometimes block your line of sight when running, leaving you to step on unseen rocks and canine deposits.

And here's a jogger's real beauty. When you want to store it in the crawl space for the winter, or take it in the car on a trip, its collapses into near nothingness for easy transport and storage. Simply pop off the wheels and fold it down into a triangular-shaped pancake. Just realize that as soon as you pack it away in the crawl space Murphy's Law says that you'll need it again the next day.

Double Your Fun

Occasionally you'll even see a double jogger commandeering a bike path. If you're feeling heroic out jogging with one kid in a jogger, wait until some mom passes you pushing a double with two beaming babies inside. Then you'll feel truly inferior.

For the most part, doubles are for those whose kids are relatively close in age, and more importantly, size. No studies exist on how well doubles track compared to the weight differentials of the riders, but get kids of dissimilar mass inside and you could well be running around in circles, just like the kids have you doing at home.

But for those with twins and others kids of similar size, a double might often be your only choice. They require a slightly wider path, and slightly more stamina and willpower, but they, too, will get you out of the house. With two riders, the only additional thing you have to deal with is the occasional fight that breaks out over a gummy bear and additional wear on the brake pads.

Casey and Brooke are three and a half years apart, so by the time Brooke grew out of her role in the jogger, Casey grew into it. Thankfully, we never needed a double. But countless families do, and the doubles work well, allowing parents to get out on their feet when their plural brood is getting underfoot.

Single or double, following are a few final pointers to their operation. 1) Make sure the tires all have equal air pressure so the jogger doesn't pull to one side. 2) Don't keep a death grip on the handle. Keep your hands lightly touching the bar. You can also switch off so you're pushing with one arm while swinging the other. 3) Schedule your jogger times to coincide with nap time. Your kids will fall asleep as soon as you leave and wake up as soon as you return for a win-win wheeled adventure all the way around.

SAN DIEGO'S STROLLER STRIDES

Sometimes necessity truly is the mother of invention—especially when it comes to mothers who find it a necessity to get outside.

Such is the case with a group of moms in San Diego taking part in a novel exercise program that has now expanded to include 600 locations nationwide and more than 20,000 participants. The sport, if you can call it that, is Stroller Striding, a postnatal stroller workout program which began in 2001 when new mom Lisa Druxman discovered a way to recreate with her newborn son by using a stroller.

Her routine has now evolved into a 60-minute class that combines a stroller walk with intervals of body toning using exercise tubing, the environment and the stroller. The long and skinny—which she hopes is the shape its practitioners become—is that it provides moms with a fun and effective way to get fit following pregnancy, as well as an opportunity to bond with their babies through exercise. "It's incredible how much the program has grown, both in size and in the opportunities it provides for new moms," says Druxman, a mother of two who founded the franchised fitness company after the birth of her first child. "Our primary mission is to expand healthy resources for new mothers across the country."

The program has caught on like wildfire, or at least Webkinz. In its first six years, Stroller Strides has stretched beyond its postnatal stroller workout program, partnering with several companies to offer prenatal fitness classes, free playgroups and clubs for moms, and— brace yourself—even its own stroller. The company has also partnered with BOB, a manufacturer of jogging strollers and stroller accessories, to offer none other than the Stroller Strides Fitness Stroller, a lightweight workout jogger that maneuvers easily, with a swiveling front wheel that can be locked into place for running or off-road use.

The device also features a Stroller Strides Fitness Kit, complete with a storage console for water, exercise tubing and a manual to assist moms in turning their routine stroller walk into a workout. The company has also branched into prenatal fitness, partnering with Fit to Deliver, a program designed to keep moms active during pregnancy via 60-minute classes. It's also debuted the LUNA Moms' Club, a free program offering weekly playgroups and mom's night out events at Stroller Strides locations to create a supportive community for moms.

Druxman, the Über-mom, also just released *Lean Mommy*, a book incorporating the Stroller Strides workout to guide new mothers down a healthy postpartum path, maximize their free time, and bond with their baby through exercise. The workouts simply require a stroller, front pack carrier, exercise tubing and requisite baby.

If you have additional spare time (insert laugh track here) and want to take on a side job, it's also not a bad place to work. It's the 17th fastest-growing franchise in the country and, according to *Working Mother Magazine*, is one of the top 25 small companies to work for in the country. And all from a mom jonesing for exercise. "Our goal is to provide moms with every opportunity to be happy and healthy in motherhood," says Druxman. Info: www.strollerstrides.com.

RUNNING WITH KIDS

Okay, enough of the jogger. What about getting your kids into the action?

While not many parents actually go jogging *with* their kids, that doesn't mean you shouldn't encourage them to run on their own. Kids are natural runners—just look at any recess at school. But they don't necessarily like it to be an organized activity in itself, especially with their parents. They want to play, not get exercise; and they like doing so with friends, not family.

Deep down inside, even kids realize they need to burn off a little energy every day—especially after that third bowlful of Trix. But to do so by going for a jog? That has as much appeal as overcooked Brussels sprouts.

If you have healthy, active kids, you don't really need to encourage them to run. It's not like riding a bike. They figure it out themselves pretty easily...like the first time they hurt their older brother and have to run away. I don't think there's such a thing as a how-to video on teaching your child to run, and I've never witnessed a parent saying, "Okay sweetie, just move your legs back and forth real fast...now swing your arms a little. No, the arm opposite from your leg."

Running is programmed in as a survival skill, and comes in handy throughout their lives, whether it's girls running away from boys, boys avoiding cooties, and kids of all ilk running away from their parents at suppertime.

One of Casey's proudest running moments—one that she still talks about to this day—came as an underage 4-year-old when she went out with the 5-year-olds at the local rodeo halftime to grab a ribbon from the tail of a sheep. It was sheer mayhem, a giant amoeba of kids oozing this way and that, some falling in manure, some lagging behind, some portending a future as track stars. Caught up in our peanuts and Budweiser, we barely heard the announcer say, "We have a winner."

"What's your name?" he asked the girl holding the ribbon.

"Casey," she replied meekly, holding up the ribbon with a sheepish grin of her own.

That day instilled in her the importance of running, and running fast. From then on, she hasn't been afraid to try and perfect it.

I can only remember one time when we went out for a family jog as kids. The only reason we did was the ulterior motive behind it. More accustomed to running for political office than doing so on pavement, my mom was vying for a seat on U.S. Senate. In filming a TV commercial showing her wholesomeness, her campaign manager had all six of us Buchanan kids jogging, Blue Angel-style, behind her, following a van with a cameraman filming out the back door while driving up 13th Street. It was meant to look like we always went out jogging as a family together, but in reality we were breathing exhaust and staring into a camera lens. But at least it was more realistic than the later clip showing us playing football as a family, Mom handing me the ball and me throwing a lame-duck pass to my brother, Bruce.

We were, however, lucky enough to run with another person under our roof.

When he won the gold medal in the marathon in the 1972 Olympics in Munich, Frank Shorter was living in the basement apartment of our house. We loved the arrangement for the giant vats of gorp he kept in his kitchen, which we'd sneak religiously, but we also enjoyed running with him. Even if we only tagged along for the first half-mile of his 28-mile training route, he was a bona fide grown-up and by golly, we relished running with him.

My dad, bless his blister-causing soul, encouraged running also, only it was a punishment called Road Work. If we started acting up in the back seat of the family station wagon on road trips to the family ranch in Cody, Wyoming, he'd pull over and make us get out in the middle of flatland nowhere and slowly drive away, leaving us to run after the car.

He'd usually give us a warning or two first. But then the inevitable "All right, Road Work!" sentence would be handed down from the front seat if we kept acting up. Do something really bad, like throw something that lands in the front seat or make your sibling cry, and the castigation might last a mile or two—long enough for you to barely make out the car's license plate as it slowly disappeared down the road. Lesser infractions might have us pounding the pavement for a few hundred yards. Thankfully, it happened to my two older brothers more than it did to me. But no matter the victim, it

instilled the concept that running for the sake of running isn't always fun and is indeed exercise.

While you don't necessarily have to resort to Road Work, encourage your kids to run as much as you and they can, with or without you as a chaperone. Chances are that unless it involves balls, games or other apparatus, it'll end up on the back burner as an all-family activity. But it doesn't matter. Rubbing the sole raw on a pair of sneakers is the best way to metabolize Sugar Smacks. And you can always revisit running with your kids when they're teenagers—as long as you text-message them the time and place.

STROLLER SHOPPING

Please, say it isn't true. Unlike the olden days when a stroller was a stroller was a stroller, now you have to actually go shopping for them. If it isn't enough to choose between drapes to diapers, now you have to do so for strollers.

Fathers who abhor this waste of a weekend take note: the best way around it is to hint at all baby showers that a jogger, or stroller, would be much better than another peach-colored blanket. Whatever you get you'll make do with, from the airport concourse to the shopping mall.

It's another matter if you're going to run with your child multiple times per week. Then, if baby shower hints have fallen on deaf ears, you'll have to buck up for a serious jogger. A few things to look for: it should track straight; roll almost effortlessly with the slightest nudge, and your kid should be cozy and safe inside, with both a waist belt and shoulder straps. The good ones weigh anywhere from 20-25 lbs. and offer some sort of suspension to help with maneuverability and response. Wheel size hovers around 16-inches, with the better ones coming with high-pressure, road tires for a smooth roll. Also look for such frills as cup holders and storage space.

Like a gas grill, don't compromise. And brace yourself for some sticker shock at the register. High-tech versions like the BOB Ironman Sport Utility Stroller—there they go, cashing in on the popular Sport Utility moniker--can run up to $350 or more. Heck, you can push your kid around for free at home. The company even offers an Ironman Sport Utility Stroller with extra seat padding and an extended recliner feature with a whopping 70-degree tilt.

But consider it an investment in your freedom.

Chapter 7

PADDLING WITH KIDS

"There is nothing–absolutely nothing–half so much worth doing as simply messing about in boats."
—Kenneth Grahame, *The Wind in the Willows*

THE COMMENTS STARTED EARLY MONDAY morning as I walked into Mocha Molly's for a ritualistic cup of coffee. "Hey," said one passerby, "nice photo in the paper." Dropping a buck in the Coffee Karma Can and pressing the button on the almighty urn, I heard someone else offer, "Nice shot of Brooke...too bad you were in it."

The ribbing revolved around the day's cover shot in our local paper. Plastered all over town, and later making its way to relatives across the country, was a picture of my two-year-old daughter and me maneuvering an inflatable kayak (okay, okay...a ducky) down the Yampa River. The date was Oct. 27, a little late for such a trip in the Rockies, but it was warm enough to pull the craft out of hibernation.

It was my turn to watch Brooke for the afternoon (I almost said "baby-sit," but you don't "baby-sit" your own kids, you watch them). My wife, bless her soul, was off on a mountain bike ride with friends. Walking back from the park, we stopped to throw rocks in the river and build sand castles on shore. As quickly as the latter were smashed, my daughter, feeling the sun on her now-naked bottom, blurted out ten percent of her vocabulary: "I wanna' go rafting."

She learned the word a full year and a half earlier when we took her as a nine-month-old on a three-day trip down the Colorado River's Ruby-Horsethief Canyon. And it was then we realized that—aside from the scorpions, rattlesnakes, cactus, fire ants, poison ivy, sunburn, cliffs and rapids—paddling with kids is one of the best things in the world that you can do as a family. It doesn't matter if you go with an outfitter or brave it on your own, go for a single day or a week, or take to the waterways in a canoe, kayak or raft. Getting out on the water as a family will float your spirits just as it does your craft.

Of course, it's not always effortless—especially if you're venturing out for more than one day. Diaper changes, pacifier cleaning, cry arbitration and crib packing all compete with everything else you normally need to do to get ready for such a trip. You'll also learn that crack-of-dawn starts will be a thing of the past; a trip's success is measured by smileage more than mileage; and your kids will command more attention than the waterway you're navigating.

But you'll also learn something far more important. When you're making mud pies, skipping rocks and feeding ants to ant lions, none of these other gauges of success matter anymore. There's far more to a paddling trip than meets the grown-up eye.

Once we realized this, we started taking our kids on river trips regularly, convincing other gullible families to join in. Kids became an integral part of these excursions, from the logistics of running shuttle ("Okay, we'll leave your rig at the take-out, but we have to shuttle three car seats down") to rigging for the different ages ("Okay, let's tie the Pak n'Play and umbrella on the back of the blue raft for Abbi, and keep the bow of the red raft free for Stuey, Jack, Lexi, Emily and Carson"). We also learned a few more unorthodox things. If you're telling a bedtime story in the tent, make sure your spouse didn't bring the baby monitor out to the campfire where everyone else can hear you; and a toddler placing a headlamp over her diaper and dancing around the fire rivals the best entertainment you can find anywhere ("I said make it a Bud Lite, not a butt light").

Armed with these experiences that October day on the Yampa, Brooke and I set off for our final voyage of the year. And this time I was Solo Dad—no mom packing sunscreen, sunhat, water shoes or water wings. Any mistakes would be on my shoulders.

After filling the car with gear, we set off for the take-out, where I left the baby jogger, her take-everywhere stuffed camel, a pair of running shoes, towel and change of clothes for each of us. "Why are you doing?" Brooke asked from the car seat. And thus began her first lesson in shuttles, if not pronouns.

"Well, we have to leave the jogger here so we can drive up there and float back here and then jog back up there to get the car to drive back here," I explained. "Oh," she replied, accepting the dissertation readily.

Explanation complete, we made our way to the put-in and paddled away. Halfway down, after soaking at a riverside hot spring where Brooke caught two snakes, a man waved us over from shore. It was the photographer from the newspaper, looking to epitomize the unseasonably warm weather. He found it in us, dad and daughter, each with ear-to-ear grins and goose-bumped butts.

Despite the coffee shop heckling it created, the photo clearly captured the fun you can have paddling as a family. Our Year of the Flatwater Trip evolved every year thereafter, and now we make paddling—be it on rivers, lakes or the ocean—an annual activity. Add water to your children's upbringing and they'll likely remember it when they're well down the river of life on their own.

WHAT MOTIVATES KIDS
By Bruce Lessels

What motivates kids to paddle varies tremendously from one child to the next. Figuring out why they're in a boat to begin with is the first step to being able to start them down the path to becoming lifelong paddlers. Most kids won't tell you what makes them tick. You have to play detective.

Take our two daughters, for example. Our 8-year-old is something of a risk taker and very comfortable in the water. She's task oriented—she does things for the sake of doing them, and maybe even for the adrenaline rush. She wants to learn skills—the how's and why's are important to her. This winter, she asked to go to an indoor pool with me to learn to roll a kayak. Shortly after I taught her to wet exit, she was playing around with getting back into the boat underwater. A little while later, she asked another adult to teach her to roll, and she was hip snapping against the side of the pool in no time. Another couple of sessions and she mastered the roll. She likes whitewater, just as she finds snowboarding more interesting than skiing. She's fascinated by the styles, the personalities, the excitement of whitewater, and she thinks Mohawk hairstyles are really cool.

Our 11-year-old is more interested in horses than in kayaks. She's a very good paddler and can move a kayak effectively, but to convince her to come on a paddling trip, we have to invite the right friend along. Then it becomes a social thing. She and the friend might paddle ahead and challenge each other to see who can stand up in the cockpit longer before falling in, or just float down the river lounging on their back decks and telling jokes. She's competitive, so if she and the friend decide to see who can get from point A to point B faster, she'll figure out how to paddle as fast as she can, and might even ask us for some advice about how to go faster. But take the friend out of the equation, and her motivation to paddle plummets.

A few years ago, she and I paddled an early-spring run on a local Class II-III creek with her schoolmate and his dad. We paddled two tandem canoes with dads in the stern and kids up front. My daughter wasn't thrilled about the trip, but she was curious enough to see what it was all about that she went along with it. The other boat flipped a couple of times and we quickly rescued them.

As we continued downriver after helping them recover from the second flip, my daughter stopped paddling in the bow and turned to face backwards and look back at the other canoe. It was OK; I didn't need her to paddle, but I could see she wasn't enjoying herself. I asked her what was the matter and she started crying and said she wanted to pull over and stop the trip. "But we haven't even gotten wet," I said.

"I don't care. I just hate watching Daniel get cold," she replied.

I tried to reassure her, reminding her that he was wearing a wetsuit, but she wasn't buying it. Finally both boats pulled off the river, having only completed a third of the run, and called it a day.

I learned a lot about motivation that day. For one thing, the motivation for that trip had come more from the dads than from the kids. I should have seen this at the beginning, but I was so intent on paddling the river that I missed the obvious signals she was sending me. For another thing, my older daughter is a people person and very empathetic. She can't have fun if she thinks someone else is not having fun. It's a great quality about her and one I hadn't fully appreciated until that day.

Our kids might turn into fanatical paddlers, horseback riders, or snowboarders, and in my more lucid moments, I'm fine with any of those choices. But when I'm feeling the urge to get in a boat, I can convince myself that they think just as I do. Nothing could be further from the truth. And it's a good thing, too. If I can expose them to paddling in a positive way, give them some basic skills and safety information, and help them have some good times in a boat, then I've done my job. It's up to them to decide whether and how to continue.

—Bruce Lessels is the author of "Paddling with Kids" (Appalachian Mountain Club), a former U.S. Team Slalom racer and owner of Massachusetts' Zoar Outdoor Center. He lives with his wife and two daughters on a small creek that feeds his hometown Deerfield River.

EQUIP THY BROOD

Before you get started, memorize the number one rule when paddling with kids: always make sure both you and your child are wearing a properly fitted life jacket at all times when on the water. Though sometimes you might want to put them in a straight jacket instead, never stray from this golden rule.

It doesn't matter if you're in a canoe, kayak, raft or even a pedal boat at the local lake. If you take home nothing else from this chapter, sear this into your skull like the pancakes you burn after distractedly cleaning up a glass of spilt milk. Today's Coast Guard-approved Type III life jackets fit better and are more comfortable than ever, and there's no excuse not to wear one.

PFDS FOR HALFPINTS

We tested the following PFDs for tykes on a multi-day spring rafting trip with six kids, ages 2-7. While the canyons provided the perfect testing grounds for our little guinea-piglets, the real laboratory came during cannon-balling cliff jumps into side pools, where every PFD worked flawlessly. Shoulders stayed tight thanks to crotch and side straps, and the jackets didn't rise to the ears while raising our subjects back to the surface. Sure, our little vole-sized volunteers might have gotten cold in the process. But it was a small sacrifice to pay for science, and nothing a Fruit Roll couldn't cure.

Extrasport Volks Child, Junior and Inlet Junior

A deep-cut neckline and open arm holes are designed to make Extrasport's Type III Volks Child and Junior PFDs as comfortable as footie pajamas, so your kids will put them on and keep them on. Both are made from a 210-denier fabric that should withstand most errant land-based tumbles. The Child ($50) is for toddlers weighing 30-50 lbs., with dual leg straps that keep the jacket where it belongs. The Junior ($54) is for kids weighing 50-90 lbs. Extrasport also makes a full-featured youth PFD called the Inlet Junior ($80), with a center-zip design, fleece-lined hand-warmer pockets, adjustable neoprene waist belt, and reflective shoulders and logo. www.extrasport.com.

MTI Infant, Child, Youth Reflex/Discovery

With PFDs for tykes of all walks—including those who can't walk—MTI makes a life jacket for everyone in the mini-van. The Infant (0-30 lbs.) and Child (30-50 lbs.) come with large high visibility colored grab loops on head supports for easy retrieval, crotch straps, buckle waists and center zippers. The Youth Reflex and Youth Discovery are designed for children 50-90 lbs., with a center zipper, duel side straps and adjustable shoulders for matching the growth of your child's torso. www.mtiadventurewear.com.

NRS Crew Universal, Youth Vista

Northwest River Supplies has solidified its child PFD presence with the Crew Universal, a Type III that's ideal for flatwater and close-to-shore safety. It doesn't offer frills and other fancy bells, just safety and all-day comfort. The jacket has lots of flotation, four side adjustments and a waist strap for a comfortable fit. A tough 400-denier nylon shell stands up to years of use. Sizes: Youth (50-90 lbs.), Child (30-50 lbs.). The company also has the Youth Vista, a medium-profile PFD that offers everything you need for river, lake or ocean safety. Size: Youth (50-90 lbs.). www.nrsweb.com.

Stearns Infant, Heads-up and Puddle Jumper

Scooby-Doo. Tweety Bird. Taz. Sea Creatures. Iguana. If you can't get your kids into a Stearns PFD, you probably won't be able to get them into their favorite PJs, either. Offering more kid-model PFDs than any other manufacturer, Stearns is the front-runner in the kid's life-jacket market. With adjustable belt and leg strap, zippered front and rounded flotation collar with grab strap, the Heads-up line includes models for infants less than 30 lbs., and children 30-50 lbs., all with cartoon caricatures that will make them want to wear them to bed after they're done boating. www.stearnsflotation.com.

Lifejacket lesson drilled home, when it comes to crafts—not needlepoint and pottery, but paddlecraft —there are as many alternatives to choose from as there are birthday present options at Toys R Us. In Colorado, we often take to the local waterways and lakes in rafts, canoes and inflatable kayaks (not too much use for sea kayaks for us landlubbers). In the Midwest and along the coasts, families break out canoes, sea kayaks and rec kayaks for their watertime fun. Even taking the family rowboat on Golden Pond instills the magic of water, as does hopping in an inner tube down a slow-moving creek.

Craft chosen, there are two ways to get your feet wet: either line up the necessary gear and John Wesley Powell it by yourself, or hook up with an outfitter to show you the ropes. For those unfamiliar with the discipline, for any real trip, and especially overnight ones, going with an outfitter is the best bet. They have the gear and skills to ensure your indoctrination into paddling doesn't become an indunktrination (no, that's not a word, but it could be).

Unsure? Take an outfitted trip first and then play Huck Finn. As they say, better safe than soggy. Either way, realize that paddling with your kids is a way to come together on a medium that's responsible for all life itself—which means it's bound to help your family life as well. If that's not enough to stop your kids from fighting, perhaps it's time for Dr. Phil.

For me, it started when I was a water droplet of a man myself and joined my family as a fifth-grader on a five-day float down Colorado's Yampa River. Whether that trip influenced me to eventually raise my own kids a block away from the same river, I'll never know. But it left an impression as indelible as the markers my daughters use on the living room walls back home.

About all I remember from the trip is the guide telling me to kiss the desert-varnish-striped Tiger Wall for good luck as we floated by (practice for my first real schmooch that I laid upon Laura Brandt just a year later), and giving my mom a bouquet of Indian Paintbrush flowers at camp, my face reddening like its petals when a female guide commented on the gesture. You never know what a child will remember from any given trip, even if the memory's buried like a plastic soldier in the bottom of the toy basket. Not to undermine my masculinity, but for me it was a flower bouquet and a kiss.

While I commend my parents for taking us out on the Yampa, and feel we're paying it forward with our own brood, some parents take it farther than we do. Joe Jacobi, who won the 1992 Olympic gold medal in two-man whitewater canoe, regularly takes his daughter, Seu (named for the course in Spain where he won the Olympics), on the back of his whitewater kayak while surfing Tennessee's Ocoee River. He started this when she was as little as six. "She loves it," he says. "She posts on it just like she's riding a horse."

Jacobi, one of the country's top kayak instructors, feels it's all about what you're comfortable with and what you know. He's more comfortable in a kayak than on a canter. After signing Seu up for horseback riding lessons later that year, he realized how other parents must feel about her kayaking. "I was as scared for Seu horseback riding as other parents would have been for kayaking," he said.

Another acquaintance, who runs the National Whitewater Center in Charlotte, N.C., regularly puts his daughter in the front of his two-person whitewater canoe and takes her down the course. Mark Singleton, executive director of American Whitewater, a nonprofit dedicated to preserving waterways, recently bought a Shredder, a two-man cataraft, for his two kids, aged 10 and 8. Jessie Stone takes it beyond family by organizing kayaking trips for inner-city kids.

All this goes to show that kids are never too young to take up paddling, and that there are a variety of craft to choose from in getting them started. Just be prepared to purchase something after they get their first taste.

WILD RIDES IN WATER WORLD

Cringe if you will, but even taking your kids to water parks will instill a love of recreating with water, one that might resurface later on a waterway without the floating Band-aids.

We're certainly not averse to having technology lend a hand. We've visited Water World in Denver, with great results, from swirling down the toilet-shaped Whirlpool ride and plopping into a pool to taking a lazy inner tube float through a man-made canal. While it's not wilderness, it's wet.

So one time it wasn't so great. It came on Disney World's It's a Small World ride when our boat stalled out just minutes from the end, bumper-to-bumper behind similar craft. Stuck like a raft on a rock, we were forced to listen to the tiny dolls repeatedly sing the ride's theme song like a twisted scene from *Clockwork Orange*. There was no escape, particularly from the two merry-go-round Indonesians who twirled nauseatingly close every third verse. Painful as it was, trapped seconds from salvation and sanity, it was a float trip. And deep inside it, too, instilled how much fun you can have on water.

This was pounded home again when we visited Disneyland in California. The kids' favorite ride wasn't the Matterhorn or Mr. Toad's Wild Ride, but Grizzly River Run, where a track hauls your "raft" up a giant mountain and then turns you loose to career with the currents. The ride's builders tried to create an aura of fun and authenticity, from ancient kayaks hanging from rafters in the entryway to round eight-person "rafts" complete with drybags, Pelican boxes, and, oddly, avalanche shovels strapped behind the seats. After buckling our seatbelts (a no-no on any real river trip), we were whisked away on the "river," passing petroglyphs, a disheveled kayak camp and tributaries littered with "real log" strainers. Then we plunged over Bear Claw Falls, into the wave-filled Eureka Mine Shaft No. 13921, and finally over an Old Faithful-like geyser that spewed and sprayed riders at random. Led by our daughters, everyone screamed with delight until the bitter end.

"Can we do it again?" they asked as soon as we disembarked.

On the next ride, after wising up and bumming cheap ponchos from people exiting their ride, Brooke wasted no time in telling our fellow passengers, "We go real rafting all the time in Colorado." She was proud of the fact, and felt prepared for whatever Disney could throw at her. In all we did the loop five times, more than Jumpin' Jellyfish and the Yellow Submarine combined (thankfully, It's a Small World was closed).

The point to our National Lampoon-like vacation? Riding atop water in any form, even if you're just seconds away from the cotton candy kiosk, can open your kids' eyes to the fun your family can have floating.

CANOEING WITH KIDS

Canoes are great watercrafts for including your brood. Not only can a single parent load, unload and carry a canoe big enough to fit the whole family, but they even offer the benefit of playpen-like walls to keep your kids in the boat.

As well as their ease of rigging comes their usefulness. There's a reason Voyageurs used them to trek over hill and dale throughout the Northland (though, admittedly, not often with kids in tow). Get to a stretch of river you don't like, or come to the end of a lake, and simply unload it, throw it over your head like a fur hat and portage away. Another benefit is their carrying capacity. They're like a floating grocery cart that can carry food and family, lacking only the wheels for a portage (and you can actually get those, too). Even a simple 16-footer can fit a family of four, as well as Rover the dog.

Here I have to confess. While I've taken several multi-day canoe trips in the Boundary Waters and Canada, I've yet to take the kids on one of these week-long forays. We've done plenty of paddle-camping trips, sure. But they've usually been in a raft, which is uniquely suited for rivers out West. We've taken our kids canoeing aplenty, but usually when base-camping at local lakes. All this is to say that I don't profess to be another Grey Owl when it comes to canoeing. But that doesn't diminish the craft's practicality for family paddling.

Countless families put canoes to great family use, piling the kids in for multi-day trips. Known for their epic photography voyages throughout the North Country, Canada's Gary and Joannie McGuffin didn't lose a stroke when their daughter, Silas, now 10, came along. She's already been on several month-long adventures with them and is wiser beyond her years because of it. Plenty of other parents regularly take their kids canoeing as well, from the Buffalo River in Arkansas to Stillwater Canyon of the Green River in Utah.

For good reason. If you know what you're doing, wear life jackets and have a modicum of balance, canoes are the perfect family camping craft. They're also perfect for simple day trips on Lake Sunday.

Our perfect family canoe manifests itself as a 15.5-foot, Royalex Old Town Osprey, as forest green as our canoeing skills. When we first got it, it was big enough to fit three-year-old Brooke five times end-to-end, with room left over for newborn Casey, and our dog, Java. Now that they've aged a few years, it still fits everyone, mom and dad taking the bow and stern, with kids and pets in the middle.

At first it didn't happen that way. As an infant, Casey became affectionately known as what my friend Mike McCrae calls a "bow baby," riding shotgun in front of the bow paddler, most often my wife. This meant my wife couldn't always be relied upon for a stroke when necessary, as one hand was constantly monitoring Casey. But the system worked and we managed to make wakes, while I handled the majority of the propulsion and steering.

Inevitably, Casey would succumb to the movement and sound of water and nod off to sleep, and we'd be back to two-paddler cruise-mode, actually getting somewhere instead of relying on my J-stroke. If there was a way to bottle the droopy-eyed feeling canoeing evokes and sell it to parents at bedtime, I'd be a millionaire.

Whenever Casey fell asleep, we had two options. Let her snooze where she lay, and hope drips from the paddle didn't fall onto her forehead and wake her up, or move her to a cozier spot amidships. Either way, it was a welcome reprieve for the baby-sitting bow paddler.

Eventually, your child will graduate from her perch in the bow to her rightful spot in the middle of the boat, where she then falls under the stern paddler's jurisdiction. Though still more of a passenger than paddler, this is when she graduates from being a bow baby to...midships munchkin. Though she won't get a boat-shaped hat and diploma for the milestone, it does represent a coming of age for aspiring canoeists. Now, like becoming capable of performing household chores, she's part of the team, especially if you outfit her with her own pint-sized paddle.

With the move to midships, however, comes the responsibility of outfitting. Lay down a simple piece of closed-cell foam to keep them warm and dry, and if possible rig some sort of shade (an umbrella or, for nappers, a towel spread across the gunwales). Whatever you use, don't tie anything down that could impede escape in event of a capsize.

When your kids get bigger, replace the pad with a seat in the form of a cushion, low beach chair, or specialty canoe seat. This will aid their paddling and keep them from becoming slumbering ballast. Another hint from McCrae: Inspect the canoe's outfitting for potential dangers. Make sure seat and thwart bolts have cap nuts and that all sharp edges are covered.

Now it's onto grad school. Once your kids actually start pulling their own weight, they might want to move back to the bow. When this happens, and there's just one grown-up along, turn the boat backwards and place your child up front and you in the rear. This gives the canoe better trim, as you'll be positioned slightly forward of where

you'd be normally.

When your kids get old—and heavy—enough, the last transition is to turn the canoe back around and paddle it normally, taking turns between occupying the bow and stern. As McCrae notes, however, this configuration is short-lived; by the time most kids are big enough for this, they'll want nothing to do with mom and dad. If the seeds have been planted correctly, they'll want a boat of their own.

As a rafter first and canoeist second, I've always drooled over canoes' simplicity, especially their ease of loading and efficiency in the water. Compared to rigging and rowing a Kilimanjaro-mounded raft, you actually go somewhere with each stroke.

For many, it's a question of storage—not how much your canoe can carry, but where to keep it when not in use. As all parents know, garage space lessens once kids enter the picture. While you can deflate a raft or inflatable kayak and store it next to the jogger in the crawl space, actually owning a canoe is like having your mother-in-law visit; you're never quite sure where to put her. Canoes—like some mothers-in-law—are big and cumbersome, and you don't fully appreciate this until you're solo-wrestling it into your garage (your canoe, not your mother-in-law). Like getting a dog, ownership bears responsibilities; you have to care for the thing, water, shelter and all.

We use our canoe most often on family trips to Hahn's Peak Lake, thirty minutes out of town. The first time we made the trip with everyone—my wife, Brooke, Casey, and dog Java — I felt a certain smugness in knowing that I had finally joined that special clique that gets to drive around with canoes atop their cars (and kids in the back). No matter that we were dwarfed by it in our Subaru, and I felt like an ant carrying a leaf — we couldn't open the hatchback, check the oil or even see the stoplight above our hood. I was officially a canoeist, giving the one-finger-off-the-steering-wheel wave to fellow canoeists as if we were connected by birth.

"Dad, why did you wiggle your finger at that car?" Brooke asked the first time I did this universal beckoning to my boating brethren.

"Because they have a canoe on their car, just like we do," I replied.

The answer didn't make much sense to her, but it didn't matter. The important thing was we were going canoeing as a family. And she'd hopefully learn a lot more from it than the finger-wiggle wave.

It was at the put-in that I fully appreciated our new family member's beauty. Compared to rafting, it was a logistical godsend—no Hypalon amoeba wrestling or rabbit-through-the-hole rigging. Simply lift it off the rack—or, in reality, herniate your disc trying to lower one end by yourself because your wife is chasing the kids — throw it in the water and paddle away, wicker basket, flannel shirt and all.

A storm cut our excursion short, but not before we found the canoe to be the perfect playpen and toddler barricade, and had fallen in love with this new addition to our clan. Of course, in so doing, we also opened a proverbial can of worms; Brooke had so much fun she wanted to go the next weekend as well, which we did, as well as the one after that. The trips weren't big, just day-long forays into the forest as part of a typical camping weekend, but they stockpiled another family activity into our arsenal.

There's a final attribute of canoe ownership as well. Because we usually had too much gear for the Subaru, what with playpens, strollers, coolers and snack baskets, we turned the canoe into a cargo box by loading it upright to accommodate the extra gear. Though no self-respecting canoeist ever does so—and might think twice about giving our family the one-finger wave upon seeing this approach—we didn't care a bit. We had a new addition to our recreation family, who was getting along with everyone just fine.

12 TIPS FOR MULTI-DAY PADDLING WITH KIDS

No matter the craft—raft, canoe or kayak—paddling with kids is an art you can continually hone. Following are a few hints to help you along the way.

1. No matter the trip, plan enough days so you can float leisurely. You'll need plenty of time for potty breaks. You'll never put in or arrive on time, so don't even try. Kids, rather than destinations, dictate lunchtime.

2. Keep plenty of water handy and stress the need to drink it. Hydration systems work well, as do bike water bottles and squirt guns.

3. For napping, inverted Crazy Creek chairs make great shade, and so do towels and umbrellas. Let your kids rest prone on a raft's bench-seat or even in a car seat resting on the floor (keeping their life jackets on).

4. Bring along some 12- and 13-year-old girls. They're worth their weight in babysitting gold.

5. Bring alternative paddling vessels (inflatable kayaks, rec kayaks, canoes, etc.), as well as an assortment of tubes and alligators that kids can float in behind your raft.

6. Give a last call for the groover (portable river toilet) a minimum of five times— and make sure every kid hears you—before packing it away.

7. Encourage sleepovers by letting kids tent-hop for the evening (it might even free up some private time for you and your spouse).

8. Sand will stick to the nose drool of a two-year-old and stay there until someone wipes it off.

9. Don't worry about preparing special meals. Even finicky eaters like Casey will eat most anything on a river trip. And keep snacks at the ready (my wife keeps them in a quick-access box under her seat)

10. A frog can be passed around to fourteen different kids without any real adverse effects, but be prepared for a coating of urine on pass Number Seven.

11. The bigger the squirt gun, the better.

12. Gummy bears melt into a blob if left exposed to the sun.

REC KAYAKING WITH KIDS

Rarely will you find a better craft for getting your kids out on the water than rec kayaks, a new breed of boat whose wide, flat bottoms make them stable enough for even the most torrential tantrum. Clad with a properly fitted PFD, children of all walks can use rec kayaks as a seamless indoctrination into the wonderful world of paddling.

Think of them like a sea kayak with training wheels. They're so stable your grandmother could hop in one and paddle away, leaving you stuck with your own kids.

Like kids themselves, these family-friendly kayaks come in a variety of styles and sizes. Two types work best for tykes: sit-on-tops, where you and your child sit on top of a depression in the kayak's hull; and uber-stable rec kayaks, which have large, open-cockpits for ease of entry and exit. Without claustrophobic cockpits to cram inside, both let you and your kids paddle away on the first try without fear of tipping, and both are perfect for paddling as a family, whether your child is in Pampers or getting a Ph.D.

Both styles are available in one-, two- and even three-person models, meaning that, like the family station wagon, you can position your kids wherever you want. In the early years, you're best putting your child directly in front of you (bring an extra life jacket for them to sit on). Then they can grab the paddle between your hands and feel the motion of propelling it forward.

If you're paddling where water and air temperatures are warm, sit-on-tops make the perfect choice. Your entire bodies are out in the open, and your child can even jump in the water to cool off and then climb back aboard. Self-bailing holes near the seat keep the water out, and in the rare event of a capsize, you can simply flip it over and climb back aboard—just like climbing back on a bike.

Rec kayaks have the same wide, stable bottom as sit-on-tops, only they add an enlarged cockpit. This keeps you and your brood out of the elements, and keeps water from puddling around your derriere. Most single-cockpit rec kayaks are big enough for you and your child, and some come with cockpits so large they can fit your mother-in-law as well (though that might be too close for comfort). There are also a variety of double models on the market, letting you position a child up front while you steer from the stern.

No matter which design you go with—sit-on-top or rec, single or tandem—the learning curve for each is akin to riding a tricycle. There's no learning, no leaning, and most importantly, no rolling. Simply hop on and go.

Inflatable Kayaks

Next up on the inflatable ladder when it comes to paddling with kids are inflatable kayaks, or duckies as they're affectionately known by those who don't mind compromising their manhood. I'm not sure who gave them the merganser moniker, but it's an apt analogy. You bob around on the water, propelled by paddles that are as good a tool for the task as webbed feet. Conjuring images of Sesame Street's Ernie in a bathtub, the nickname alone should make your kids start putting their swimsuits on backwards and packing the car.

Nomenclature aside, they're the perfect craft for introducing your young-uns to the world of water. In the first place, they're not fragile like that heirloom canoe. They're made of rubber, PVC or hypalon, just like most indestructible toys. The only way you can hurt them is to puncture them with something sharp, and most parents know to leave the scissors at home. Their make-up also means that they bounce off things rather than go "thunk," sparing your back unnecessary jars and your craft unnecessary scars.

Their best attribute comes in how they handle. Most often paddled with a double-bladed kayak paddle, duckies have wide enough bottoms—like we parents get as we mature—to make them stable, are narrow enough to keep them maneuverable, and carry enough length for the hull speed needed to get you back to shore for snack time.

All this creates a versatile craft that gives your kids a more intimate connection with the water than a raft, yet a more stable one than a traditional kayak or even a canoe. If you're messing about in boats with others, like say on a group rafting trip, they're also nimble enough to deliver things like sippy cups and juice boxes on the fly. Best yet, they can offer a kid-watching reprieve to an overworked spouse who wants to take it out solo.

A ducky also has advantages off the water. When you're through, you simply deflate it and roll it up for easy storage back home—which you most definitely need, now that your garage is littered with mounds of kid gear. Your kids can even get involved in the deflating process, sitting on the tubes to errant fart sounds emanating from the valves.

Duckies generally come in two sizes, single and double, each of which is suitable for boating with your brood. If you're planning to paddle with more than one child, a two-man might be the way to go. They're faster, have more room, and can carry gear for simple overnight excursions. Have the grown-up man the stern for steerability, spread the kids out amidships and bow, and head off into the sunset.

You can also fit one or even two kids in with you in a single, putting the smallest

up front and the largest behind you piggy-back style. You won't set any distance or speed records, but it's plenty of space for tooling around the lake beside camp. Hint: if you're in a single, try putting your child on your lap, giving her a paddle, and letting her call the shots. It'll give her ownership in the "expedition." Then you can chip in as needed if and when the steering goes awry. An alternative is to place the paddle between you and your lap-child's back, but that restricts motion.

On a recent foray down the Yampa, Casey was happy to be up front paddling and in control of her own destiny. Happy, that is, until the first ripple washed up through the self-bailing floor and saturated our respective derrières. But she laughed it off, and afterward I had her sit atop a small drybag, which kept her high, dry and Queen of Sheba mighty. And thus began the Butt Game. No matter where we went, from then on it was my butt that got wet and not her's—a fact of which she was keenly aware. When Brooke climbed aboard in the stern, her butt also bore the brunt of Casey's wrath.

We've used duckies on our local town run — as evidenced by Brooke's and my picture in the paper, thank you — on day trips down the Colorado, at lakeside campsites, and as additional craft on multi-day rafting trips. We've even used them as battering rams against tubers on a crowded Sunday afternoon, and flipped them upside-down at campsites to create waterslides into the river. No matter where we are, kids gravitate to them as they do cartoons on a Saturday morning.

How much do kids like duckies? On one raft trip, young Henry, 3, summed up his sentiment succinctly. "I want to go chicken," he said, pointing to the inflatable kayak. "Quack, quack!"

GUYS AND DOLLS

Take your kids paddling enough and it will likely infiltrate other areas of their lives. Such is certainly the case with our daughters.

Two winters ago we gave in and gave Brooke an American Girl doll for Christmas (note to self: don't tour the American Girl Doll factory in New York City right before the holidays). Her friend, Madeline, then gave her an American Girl Doll kayak to go with it. A month earlier I didn't even know what an American Girl doll was (other than that they're expensive), and now Brooke even had an American Girl Doll kayak to go with it.

Admittedly, I was impressed with its attention to detail. It comes complete with an inflatable hull and deck, storage rigging on the bow deck, a thwart for a backrest, and most importantly, a miniature life jacket that fit the doll perfectly. A sunburst design graces the top of the hull, and stenciled on the boat's side are the words "American Girl Belize Kayak Adventure." If that leads to Brooke someday wanting to sea kayak Belize, I'm all for it.

The only real differences between this model and the real McCoy lies in the paddle. The shaft has square ergo grips for the doll's hands, as well as noise-maker beads inside – features you'd never see in real life. Where its designers came up with this, I'll never know – and I doubt any real paddle manufacturers will ever follow it.

More disconcerting is the warning on the boat's bottom that says, "Doll and kayak should not be placed in water."

"How come I can't place it in the water?" asked Brooke innocently once she read it, already planning its bathtub adventure. "I want her to have as much fun paddling as we do."

SEA KAYAKING WITH KIDS

Brooke was giddy with excitement all morning. She was only four and we were leaving our bed and breakfast in Tofino, British Columbia, for a day-long sea kayaking tour of Vancouver Island's Barkley Sound. Best yet, in a land known for rain and clouds, there wasn't a cumulus in sight, the sky as blue as her Finnish-bloodline eyes.

While my wife went in a single kayak, I put Brooke up front in a double, a nylon spray skirt with suspenders going over her life jacket to keep the Pacific splashes at bay. No sooner had we put in, when she started singing, "Down by the bay, where the watermelons grow," a Raffi favorite.

She loved it from the first stroke. "I can't wait to see a starfish," she said after she finished crooning, dipping her paddle blades in alternately, just like she was supposed to. "Do you think we'll see babies, also? Maybe we'll see Baby Beluga!'"

The tour took us around the protected seaside houses of Tofino and out through a series of small islands, into the British Columbia wilderness. Brooke's strokes didn't really help, but they didn't need to. She was having a blast—especially when she figured out how easy it was to splash me in the stern. Towering cedar rose overhead, and eagles perched on branches far above. Seals poked their heads out of the water at us, as curious as children in a classroom. Then they'd disappear like kids come dinner time, Brooke scanning this way and that to see where they'd surface next.

But it was the starfish that stole the show. Rounding a rocky point, Brooke trailing her blade in the water and watching its wake, we pulled in close to a rocky shore and there they were, in all shades of purples and oranges. "Look, Dad!" Brooke exclaimed. "They're all over the place! Just like in the sky!"

I didn't need any more of a lesson to understand how valuable sea kayaks can be for family forays into the wilds.

Another time, shortly after Casey was born, we rented a houseboat on Utah's Lake Powell with two other families, and topped it with three sea kayaks. We'd take the houseboat as far up a side canyon as we could, and then break out the sea kayaks to explore it farther, putting the kids in the cockpits with us. Then we'd return to the houseboat (complete with a water slide off the roof) for dinner and accommodations. They loved it—at least up until Casey got sick and kept everyone up all night in the tight quarters. My friend Tim still talks about the rally that trip required, especially since on the way home we met another group of friends for a five-day raft trip down the San Juan (remember what I said earlier about having to have a high tolerance for cluster management).

Like Brooke and Casey, my first experience in a sea kayak came with my family—only I was a few years older. I was in high school, and my mom took four of her six kids on a seven-day, sea kayak trip in Alaska. Thankfully, the trip was outfitted, so we didn't have to rely on Mom's logistics or, worse, cooking. We took a charter boat to Culross Island in Prince William Sound, where we based while exploring tidewater glaciers, watching whales and learning all about Alaskan rain and mosquitoes.

Admittedly, it was a late start for me, especially compared to many of today's more ardent sea-faring families, who get their kids out touring while they're still toddlers. But we lived in Colorado, which is known more for its skiing than sea kayaking, and the opportunities just never arose. Still, that one trip in high school made as lasting an impression as the rock I dented my kayak on. I went on to spend two summers guiding rafts and sea kayaks in Alaska, and have been back sea kayaking in Prince William Sound multiple times since.

Unlike rafts, inflatable kayaks and even cumbersome canoes, sea kayaks are sleek and simple, little changed in design from when their Aleut inventors used them to fish and hunt whales. Unlike canoes, they're easily propelled by one person, and put your lower half out of the wind and rain. Traditional, higher-performance sea kayaks have relatively small cockpits and come with easy-to-remove nylon sprayskirts to keep the water out. They're narrower and longer than more user-friendly rec kayaks, which makes them faster, but harder to turn unless you have the help of a rudder. This makes them a better choice when you need to make distance (rarely the case when you're bringing small children along) and in colder climates, where your lower body can reside out of the cold.

They come in both plastic and fiberglass, each of which has its pros and cons. Plastic, as you know from the kids' toys littering your family room, is tougher, heavier and less expensive. Fiberglass is lighter, faster, more fragile, and more demanding on the pocketbook. Our yard at home has one of each.

Base your material and size decision on where you'll use it most. If you're serious about taking it up with your family, tandems work best for younger kids. You can command the stern position, putting your child in the bow. In the odd event you ever get a baby-sitter (hallelujah!), you and your spouse can even escape for a romantic retreat together, if you remember how.

A general rule of thumb: until your kids are capable swimmers, stay close to shore. There's more to see and it's safer than playing Pippi Longstocking on the high seas. Use your discretion, with your child's age and ability determining your route selection.

Make sure your craft has bulkheads or float bags, and that you have a rescue plan should things go awry. Above all, tell your kids what to do beforehand in the event of a flip; that way, they'll be better prepared if you do make an unannounced visit to Atlantis.

While there are several rescue techniques for getting back into a boat (most involving a paddle float and bilge pump), your best bet, especially with kids along, is staying close to shore so you can swim to land easily, and traveling with another paddler to make re-entry easier. Another hint: if your child is using a spray skirt, make sure it comes off as easily as the skirt on Barbie back home.

Some parents store gear in front of smaller children's feet so they won't slide under the deck. Others use a drybag or pad as a booster seat, having their kids straddle it

like riding a pony. The added height helps their paddles clear the sides of the boat and makes it feel like they're not gophers poking their heads out of a hole.

When it comes to paddles, don't get one sized for Yao Ming. Normal adult paddles are usually too big for children. Several companies make children-specific paddles; paddles for small adults can also work. You can also use children-sized wooden canoe paddles that, even though you're in a kayak, can instill the lesson of locomotion. Teach them the proper paddling technique by having their hands shoulder width apart (a lot of kids put them too close together), and show them how to rotate their torso with each stroke.

Then rotate sea kayaking into your list of family friendly activities.

FAMILY BONDING

Family bonding can come in many forms, from spooning the sweet potatoes on Thanksgiving to sea kayaking in Southeast Alaska. That's what we discovered, anyway, on a family reunion in Sitka.

There were thirteen of us in all, part of a get-together Mom gave everyone for Christmas one year. It promised to be a veritable float with Dr. Phil that would have us all singing Kumbayah by trip's end.

At least that's how it was supposed to work. By the time my wife and I flew in from Anchorage and met everyone in Sitka who had ferried north from Vancouver, you could cut the tension with a paddle blade. It was obvious they had spent too much time in close quarters and tight berths; people wandered off on their own for lunch, planned solo excursions, and did their best to avoid group dynamics. Time, I figured, for a little kayak therapy.

What better way than a sea kayak trip, I reasoned, to bring us back to our common umbilical cords? We'd experience every rah-rah cliché in the book: we'd only be as strong as our weakest link, together each achieves more (T.E.A.M.), and there is no "I" in team (though there is one in "family").

Unfortunately, there is also an "I" in rain, which pummeled the hotel window when infant Casey woke us at 5 a.m. With no hotel lobby to relax in, I jiggled Casey in the Snuggly under an awning in the dark, pouring rain, waiting for the local coffee shop to open. The scenario was as dismal as the weather.

Three hours and lattes later, a call to our outfitter confirmed that the trip was still on. After meeting on the hotel porch ("Does anyone have an extra rain jacket?" "Where's Lisa?" "What are you going to wear?"), we caught a cab to the put-in and the start of our Family Bonding through Boating Program. Putting down our assorted coffees, we equipped ourselves with paddles, sprayskirts and PFDs, much like Mom readying us for school in years past, and then began the task of pairing up.

A dead silence ensued before my brother, Stephen, broke the glacial-thick ice: "Who wants to go with Mom?" No hands rose. Not on the best of terms, Lisa and her teenage daughter, Sarah, split up; Helen paired with my wife's sister, Laurie; Catharine and her husband, Dave, paddled the divorcemobile; and I, brave soul, got the matriarch. Next: the bow vs. stern debate, the guide waiting for us to sort it out as patiently as the waiter who fielded our a la carte order the night before.

Paddles banging, we finally pushed off into the glory of Sitka Sound. Soon we were as scattered as on the old family outing to the grocery store, some kids homing in on the Cap'n Crunch and others the Space Food Sticks. Catharine and Dave quickly applied their Ph.D.s to marine life on shore, Helen and Laurie lagged behind discussing lack of children, 19-year-old Sarah flirted with the guide, and Lisa listened to Denise bemoan traveling with toddlers. I, meanwhile, babysat 70-year-old Mom from the stern, using the rudder to keep us on course. I was just beginning to see it as a metaphor for Mom steering us through childhood when my reverie was interrupted: "I have to pee," she said, when we were already far behind the group.

After pulling over, where I repaid her for countless pee stops in the family station wagon, we caught the group at the mouth of Indian Creek. And that's where it hit me. Reminders of family were everywhere: the procreating salmon, the eagle swooping down for a take-home supper, the starfish dog-piling on one another like siblings in a TV room, harbor seals rough-housing, and mussels bunched together as if sharing the bathroom mirror. Even the kelp beds seemingly swayed as one, growing upwards from common roots. Okay, maybe I was going overboard (what was in that latte, anyway?). And maybe it was just that I, too, was in need of a little time alone. Luckily, just as the rain started again and sibling and spouses' arms tired, before my synapses burst with similes, the trip came to an end.

Did the whole sea kayak experiment work? Did we bond better as a family? Who knows? As soon as we disembarked at Crescent Harbor, everyone went his own way again, some to gift shops and others on to Totem Pole hikes. All I know is that when we met again that evening for dinner—a waiter's nightmare with high chair, booster and thirteen story-telling paddlers—spirits were as light as our paddles' drip rings. Sure, we were still a far cry from the Waltons, with Mom dictating what we could order, seats changing mid-meal and three desserts coming with thirteen spoons. But even when fighting over the cheesecake's utensils, we were as close as we've ever been passing the peas at Thanksgiving.

RAFTING WITH RASCALS

Rafting is another great way to open your kids' eyes to the world of water. At a recent baby shower, I talked to a gentleman whose friend's daughter, Katia, already has a whopping one-thousand river rafting miles under her Barbie-sized belt by age six. That's a lot of time that could've been spent watching Barney.

But there are concessions to consider with the craft. The first is where you take it. You're not going to have much fun taking your family out in a raft on the local wind-swept lake or bay. Rafts need current to help propel them along, so the parent doesn't blow a gasket. This means they're pretty much relegated to rivers.

Now you have to find the right one—not too hard, but still with enough current to carry you and your gear along. And you can't always just go with the flow. Current can run you into things. Don't just put in Huck Finn-style, without knowing where you're going, what the trip entails, and what sort of hazards to expect.

For the most part, these hazards present themselves in the form of rapids. Until your kids are comfortable swimming on their own in a PFD, forsake rivers with white-water for those offering a more leisurely float. Rapids are rated on a scale from I to VI, with I being simple flatwater and VI being unrunnable. Think of it as the difference between raising one kid and six. When you get the hang of it, you can get by with one pretty easily. Up the ante to six, however, and you'll be scrambling for dear life. Stick to the Class I-II waterways until your kids are comfortable swimming in rapids.

Also, whether you're going for a day trip or overnight, or have one kid with you or a gaggle, have another adult on board to tend to your kids' needs while you're behind the oars. If you're bringing gear, put it in the rear compartment so the kids can be up front where you can see them.

We've learned a few tricks of the rubbery trade over the years. Like your raft in a wave train, you're going to have to roll with the punches the first few times out. You'll make mistakes and learn as you go.

Being a trip leader on such an excursion—usually the one who secures the permit and/or organizes the trip—lends itself well to being a parent. It requires the exact same skill set, from planning and logistics to exercising patience—cluster-management, in other words. You have to plan meals, hassle with equipment, load and unload cars and rafts, all while deftly dealing with different personalities. Perhaps no other outdoor activity better mimics the art of being a mom or a dad.

A few tidbits we've picked up: it's okay to pee in the raft (as long as it's a self-

bailer), and a simple pail and a shovel are just as important as a pump. Other words of wisdom: don't try to rig and baby-sit at the same time—as at home, you'll never get anything done. Also, keep half an eye on your kids at camp. On one trip, Brooke slipped out of view only to knock down the entire stove and a twenty-person vat of chili when reaching up to the table to get some water. Luckily, it didn't land on her, but plenty of hungry eyes did when we had to make do with just tortillas.

On the water, if your route is wide and free of obstructions, you can attach your craft together to create a floating barge, allowing kids to intermingle. This is also a great time to dole out snacks (and see what the other parents brought). Also keep rain gear and warm clothes accessible in a day bag, and prepare to pull over and wait out a storm if the going gets rough.

20 TIPS FROM REAL RAFTING MOTHERS

Want to really know what it's like to take a raft trip with kids? Heed the following advice compiled from real rafting mothers.

1. Group kids with compatible kids
2. Youngsters are all about snacks—keep plenty on hand (they're too busy playing at camp to eat regular meals)
3. Don't bring extraneous toys—they have all they need on hand (except, maybe, a Nerf, sand bucket and mini-costume for Costume Night)
4. Despite the extra rigging it requires, bring one "Tot Spot" chair per kid
5. Campfire stories shouldn't be too scary
6. Keep some shade going all the time (umbrellas, towels, rash guards, etc.). Hint: use poly-pro jammies on the raft
7. Get them contributing to the group as young as possible
8. Bring unsuspecting "kidless" adults (or even a couple of teenage sitters)
9. Bring ear plugs if you're a light sleeper in close proximity to a toddler's tent
10. Don't bring too many clothes—they just turn into a wet mess
11. Kids prefer campsites with the best rocks (for jumping, hiding from grown-ups, torturing siblings, etc.)
12. Don't over-commit on distance: ten miles/day is good
13. Don't bother bringing homework; it just gets wet and never gets done. Do bring a journal and book
14. Never allow them to exclude anyone
15. Feed kids during happy hour (the kitchen box makes a great table, but get everything you need out first)
16. Don't let them walk around without shoes (scorpions, cactus, etc.): bring sandals or river shoes
17. A squirt gun can make any kid cry, regardless of age
18. Be wary of all-dad trips
19. Keep the groover handy (says one Mom: "Let them get constipated.")
20. Stick to the minimum one-adult-per-kid rule

If you have to negotiate a small rapid, scoot everyone toward the center of the boat and point out appropriate anchors to hold onto. Explain what to do beforehand if you anticipate a bump, and illustrate how to hold onto a perimeter safety line and/or look for a throw rope in the event of a swim.

Above all else, have fun and don't try to stick to a pre-ordained itinerary. Go with the flow and accommodate your kids' needs, whether it's potty breaks, snack stops or pulling over for a game of tag on a sandy beach. A final word to the wise? Pack an extra box of fruit rolls.

The San Juan: A Case Study

My wife's eyes bored deep into the back of my head— as deeply as the river had bored the canyon far below.

What's the big deal? I thought. I had gotten the beta on the secret trail leading to a swimming pool up a side canyon on the San Juan River, and so far it was panning out perfectly. Don't take the obvious trail from camp to the waterfall coming out of John's Canyon; it cliffs out. Instead, hike downstream a few hundred yards, scramble up a cliff band, and then traverse a ledge back upstream to the swimming hole.

We were on the 'scramble up a cliff band' part. The problem was, we had ten kids in tow, ages 4 to 12, who we were belaying up a crack with a throw rope. That's what got my wife's motherly instincts flowing, manifested in her laser-like glare.

Still, only a short vertical crack separated us from a catwalk of sorts leading to one of the best swimming holes in the Southwest. I was sticking to my plan. A friend, an ex-raft guide named Heidi, had told me the hike was fine for kids, and that the cannon-balling ends more than justified the means.

Armed with that ammo, I did what husbands worldwide have done for eons—I ignored my wife. And then we helped every last Who up the crevasse, boosting rumps from the bottom and extending hands from above. Now all that remained between us and a gin-clear swimming pool was a traverse along a cliff-lined trail no wider than their school sidewalk.

This is one of the great things about doing such a trip privately rather than with an outfitter. You have to know what you're doing, from lining up the proper permits beforehand to having the right paddling skills, but you get to call the shots yourself, whether it's preparing meals, selecting campsites or heading off on spouse-glaring side hikes. While kids add another layer of complexity — like throwing boulders into a simple stretch of moving water — for us, the organizational part came relatively easy. I'd led trips for years before kids – on the Selway, Middle Fork, Grand Canyon, Green and others— and kids were just like any other passengers, only smaller, snackier and more energetic.

The upshot is that beyond the additional logistics they create, kids open your eyes to a micro-world you never paid attention to before. They chase frogs and lizards, make paint out of mud, and crawl through tamarisk tunnels — having a blast with things you never realized were even there. And taking the floating playroom of a raft lets you bring everything you need to make the journey as hassle-free as possible.

Our trip on the San Juan would take us fifty-seven miles in six days, from Mexican Hat to Clay Hills Crossing. Most of it is easy Class I-II, save for II-plus Government Rapid, which kids can easily walk. Dorky dad that I am, I began referring to the rapid as Government (insert evil voice here) Muuuhaha Rapid, which the kids repeated all trip, much to the dismay of the other parents.

In all, we had five families along, with fourteen kids and nine adults. On the solo side were Greg and his sons Danny, 10, and David, 7; Sally, with offspring Kelly, 11, Joe, 9 and Luke, 7; and divorcé Dan, with daughter Anika, 6. Then came the couples: Pete and Gretchen and their two sons Otis, 4, and Oliver, 2; the O'Connells, including twins Finn and Kathleen, 8, Meg, 11, and Mary, 13; and my wife, Denise, and I and daughters Brooke, 7, and Casey, 4.

This ratio broke every rule in the book. The kids had us outnumbered 1.5 to one. They could mutiny if they wanted to—but then who would marshmallow their sticks? Like Captain Bligh, we also had experience on our side. Everyone but Dan had their own raft, and Greg had a massive trailer for shuttling the gear. Though their parents were seasoned river rats, Otis and Oliver were the only first-time river runners.

None of this overshadows the workload such a trip entails, from divvying up meals (everyone was responsible for shopping and preparing one dinner, lunch and breakfast) to orchestrating rides and packing. Take getting ready on the typical school morning and multiply it a thousandfold to emulate the preparation needed to take kids on a multi-day paddling trip.

Coinciding with the kids' late April Blues Break vacation from school, the adventure started with the drive. Aside from obligatory potty breaks, we made stops at Arches National Park and Hole in the Wall near Moab, which includes a petting zoo with ostriches and a sandstone cave that homesteaders had converted into a house. A tour shows the pioneers' living room, kitchen and children's bedrooms.

"They lived there?" asked Casey, incredulous. "I want to live in a cave."

From there, it was on past the Anasazi art at Newspaper Rock before arriving, more than eight hours and twice as many gummy bears later, at the Recapture Lodge in Bluff, Utah.

A sign for the nearby Sand Island put-in helped recapture my misspent youth as well. It was here, twenty years earlier, that I organized my first-ever river trip for spring break, during my final year of college. Kids were replaced with co-eds, Barney dolls with a barrel of beer, and tuck-in time with late-night toga parties. We rented rafts, pilfered food from our campus meal plan, and played Fear and Loathing for seven, sun-drenched, debauchery-filled days. We were so Hunter S. Happy that we even lost our bearings on the map and floated into the take-out a full day too soon.

You'd never make that mistake with kids. If anything, you're always slower than expected, not faster. And you have your wits about you better, too.

As we pulled into the parking lot, a fight from the back seat interrupted my reverie. This trip, I realized, would be markedly different. This became more than apparent as soon as we opened the car doors at the motel. It was like opening a jar of bees: the kids exploded in all directions, eventually rendezvousing at the playground, bordered by a massive, fallen cottonwood that served as even more of playground. Like exercising your dog, we let them expend their pent-up energy and used the freedom to repack gear, figure out the shuttle and fill water jugs.

Rain dampened the ground the next morning, but not our moods. The kids were up before we were, eager to get to the river. To keep them out of our already matted hair, the moms took them to a nearby cliff to view Indian petroglyphs while the rest of us headed to the put-in at Mexican Hat to ready the rafts. When they showed up after their anthropology lesson, the rafts were loaded and water and lunch laid out in the trailer.

If you were to equate our trip to a novel, ours was a true Grapes of Raft. Like climbing Everest—which our pile of gear resembled—bringing kids takes some acclimating. The biggest hurdle is simply making everything fit. As well as the typical firepans, tables, horseshoes, flamingos and lawn chairs you bring on a river trip come the accoutrements of youth: industrial-sized tents, car seats, kid chairs, bassinettes, fold-a-cribs, and more toys than you can shake a rattle at. Pete's raft had a Pack n' Play crib strapped atop an anthill of drybags in the stern; and ours had a car seat for naps below the oarsman, with an inverted Crazy Creek chair offering shade. Smaller bags harboring rain gear lay clipped about; sand buckets, squirt guns and footballs littered the rafts' floors, and snacks found shelter in a variety of coolers and plastic boxes. Inner tubes and inflatable kayaks trailed like dreadlocks behind the rafts, getting ready to annoy oarsmen by pendulumming into their oars. Rafting with kids isn't for Type As.

There's also added calculus to the shuttle conundrum. Not only do you have to get the right number of cars to the take-out, but also the correct number of car seats, which takes Ringling Brothers-type juggling. "Okay," we calculated. "We'll have to make sure seven car seats make it into those two cars."

Thankfully, we had help on this trip. If our gear wasn't neat and tidy, at least our shuttle was. We hired it out to Kansas transplant Richard Neff from Valles Shuttle Service, who would baby-sit our vehicles and car seats and have them all waiting for us at the Clay Hills take-out in six day's time.

If you've ever tried to actually accomplish anything at home while watching kids, multiply the hassle when rigging a raft. While having a beach makes it easier—for the most part they'll busy themselves with sand castles and mud pies, while avoiding a fleet of sunscreen-carrying moms—Murphy's Law dictates that they'll get underfoot right when you move the trip's heaviest, most awkward piece of gear: the drybox.

Eventually you'll get everything sorted out and shove off—hopefully, not leaving anyone orphaned ashore.

While the San Juan traverses some of the best canyon wilderness in the country, somewhere above the canyon rim near Mexican Hat is an Air Force base. The last time we were here, three fighter jets buzzed the rim with a loud sonic boom. "River trip, loud airplane," Brooke muttered in association for months afterward. Luckily, she grew out of it and we won't be taking her mumbling to a sanitarium. Today, as we the shoved off, the only sound was the lap of the river.

The kids quickly settled into their new floating home. We rigged the gear in the stern, freeing up each raft's front as a walled-in playroom. They could sit on a bench covering the thwart, or stand on the floor, waist-deep to the tubes. It was the perfect kid barrier.

The comments the first hour alone reaffirmed our choice of vacation.

"Look what we found...a real-live lizard!" Anika, 6, said right before we shoved off.

"I got splashed and got wet!" added another as we rounded our first bend.

"Can we go home and get my slippers?" asked four-year-old Otis.

The comments were as innocent as the river supporting our rafts. Day one and already the dividends were piling as high as our gear. Realizing them, of course, requires an investment in everything from patience to sleep deprivation. But once the returns start trickling in—my daughters saying "This is my best day ever," and "I want to live here"—the rewards of floating with kids outweigh even your loaded-down craft.

Our first stop came at the neck of mile-long Mendenhall Loop, a bend where we let all the kids except Oliver—under adult supervision, of course—hike over a low-lying saddle and back down to the river on the other side. The shortcut served a lesson in geology as well as history. At the top was an abandoned stone cabin once lived in by pioneer Walter Mendenhall, spawning questions about him the rest of the day.

"Did he have kids?" asked Luke.

"What did he eat?" asked Brooke.

"I'm hungry," said Casey.

We picked up the kids hitch-hiking on shore a half-hour later, Brooke leading the charge with a Sissy Spacek thumb held high.

Camp came just as the sun was nodding behind the canyon rim. We pulled over at the upper of several spots we had marked on the map, but sent a scout down in an inflatable kayak to make sure we weren't missing out on Shangri-La just downstream. Sure enough, he radioed back that the next camp was even better. So we herded the kids back into the boats and shoved off. It was a good call. A path led to a playground-sized sandbox on a bench above the beach, with a Hobbit-sized maze filled with butt-slides leading through the tamarisk from the upper veranda back down to the bank-side kitchen.

You couldn't script a better place for kids to burn pent-up energy. It was Kids Gone Wild from the moment they stepped ashore, with children darting in all directions, painting dirt-water on cave walls, chasing lizards and wallowing in mud. And it offered the beginnings of their education at Outside U. Among the lessons: cacti hurt, yucca are pointy, and red ants bite.

Eventually we gonged the dinner bell—in this case an upside-down spaghetti pot—and rounded the kids up from their assorted adventures, which let us grown-ups finally relax. A campfire and marshmallows, followed by a few rounds of This Land is Your Land, Baby Beluga and Down by the Bay on guitar, soon led to story time and, thankfully, bed, with the Exhausted Caretaker Principle ensuring only half the parents re-emerged after tuck-in.

In the morning, the kids gained a lesson in canyon erosion by building a water canal from the upper sandbox down to the beach. While we carried bags down to the rafts, they dumped water into it and watched it schuss through the sand until it created a mini-ravine filled with pools and drops just like the side canyons pouring into the San Juan.

The random comments made over the next few days confirmed that everyone was quickly adapting to life on the river.

"Hey, I made the perfect sandwich," said Kathleen at lunch.

"Anyone want to play 500?" asked Finn with a Frisbee, at a rest stop on a broad sandbar.

"Hey, a lizard!" announced Casey before scampering off to give chase.

"I'm firster," said Otis, when the kids lined up to slide down a rock into the river.

They adopted pet caterpillars and frogs, chased garter snakes out of their skins, built forts of driftwood, and blasted the unsuspecting with the old 90-degree trick squirt gun. At one camp, Casey started crying after she lost her pet caterpillar and all the other kids still had theirs. But the tantrum was quickly sidetracked by another river offering.

"Hey, look, a ladybug!" she exclaimed, catching it and rushing over to show the other kids her newest find. The lost pet caterpillar was officially old news.

I don't know of any caterpillar cartoons—perhaps they're just not personable enough to lend themselves to Disney — but it was caterpillar city on the San Juan. One day, I steered the raft close to shore, where we passed village after village of cocoons high in the willows. The nine kids who somehow migrated onto my raft commented on each one, letting their imaginations run wild. My wife commented also, especially when we got too close to a branch and it whipped one of the cocoons into her hair, sticking there like a marshmallow. But that's another story.

Later, passing close to the bushes again, we picked up a lone caterpillar hitchhiker on the front tube, a castaway from a cocoon. Resembling Cindy Lu Who, down to her feet snuggled into a sack, the poor thing was left high and dry on our raft, as alone as a soloist in a third-grade choir concert.

Everyone quickly scooted over to make room and voted to name it Freddy Freckles. Protecting him against the wind, the kids then passed him around in their cupped hands as we gave him a ride downstream, past row after row of other cocoons. Eventually, goodwill got the better of everyone and we dropped him off at his friend, Patty's cocoon a mile or two downstream.

"Bye-bye, Freckles," waved Casey as we floated away. "Have fun at your friend's house."

Just like each bend during the day, each camp brought a different playground. One night led to an impromptu costume contest using whatever you could find. The winners were Otis the Beer Salesman and "Huck" Finn as a bandana-on-a-stick hobo. The parents' costumes paled in imagination.

We churned out our mileage in bite-sized portions, just like the mini-Snickers we broke out for snacks. We made 9, 9, 13, 7, 12 and 7 each of the six days, leaving plenty of time for breaks, side hikes and obligatory mud baths. Standing knee-deep in one mud pit, I told the kids to turn around and then topped it with my hat and sunglasses when their backs were turned. I then hid behind a nearby rock, offering a quick lesson in the powers of quicksand. Jaws dropped when they turned around, before Casey saw my butt sticking out from behind a boulder.

Another camp was littered with the conical depressions of ant lions, so we played Gladiator by feeding them ants and watching the predators' claws snap the offerings out of the bottom of their lairs. Later, a discussion on desert varnish streaking down the cliffs led to the girls talking about streaking their hair. Some kids built sand castles, while others made paint brushes from sage and paint from red mud. In my notebook, Brooke drew a smiling picture of herself sleeping in a tent with a dream bubble showing her mom, dad and sister in similarly peaceful slumbers by the river. There was no loud

airplane anywhere.

Throughout it all, the grown-ups learned as much as the kids. Perhaps the most important lesson concerned time. Don't push schedules when you have kids along. Be like your raft and go with the flow. You'll never put in when you think you will, so don't stress out about it. Also, when it comes to food, stomachs, rather than destinations, dictate lunchtime. So what if you don't make it to that side creek for lunch? If your kids are hungry, have a sandwich at the nearest sandbar.

We also found that scouting for sleepers is as important as scouting for sweepers (trees overhanging the banks that can create entrapment dangers). Just like dodging river obstacles, you have to anticipate when the naps are coming and make adjustments. Instead of ferrying away from a wave's pillow, you're constantly fluffing one, trying to create the perfect quarters for a snooze, be it in a car seat underfoot, a pack n' play strapped atop the gear, or the seat up front. If it works, it's all quiet on the Western float—for as long as naptime lasts, anyway. And with mileage compromised with snack, beach and bathroom breaks, that's when you'll actually make progress.

Like any trip with kids, it wasn't all Leave it to Beaverville, especially when I was forced to listen to Brooke, Casey and their friends sing "I'm a Barbie girl..." one day for three miles. "I'm a Barbie gii-rrrl, in my Barbie wor-rrrld." I felt like adding a lyric that rhymed with "hurl." But they were having fun, and that's the bottom line.

The kids cried at times, too, during which we discovered that bawls create the perfect wave length for echoes. They also got scrapes, tantrummed and fought over everything from Nerf balls to Cheerios. In our tent one morning, Casey said, "There are three things I don't like about this camp...stickers, splinters, and your hair gets tangly."

But aside from dealing with the legitimate scrapes, the tantrums and fights don't happen nearly as much as they do back home. And in the end, these disagreements dissolve just like the sediment in the river, upstaged by an experience that will be remembered for life.

Of course, like my wall-kissing trip on the Yampa all those years ago, you never know what they'll remember, either. A few days into the trip I asked Casey what her favorite part was so far. Her reply? "Sleeping with Anika and the blue drinks."

For Brooke, it was the blue pools we plunged into—which brings me back to the cliff. When everyone made it safely up, we told the kids to look straight ahead, not down, as we traversed a trail crossing a gradual slope leading to the swimming pool. Since Casey was the youngest, I followed closely, with other parents scattered about to lend helping hands. Soon we arrived at a short down climb that led to a pristine pool, dimpled into a cauldron of slickrock, perched high above the river. For the kids, it was a natural Water World.

Wearing her life jacket, Brooke was the first one in, cannon-balling off a ten-foot cliff into the pool. Then she swam to a sandy beach marking the only break in an amphitheater of sandstone. One by one, the other kids followed suit, having a swimmingly good time. If they weren't jumping off the cliff, they were running around the inside of the cauldron, seeing how centrifugal force could carry them before they fell in.

"This is so cool," said Kathleen, 8, a star on her swim team back home.

"Cowabunga!" shouted Casey, before arcing into a parent-cringing belly flop.

Afterwards, we made our way back down to camp, whose giant boulders, bushes, and beaches led to a sunset game of Capture the Flag. Grown-ups and kids got split up randomly, and it didn't take long for me to get captured. It was my penance, I surmised, for ignoring my wife's glare earlier. But it didn't take long for one of the kids I had helped up to the pool to run by and free me.

WHITEWATER KAYAKING AND KIDS

Whitewater kayaking isn't one of those sports your kids are likely to take to at a young age. There's something about being trapped upside-down under water that goes against everyone's innate sense of Darwinism. And that's probably a good thing. Nevertheless, if you can instill a love for paddling in other craft, they might graduate to whitewater kayaks in their own sweet time.

Companies like Jackson Kayaks are making it easier than ever for kids these days by manufacturing pint-sized boats, paddles, spray skirts and even helmets, most of which look like you could hang them from your rearview mirror. If you have the expertise to get them involved—or better yet, access to certified instruction—and your kids have the desire, by all means do so.

We got Brooke a Jackson Fun1 kayak for Christmas one year and her eyes got as round as the sledding saucer next to it. Then she quickly launched into her spastic, high-pitched "I got a kayak" dance. I don't know if she liked it more because she could tell her friends she got a kayak, or because she actually wanted to learn how to paddle it. If it had fit under her pillow, it would have been there that night.

To her credit, since everything is kid-sized, from paddle to boat, she loves paddling it. As a learning tool, she can actually fit inside it without feeling dwarfed and can feel how different strokes affect the boat. A wide sweep on the right turns it left, and a rudder on the right steers it to the right. Such strokes in a bigger boat would have the effect of a kid punching an elephant.

Still, be careful not to jump the gun when it comes to getting them out on a river. I might have made just that mistake with Brooke.

It happened while testing a Topo Duo, a two-person whitewater kayak from a company called Eskimo. A magazine wanted me to assess its value as a teaching tool, so naturally I enlisted the unsuspecting help of my daughter, then aged eight.

Stupid is as stupid does, but I wasn't entirely stupid. Before putting in on our local town run, we headed to the pond, where I fitted her in a spray skirt and we paddled around flawlessly. I hedged our bet by performing a practice Eskimo roll, telling her to simply hold onto the boat's sides while upside-down and I'd roll it up. It worked perfectly (save from her nose hurting from getting hit in the face with a soccer ball the day

before), and she emerged dripping and smiling.

From there it was on to the river, where I'd already scripted how well the story would play out. In fact, her first mutterings as we floated downriver were filled with blissful innocence. "My leg itches," she said matter-of-factly, her appendage out of reach below her spray skirt. "Hmmmm...how do I scratch it? Oh, I'll just use my other leg. Aaahhhhh! I like this...no mosquitoes can get inside."

In the midst of this idle chit-chat, I failed to see a submerged rock that hit our bow, prompting Brooke to reflexively lean upstream. Uh-oh. I didn't count on this. Over we went before I had a chance to brace us back upright. While under water, I instantly remembered my only other time in a Topo Duo years earlier, when I had taken a friend out on the Class III Blue River. When we tipped then, I rolled it back up only to find him already out and swimming. Not wanting that to happen to Brooke, I changed plans mid-gulp. Afraid Brooke had already abandoned ship, instead of trying to roll I bailed also.

Chagrin time. When I popped to the surface a split second later, Brooke was still in the boat, now upside-down (social services, stop reading here). I righted it instantly and calmed her down. While she was only under water for a second or two, and was mainly upset because her nose hurt, now I was the one swimming while she was floating downstream in the kayak. Hadn't planned on this.

Both paddles long gone, I scissor-kicked us to shore and speared the boat into a bush to regroup. Then I pushed Brooke up a steep embankment to a road across the river from where we parked. We had made it a total of a hundred yards. And there was Brooke, a little eight-year-old girl standing by herself, dripping wet in helmet, life jacket, paddle jacket and sprayskirt, when a passing motorist rolled down his window and asked if she was okay. "Yeah," she replied. "My dad's down there."

Out of sight, and still dealing with the kayak down below, I could only muster a feeble "I'm down here!" from my out-of-sight perch in the bushes below.

When I pulled the kayak up and joined her on the road, she looked at me with a "You've really done it this time, Dad" type look.

"Well, you wanted a story," she said, keeping her sense of humor. "Now you have an embarrassing one."

I sure did. And her lesson wasn't over. With our car on the other side of the river, paddles washed down to the Sea of Cortez, and no bridges upstream or down for miles, I had to impart yet another tutorial: how to hitchhike shuttle. So we stuck out our thumbs and started the walk of shame. Luckily, a friend drove by in his van shortly after.

"You guys need a lift? What the heck happened?"

I fessed up as we piled in, stowing the boat beneath the bed in his van until one end was sticking out a few feet past the bumper. As he drove us back to our car, I was certain the tale would reach my kayaking buddies downstream before even our paddles did.

Brooke was well-deserving of a chocolate-vanilla twirl ice cream cone on the way home afterward, and I was equally deserving of the tongue-lashing I got from my wife, Denise. "You what?" she said when the story unfolded, the only thing missing, a rolling pin in her hand. "What are you doing taking her in the river at this time of year?"

Brooke had her ice cream, and I had my humble pie. While we were never in danger, the lesson I learned is, don't push it. If you're bent on introducing your kids to whitewater kayaking, start on a shallow, slow-moving river, not the Yampa in spring. Another pointer: don't use a grown-up, neoprene spray skirt. That's what I had on Brooke, which was wrong. They can't pull the rip-cord as easily as adults can. Use a nylon skirt that's easier to pop off.

Of course, a lot of it might well have just been my own ineptitude. Later, another kayaking friend, Rick Frankin, borrowed the Topo Duo and took his five-year-old son, Kai, down Class III-IV Cross Mountain with nary a problem. Under his dad's more expert guidance, Kai also kayaked solo through the C-hole downtown, punching through a wave that frightens many adults. The trick, says Rick, is teaching them how to happily wet exit on their own, and using a nylon skirt. Otherwise, there's no skirting the reprimand waiting for you back home.

A True Paddling Prodigy

Some kids have it easier whitewater kayaking. It's in their genes.

Dane Jackson, who turned sixteen in the summer of 2009, is the son of four-time, world freestyle kayak champion and Olympian Eric "EJ" Jackson, president of a kayak manufacturer called Jackson Kayaks. While the company has done wonders for getting kids on the water through its innovative line of kid-sized kayaks, EJ has done even more to get his own kids, including Emily, now nineteen, involved.

Both kids are phenoms. Dane is a two-time national junior men's champion in freestyle kayaking, and placed third in the men's pro division of the Teva Mountain Games in Vail, Colorado. At age eleven, he became the youngest person ever to run Africa's Nile and Zambezi rivers. Older sister Emily, meanwhile, won the women's pro

World Cup in freestyle kayaking in 2008, is the junior world champion, and is the four-time reigning Teva Mountain Games women's champion. At age thirteen, she became the youngest woman to ever paddle the Nile and Zambezi. They're not just kids; they're full-on kayaking kids.

Of course, it helps to have genes only one step removed from gills. EJ is one of the most passionate, energetic and best paddlers on the planet, and his enthusiasm has rubbed off like chalk on a sidewalk.

When Dane was just four, EJ loaded his family into an RV for five years so he could train, teach and compete at kayaking events throughout North America. It meant that his wife, Kristine, home-schooled Dane and Emily at a fold-down desk above the drive train. But, combined with the family's international travels, they learned even more about the world around them. By age nine, when other fourth-graders were writing about summer trips to the zoo, Dane could give oral reports on Africa, Chile, New Zealand, Spain, England, Austria, Australia and Germany.

Though it might have detracted from such conventional father-son bonding opportunities as playing catch, EJ was dedicated to teaching Dane how to kayak, the effort producing a Mozart-caliber prodigy in paddling instead of piano. "He got way better than I ever was at his age," maintains Dad.

Like Mozart, Dane developed a knack for it early. As a toddler, his favorite pastime was dragging his dad's kayaks from the back of the house to the front again. When it came to bathing, he'd play with homemade foam kayaks for hours on end. "He never watched Barney," says mother Kristine. "Only kayak videos."

While most toddlers were mastering stairs, Dane was mastering staircases of rapids. His first real taste of whitewater came by accident. Just two weeks shy of his third birthday, when trying to follow his dad, he accidentally ran Class IV Little Falls on Washington, D.C.'s Potomac River, emerging shaken but upright down below. It was like any other kid accidentally going down a steep hill on a bike, only he was in a kayak. "He went the wrong way around an island when Eric told him to go right," says Kristine. "He hadn't learned his lefts and rights yet."

As soon as he did, and also learned how to right the boat with a roll, he began upping the bar substantially, paddling such runs as Class IV-V Upper Gauley, Upper Youghiogheny, New, Ottawa and Ocoee rivers before even reaching his teens. He won slalom and freestyle events against competitors who were twice his weight and graduating from high school while he was still learning multiplication tables.

Photographer Luke Hopkins, who tried to capture him in action at an event called the Red Bull Challenge on Dane's hometown Caney Fork River in Tennessee, sums it up this way: "I couldn't even get a good shot of him—he was so small that he was always disappearing behind the waves."

Coupled with the socially confining aspects of home school, all this paddling time meant an absence of peers in his formative years. But Dane didn't seem to mind. Instead of hanging out with similarly aged schoolmates, Dane's friends "his age," says Kristine, were often five to ten years older. "They goof around with him almost as well as kids his own age, but he did miss out on other ten- year-olds," she says. For Dane, the age gap reason was simple: "I didn't have very many friends my age who paddle."

Now that they're out of the RV and in a house in Tennessee, home schooling still has its diversions. "Rain is distracting because it means the river's coming up," says Mom. "That's all it takes to get him thinking about kayaking."

Being so good so young in a sport like kayaking also created additional problems. While Michelle Wie and Freddy Adu are redefining golf and soccer, their sports aren't life-threatening. The problem in the early years for Dane, says former world champion Clay Wright, wasn't one of skill, but of experience. "Every once in a while it hit you that he was just a kid," he says. "You'd be out there paddling and everything would be fine, but then you'd get in a judgment situation and you could tell that he was only ten. He had no idea anything could ever go wrong."

EJ knows he was often paddling a thin line taking his son out so early. "I was on guard all the time," he says, "not because his skills weren't up to par, but because of all of the little things that could've gone wrong to create a bad experience."

But Mom realizes there are rewards from running rivers that can't be taught in a classroom. "He loves it, and one of the greatest gifts we can give our children is the tools to combine a lifetime of health and fitness with a love of the outdoors," she says.

Dane's big sister, Emily, attests to Dane's talent and drive. Like other siblings taking piano lessons, she and Dane have seen each other through countless triumphs and tribulations on the river. "It drives me crazy that he could often go out there and not be scared when I'm the older sister," she says. "But he's always been pretty level-headed paddling. One time we were on the river together and he said, 'Don't cry, it's not as big as it seems,' and it really helped."

I experienced Dane's attitude and uncanny ability firsthand when I joined him on a trip down the Great Falls of the Potomac, outside Washington D.C. Dane, who a week earlier became the youngest person to ever run the falls ("I wasn't too scared," he says. "My dad told me right where to go"), was just ten at the time, but as confident as paddlers twice his age.

Luckily for my own confidence, the week's rains had brought the water level up to flood stage, forcing us to run the easier Class IV Fish Ladder section one channel over.

"Same place as last time?" Dane asked as he shouldered his boat and disappeared down the bank.

"No," shouted Eric after him. "It's someplace different. Wait for us."

The conversation could have occurred between a father and ten-year-old son anywhere, whether finding seats at a baseball game or fishing at a local pond. The only difference: we were about to paddle a Class IV rapid.

Down at the bank, Dane wrestled his spray skirt onto his customized kayak, whose ends had been cut off, squished and re-welded to fit his diminutive frame. Adjusting his tiny composite helmet, he then peeled out into the roiling current. "Come on, Dad!" he yelled over the river.

Soon EJ joined him in an eddy, executed a few freestyle moves in a hydraulic and then floated downstream. Like father, like son; Dane did so next, spinning his boat as effortlessly as a leaf in a cross-current.

Next, we eddied out above a log-filled cataract to portage. Taking two steps for every one of ours, Dane drew stares from passersby as we strolled the boardwalk to the Great Falls overlook. An elderly couple who could be his great-grandparents followed us to the vista.

Then, while other kids his age were playing the Chutes and Ladders board game, we put back in and did the same in real life, ferrying through a maze of Class IV ramps and slides. After listening to EJ describe the route, Dane watched his father disappear over the horizon line before mimicking him stroke for stroke. At the bottom, I missed an eddy on the right while Dane ended up right by his father's side. His only weakness showed downstream where his relative weightlessness made it difficult for him to punch through a wave crest to access a surf spot.

Diligent mom as always, Kristine was waiting with the car at the take-out, like a soccer mom after a game. As if he'd been doing it all his life, Dane wrapped a towel around his midsection, undressed and hurriedly changed clothes, "Come on, Dad!" he yelled again, for good reason. It was Halloween and he was joining friends to go trick-or-treating in nearby Brookmont. He was going as Scream from Scary Movie III, even though his Mom wouldn't let him see it.

It was a rare moment when he would be doing something with kids his age, and he wasn't about to let the chance to perform land-based tricks slip away.

WATER GAMES FOR KIDS

Not that any paddling trip is ever boring, but sometimes watching the world go by isn't quite enough. Whether in the boats or at camp, there are times when kids—and even the most serene adults—need a little entertainment, challenge and competition. That's when a good game can come in handy - not Twister or Candy Land, but games you can do with whatever is on hand. The beauty of this type of game lies in using what you have and making it simple enough that anyone, any age, can play. Following are a few favorites:

Games for Camp

Water Walking: Put PFDs on your kids and then find a rock-free clear spot to enter the river. Next, draw a start line in the sand. The winner is the one who goes over the water the farthest before falling in. As long as it's warm, this can kill hours of time while you're attending to camp chores. An advanced version involves sleeping pads. Clip two or three together end to end. The goal: see how far onto the pads you can run before falling in.

Ammo Can Tug of War: Most tug of war games are brutish affairs, involving the nerd team from Camp Woebegone getting pulled into the mud by the blond, buffed jocks. Not this one, which is more about balance and cunning than strength. Place two ammo cans (or any other one-foot-square objects) in the sand about six feet apart and have participants balance atop them facing each other. Lay a rope on the ground between them and have each player hold onto an end. On the count of three, the participants pull in the rope as fast as they can. When they get to the point where there is no slack left, someone gets popped off. Skilled players will balance for long stretches, taking in and playing out rope in a series of feints and charges designed either to gather in all the rope or topple their opponent.

Gordian Knot: An age-old activity for any age, the Gordian Knot is simple, requires no props and can be played just about anywhere. Have everyone stand in a circle, raise their right hand, reach across the circle and grasp the hand of someone opposite them. Then, do the same with your left hand. Two clues: Don't hold both hands of the same person, and don't hold the hand of the person next to you (this will cause a sure disaster, if not a dislocated shoulder). Once everyone is holding hands, try to untangle yourselves without letting go of any hands (although you may readjust for safety's sake). Next, add challenges like silence or blindfolds.

River Madness: A combination of croquet, putt-putt and bocce ball, all this game requires are rocks and a campsite. There are only two rules: each person gets three throwing stones smaller than a baseball, and the winner of each round makes up the next "challenge." One person decides the challenge by creating an obstacle (a pile of sticks, a cave, an island, a tree, etc.). Each person scores points for a full or partial success (points are determined by the creator). This can be played for hours on end, challenging folks to not only succeed at the obstacle presented to them, but also to use their imaginations in upping the ante each time around.

Washers: Invented by rafting mother Heidi Hanna of Steamboat Springs, Colo., Washers came about after she saw too many husbands sidetracked from chores and too many kids having close calls by wandering across the trajectory of horseshoes. So she designed a new game for kids consisting of two "coins" of PVC piping and 16 color-coded washers. With the pipe coins buried in wet sand to their rims and placed about 12 feet apart, kids divide into teams of two and play their own game of harmless shoes, throwing four washers each toward the hole. You get three points for landing in the hole, two for hanging over the rim and one for closest. Good for ages 5 and up, and keeps kids busy while you're pursuing more important matters.

Easter Egg Hunt: This is a great one for camp. Bring plastic eggs from home, and fill them with treasures found on the trip. The prize isn't as important as the search. Then tell your kids that the Easter/Spring/Solstice/Desert/River Bunny has paid the trip a visit.

Games for the River

I Spy: This classic is perfect for the river ("I spy something green, something wet, etc"). Make a rule that it can only be something people see in the natural surroundings.

Pattern-Not-Logic Puzzler: One person starts by saying something like, "I'm going on a trip and I'm bringing a book but not a magazine, a tool but not a saw, the moon but not the stars..." Everyone then has to guess at the secret to "packing" by coming up with similar examples. "A knife but not a fork" is incorrect, but "a spoon but not a fork" is correct. (Hint: think double letters).

Story Game: One person thinks of a story while the others try to figure it out by asking yes or no questions. "Is it about a person?" "Yes." "Is it about you?" "No." "Is it something that happened today?" "Maybe." The trick is that there is no story. When people ask the questions, if the last letter in the question is a consonant, the answer is yes, if it is a vowel, the answer is no, and if it ends in a "Y," then the answer is maybe. The stories created are usually better than anything that anyone could possibly think up on their own (and are often quite scandalous).

Kayak Star: This is for those paddling their own boat (i.e. canoe, kayak, ducky, etc.). While floating, get everyone together in a row, holding onto the sides of each other's boats. Once everyone's secure, have the two outside people paddle on the outside of their boats. As they do, the boats' noses will converge and the two opposite sides will come together, creating a perfect star. Float down the river this way as long as you can hold on.

FATHER'S DAY FLOAT

Every Father's Day, we road trip down to my cousin's house in Salida, Colorado, for the Arkansas River's annual FIBArk festival, where we try to prove that the 60-year-old acronym doesn't stand for Fathers in Boats Always Regret Kids (it actually stands for First in Boating on the Arkansas). We do this by sneaking out for short kayaking excursions when family duties allow, and by staging a family float Sunday afternoon.

I'm surprised they invited us back, after Casey waking up our host's household at 5 a.m. every year. But our cousins, whose daughter was a teenager, happily put up with it. Been there, done that, we could read in their baggy-eyed faces.

An I.V. of coffee later, we'd head to the event site to stroll the bike path. There we saw other blissful fathers also enjoying their special day, wheeling strollers, walking hand-in-hand with their daughters, and otherwise taking the burden of kid-raising off their spouses for a spell.

Once, when I stopped at the announcer's stand to borrow two kid life jackets for the afternoon's float, father Mike Harvey keyed the microphone and proclaimed, "Let's give it up for all the hard-working dads out there today…" Unfortunately, I gave up something more important: Casey's pacifier. A tantrum later his voice echoed over the speakers again: "Attention boaters, we have a lost binky up here. Please come up to identify." I quickly described its drool marks, and harmony was restored.

My fatherly travails got a wider airing when I had to do a quick riverside interview with mohawked ski star Glenn Plake for RSN Television's Reel Thrills. From the security of my arms, Casey dispelled any chance I had to project a cool-guy image to the Gen-X crowd by looking straight into the camera and shouting, "Hi Barney!"

That afternoon it was finally time for our fatherly float. I drew the short straw and got to head out in my kayak while Homer took the oars of the dory. Drifting a few yards away from him and all the kids piled on the bow, the sight warmed my heart. The kids were having a blast, especially since having me separate gave them a target for their water guns.

In all, we had five dads along with their kids in our flotilla, including one who open-canoed the stretch with his five-year-old daughter. As I watched my family float by from an eddy, I realized there was no way I'd rather spend Father's Day.

It was Shakespeare who said, "It's a wise father that knows his own child." At that night's barbecue, I asked Brooke what her favorite part of the weekend was. Far from the hopeful "Just being with you, Dad" or "Floating on the dory," she responded: "Watching you mess up kayaking and go upside-down a lot."

ALTERNATE PADDLING PASTIMES

Paddleboarding with Kids

There's a new craze in town.

Paddleboards are a sort of extra-buoyant surfboard that you paddle standing up with an elongated paddle. This makes them the kid equivalent of a paddle-able, floating dock. Of all paddlecraft, they're the easiest to cannonball off and climb back on, and are the most conducive to massive, water-plunging games of King of the Hill.

I became sold on them when camping with my family and heading out on mist-covered Pearl Lake early one fall morning with Casey balancing on the bow, hands outstretched in a perfect Big Kauhna surf pose. Between us, perched atop the board, rested my cup of Kona coffee, its steam mirroring the mist coming off the lake.

Without even getting our feet wet, we climbed aboard and shoved off, the mist up to my shins and Casey's waist. Propelled by my paddle from the stern, the board knifed across the lake completely under the wispy, early morning fog, our feet disappearing below. It was as if we were gliding through a sea of clouds, with golden aspen trees and mountains rising above. Occasionally, Casey would poke her head under and vanish, only to reappear beaming.

Of course, as far as kids are concerned, that's not the real beauty of a paddleboard. When we first tried one—a converted Windsurfer a friend had turned into a makeshift paddleboard—on a lakeside summer camping trip, I was skeptical. Nevertheless, we loaded it onto the trailer next to an assortment of every other paddlecraft under the sun: a canoe, sea kayak, inflatable kayak, rec kayak, even a bona fide kid's kayak. Its rank in the line-up surfaced quickly.

As soon as we hauled them all down to the lakeshore, all those other boats could only look on with envy as the paddleboard commanded the kids' affection. They were on it and off it eight hours a day, while the other boats barely got wet. They'd run down its plank and dive into the lake, push each other into the drink, and paddle it five in tandem, sometimes on their knees and others standing with paddles in hand. We had to coerce them back to shore for dinner.

Invented as a Hawaiian surf tool, a way for surfers to tinker with better leverage on waves and still get out on the water whenever the swell died down, paddleboards have since emerged as a quintessential family craft, suitable for lakes, oceans and even mild river travel. Sure, they require a modicum of balance. You'll feel like a toddler taking his first steps the first time you try to stand on one. But any kid who can walk can balance on one. When he does, be prepared for homework to take the back burner.

As with other paddlecraft, paddleboards vary depending on their intended use. Some are meant for surfing, others for cruising the flats along shore. There's even an inflatable one called the Uli, which we now have in our arsenal. When not in use you can roll it up and store it in your garage—and even transport it in your car—and then simply pump it up and watch it get as rigid as a surf board worthy of Laird Hamilton heroics.

With its softer, rock-absorbing hull, the inflatable version is also perfect for river travel. This past summer, Casey and I surfed the Yampa River through town, with her playing Kelly Slater up front while I steered from the stern. It was a cross between kayaking, surfing and snowboarding, and if the going ever got rough, she'd simply jump down to all fours for better stability and then pop back up again once the river settled down. We even got applause from diners on the riverside deck of the Yacht Club restaurant when we surfed by.

I have a photo of that excursion saved as wallpaper on my laptop, Casey crouched low with arms extended in surf pose and I less-perfectly positioned in the stern. And it's the look on her face ("Hey, look at me, I'm surfing the river! Wahoo!") that makes the paddleboard another welcome addition to our paddlecraft clan.

Inner Tubes

Near the end of one of our inflatable kayak trips with Brooke, we passed a gaggle of inner-tubers near our take-out. They, too, were taking advantage of the warm weather.

I felt like we were overdoing it equipment-wise in comparison. While we were armed with a high-end inflatable kayak, paddles, helmets and life jackets, they wore nothing but shorts and were sitting atop Goodyears. We were in tuxedos at a tailgate party. Adding to my sense of overkill, the water was only ankle deep. Should we tip, I'd stand up to my calf hairs, my helmet a good five feet away. But you never take chances with kids along, and I wasn't faulting the black circle-riding cowboys bobbing in the eddy. They had as much right to be there as we did, chafed armpits, bluejean cutoffs and all.

Inner tubes, in fact, represent a great proportion of families' indoctrination into river travel. From the Delaware River in New Jersey to the Salt River in Arizona, mild

rivers throughout the country play host to liveries that rent tubes to families and offer shuttle services after the day's run. Pay your tube rental fee, slap on the sunscreen and away you go down the river. Sure, it technically might not be "paddling" per se, but it exposes you and your brood to the basics of navigating a natural waterway, from staying in the current to getting caught in eddies and even suffering the inevitable butt bruise.

Even the Yampa River in Steamboat goes through the Great Transition every year when the waterway slows down in mid-summer and becomes the domain of tubers. When the water gets too low for rafters, kayakers and canoeists (note it's "canoeists," not "canoers"), as the rocks re-appear so does the rubber. Tubers come out in force to frolic in its gentle waters.

If only my indoctrination were as happy-go-lucky.

While inner-tubes represented my first foray into paddling moving water, I wasn't so fortunate as to pursue it on flatwater. While they're virtually idiot-proof, as evidenced by the arm-circling masses that use them, they're not necessarily designed for more difficult water.

We found this out the hard way, whiling away the hot Front Range afternoons in Boulder by rounding up tubes from gas stations and coursing down rock-strewn Boulder Creek. It didn't take long to discover where both the town and the creek got their names. My derrière still bears scars from sinking a little bit too low through the center hole and having gluteus meet granite without any formal introductions.

There are certainly better ways to get indoctrinated to tubing than the way we did. We'd emerge battered and bruised back home, with welts on our rears, puncture marks along our ribs from the metal valves that always seemed to be in the way, and the insides of our arms chafed red from the hapless arm circles we employed to dodge the butt-bruising boulders.

Pick the right waterway, however, ones that are slower and deeper, and inner-tubing can provide the perfect outdoor venture for your family.

Unbeknownst to most tubers, there's a stigma attached to the activity. For some reason, more accomplished paddlers tend to look down on practitioners of the pastime as somehow being inferior. Oftentimes, their spurn has merit. They took the time to learn the sport, get properly equipped and even take a safety lesson or two, only to see someone bounce by in cutoffs, holding a can of Budweiser.

Kayakers, especially, seem to treat tubers with suspect, as somehow inferior to the water warriors clad in helmets, PFDs, paddling jackets, spray skirts, and wielding joust-like paddles. Tubers, meanwhile, giggle by in bikinis and board shorts. They're sunburned. They have mullets and gold chains. They trail coolers of beer behind them, complete with their own tubes. Worst of all, they can't control where they're going. When our river is low, kayakers surfing the lone wave that's left are forced to play Space Invaders with these saucer riders. The uncontrolled asteroids force them to bob and weave, lest they shish kebob said tubers in an explosion of rubber and beer belly.

But the tubers are having fun outdoors, and that's all that matters. It's also big business. While I'm not aware of any tubing associations monitoring numbers or lobbying Capitol Hill, some of the more popular operations put tens, if not hundreds, of thousands of tubers on the water each season. Carry those numbers throughout the country and you have an activity that exposes a lot of people to outdoor recreation. It might expose their rears to rocks and shoulders to sunburn at the same time, but it gets them outside.

Come low water at home, eventually I'll join them, putting one of my daughters (wearing a life jacket, of course) on my lap while wind-milling my shoulders as the newest member of Armcircling Americana. And our kids love it. We pinball off rocks, careen this way and that, and stop for ice cream cones en route. And the days of butt bruises are long gone with today's fancier fanny-protecting models, complete with webbed suspension.

Hint: it helps if you know how to paddle so you aren't just floating listlessly like a piece of driftwood. You see those types all the time, unable to escape the clutches of eddies, stranded high and dry on outcroppings of rock, and losing sunglasses and ballcaps to the whims of the water. With a little knowledge of how to read moving water, you can ferry away from obstacles, avoid the shallows, and even manage last-minute lily-dips to punch through tiny hydraulics that might flip the more mullet-clad.

One time we passed someone's daughter screaming on a rock while her father waited helplessly below.

"How'd she get there?" asked Brooke as we floated by, easily missing the obstacle. "She bonked right into that rock."

Depending on the waterway, you don't even have to use a tube. Come late summer, we'll see families frolic by on inflatable mattresses, vinyl alligators straight from Whamco, and even inflatable swimming pools, using paddles the size of their forearms. The riders will lounge around on their stomachs, trail fingers in the water, and inevitably get swallowed whole by a wave called the C-Hole adjacent to the library. But it doesn't matter. It's low water so it's safe, and tubes and these other inflatable aberrations are a great way to get outdoors as a family, despite their less than hard-guy reputation.

This standing was hammered home on our maiden tubing voyage last year. Near the end of our run, I let Casey off before charging through the C-Hole blocking passage downstream. There were still a few kayakers milling about, and now I was the semi in Frogger, mowing them down as they tried to cross the freeway. Hoping no one recognized me, I punched through the hydraulic and made it to shore, where a college student was holding a snorkel and mask. He was diving for tuber bootie, making money for summer. "Four pairs of sunglasses, a Nets visor and a half bottle of cinnamon schnapps," he bragged, holding up his trophies.

Then I got out, shook my hair dry and rejoined my daughter on the bike path.

"My dad's a tuber," she told the first passerby as we made our way back upstream to our car.

While I tried to correct her and say that I wasn't really a tuber, but a rafter and a kayaker, my pleas fell short. To the tourists and other families out and about having a good time on their Goodyears, there's not much difference. It's all enjoying yourself on the river.

Chapter 8

CLIMBING WITH KIDS

"Truly it may be said that the outside of a mountain is good for the inside of a man."
—George Wherry

FROM THE MOMENT THEY COME into the world, children are perhaps more familiar with climbing than they are any other recreational pursuit. Consider their days in the uterus. Before even being born into this world, they spend their first nine months tied to an umbilical cord, giving them a head start on anything to do with ropes. A few even manage to practice knots. They might not be figure-eights or bowlines, but it's a start. Others are content with residing alongside perfect coils, another attribute of successful climbers.

They also have an early start at learning to trust their anchors. There's no better anchor than the umbilical cord to Mom. Being tied off to such a bombproof attachment point—even while bivouacking inside Mom's belly—creates an inherent trust of cords and their connection to life.

Though more of a stretch—like modern synthetic ropes to the gold lines of yester-year—the analogy can be carried even further. The first thing they hear are words like "Push" and "Breathe," much like egging on a partner on a climb. They even get delivered onto a bouldering pad of sorts, complete with spotters to make sure no one gets hurt. After this, the fathers get to play Simon Yates in Joe Simpson's *Touching the Void*, when Yates cut his partner's rope while climbing Peru's 20,813-foot Siula Grande in 1985. The umbilical cord gets snipped, and the kid gets held upside-down and spanked, just like climbers who blow their routes.

In all seriousness, kids are natural climbers. From first learning to crawl to pulling up on crib bars or grasping a grown-up's pant leg, the art of ascension is ingrained as deeply as the art of drooling. The trait likely hearkens back to escaping predators way back on the evolutionary ladder. Without a ladder to escape a crocodile's overbite, youngsters learned to climb whatever was around.

At home in our more civilized times, these items manifest themselves as railings, coffee tables and chairs—basically anything within reach that kids are not supposed to ascend. And everything, it seems, is fair game. Turn your eyes for an instant and they're up, up and away like UnderDog. Only instead of setting their sights on Simon Bar Sinister, they're fixing them on bars and banisters.

From the first time they pull themselves up on a coffee table to figuring out stairs and the backwards, shirt-lifting stomach-slide down them, kids progress along a natural climbing curve that lends itself to pursuing the sport later in life. They know their balance points and strength, and how to weigh those against the ground-thudding consequences. On our local park's aptly named monkey bars, Casey instinctively knows how strong her grip is and how far she can trust it. Whenever I jump up to go to her rescue thinking she's about to fall, she shoos me off and calculatingly swings forward to the next bar, her fingertips barely enveloping it.

One of our kids' favorite props used to be the refrigerator, a more vertical stepping stone in the climbing process than the staircase. Shift your glance elsewhere for a second and the door would be open with tiny toes clinging to the first shelf, nudging the half-cantaloupe farther inside by the cottage cheese. Then the feet would move up a rung, to the shelf with the lunch meats and cheese, finally allowing the young Yvon Chouinard to grab the top milk shelf in a desperate, dyno move to reach the Go-gurt secreted on top (which is exactly why we moved the Go-gurt to the bottom shelf of our fridge).

When Casey did this, she looked such the part of a climber that I half expected her to dip her hand in the powdered sugar as chalk, and clip into the door shelf with a leftover spaghetti noodle, before continuing on her way. Of course, this was our own fault for keeping the food she liked up top. One fall, she even figured out how to negotiate the overhang to reach the fridge's top, where we hide the Halloween candy.

During this phase you'll notice certain things about childcare that hone your own climbing skills as well. One is buckling a car seat. Perhaps no other parenting task better emulates a skill you need for climbing than this rear seat ritual. It's the perfect practice for placing or clipping into a piece of protection.

Consider the steps involved. First you have to pull the belt out of its holster near the car's ceiling. Then you bite it as you would a rope to keep tension on the spring so it doesn't lock, all while in an awkward climbing position—hunched over at the waist, with arms splayed in all directions. Then you have to thread the remaining slack through the slot behind the seat and finally over to the other side, where you can finally fasten the seat belt buckle. It's a dyno move, requiring one last lunge to clip in while your other hand is busy keeping tension on the belt.

Like not pulling enough rope up to clip in, sometimes you don't have enough slack to make that final clip, in which case you have to start all over again. Do that climbing and you're either falling through the air or getting a whopping case of sewing machine leg. Here, you just get an impatient look from your child, who's wondering why you're hunching over him for so long, and from your spouse up front who's anxiously waiting to go to wherever you're late getting to.

Other things about the car seat also have ties to climbing, from fastening the harness's buckles to constantly fitting and readjusting its straps. In the early years you're putting kids in all sorts of harnesses, whether they're in burleys, backpacks or baby joggers. This gets you acclimated to fussing with them, and your kids accustomed to wearing them. By the time children are adolescents they're often more used to wearing harnesses than some of the top climbers in the country.

Changing diapers also prepares you for climbing. You're often holding ointment in your teeth and juggling talcum bottles and wipes with your hands, all while fastening Velcro straps as quickly as you can. It might not be quite as consequential as clipping into a piece of pro halfway up the Half Dome, but it all helps. Some say raising kids gets you farther away from sports like climbing. I say it just helps you practice.

CLIMBING GYMS (AKA ROMPER ROOMS)

Whoever invented the indoor climbing gym did parents a huge favor. In fact, he or she should get a Pulitzer for Parenting. Climbing gyms are nothing more than giant, padded babysitter rooms, where kids can't get hurt if they try. But more importantly, they're the perfect place to expose children to a sport they can pursue their whole lives.

Like kids, climbing gyms come in all shapes and sizes, some doing a great job at mimicking Mother Nature and others content to simply let people climb. Responsible for introducing the most number of kids to the sport are those giant inflatable climbing walls you see at carnivals and fairs. They have a sloping ramp dotted with square handholds, a summit offering a sense of accomplishment, and a slide down on the opposite side as a reward.

When Casey discovered one of these inflata-rocks outside a convention hall in Las Vegas, it was harder to get her out of there than it was getting our co-workers out of the Hard Rock Café. Sometimes she'd fall back onto the three-foot-thick air pad, and others she'd top out like Chris Sharma, slide down the far end and race back around to do it again. With kettle corn always just a rope length's away, it was safe, fun and, most importantly, instilled the sense of what the sport's all about. Many even have an inflatable corral so kids can't escape (if only all kid activities shared this feature).

The next step up from these air-blown pseudo walls is the real climbing gym. Like their name implies, climbing gyms are gyms where you can climb. Artificial "rock" walls are adorned with a variety of artificial handholds, with belay stations positioned throughout to let customers rope up safely. Most cities now have one or two such indoor gyms, and there are also now portable climbing "towers" that people set up at festivals and fairs.

While in the olden days such facilities often required two people to climb a route—one to climb and one to belay—today's automatic belaying devices let you simply clip in and go. Once at the top, the belay device lowers you automatically, gauging your weight with more precision than a mustached booth worker at a carnival.

Take your kids to such a gym and the inside will resemble a carnival. On a busy day it will be filled with lycra-clad climbers, jamming to tunes while jamming their hands into cracks and onto holds. Therein lies the gyms' only downfall; unless you're on a tower outside, it's not really an "outdoor" experience. You pay at a desk, change in a locker room, and then head to an open station or bouldering area.

Both rope stations and bouldering areas work great for kids. Outfitted with a proper harness (available at most gyms), kids can clip into an auto-belaying rope at an easy route, use any handholds they please, and do the exact same thing the grown-ups are doing next to them. They can go as high as they like, and yell "whee!" as loudly as they like on the way down.

Bouldering stations are equally well-suited for kids. Giant foam pads as bouncy as any hotel bed let kids traverse across walls until they fall back onto the pad, where they'll likely wrestle and tumble for a few minutes before trying it again.

Where the heck were these things when I was growing up? We had a 5.9 move up our rusted gutter to get in my bedroom window, an overhang from my mom's balcony to get on the loose, Spanish-tiled roof, a frayed rope to ascend a deck in back, and a thick mat of vines on the north side of the house, leading up to the top of the chimney. Doctors would have saved a lot of stitches had climbing gyms been around.

We took our daughters to our local gym as often as we could when they were young. (Later, the middle school put a similar wall up in its main hallway inside, and now there's even one at the local hot springs pool, where kids can climb as high as they can before plunging back into the water.) It allowed us to get a work-out in while we were watching our kids, and they loved it because, well, kids love climbing. We'd outfit them with harnesses, clip them into the rope and watch them Spiderman up the walls, beaming with every foot gained.

Whether on an automatic system or belayed by us, falls never amounted to more than the stretch of the rope, which was paltry given their bag-of-feathers weight. When tired, they'd go jump on the pads while we climbed. And then they'd encourage us, just as we did to them.

"Come-on Dad," I remember Brooke saying. "Just a little higher. Don't fall, or you owe me a quarter."

It's hard to tell if they liked the climbing or belay stations better. Descending to the ground was every bit as much fun as going up. The only problem is that the automatic belay stations almost made them want to fall, which isn't the object of climbing. It was also demoralizing to realize that they trusted the automatic belay station more than they did us. With me at the end of the line, they'd shake in fear before falling, asking repeatedly if I had them. With auto at the controls, they'd jump off the wall willingly, sometimes even employing freestyle moves on the way down.

Of course, the true benefit of auto-belay stations is that they double as baby-sitters; once you tie your kids in, you can leave them there while you get your own workout in. They can climb up and get lowered down all on their own, never even recognizing that you're secretly climbing yourself. All you have to do is come back every so often to see if they need to go to the bathroom. Otherwise, you can essentially ignore them, knowing that they can't get into too much trouble.

Our climbing gym was such a perfect place to take kids that parents often held birthday parties there, much like others do at Chuck E. Cheese. Kids would eat cake, open presents and then climb, burning off the sugar high as quickly as it came on. And the gym offered one benefit more conventional party locations don't—the ability to climb up and retrieve balloons that had drifted away during the festivities.

THE REAL MCCOY – CLIMBING OUTDOORS

If your kids are comfortable with climbing in a gym, the transition to real rock outdoors will be baby-bottom smooth.

Climbing outdoors is where the sport began, and where it truly belongs. You don't have to flash 5.14 to reap a lifetime of benefits from the simple act of scaling a rock. Just climbing to your own ability teaches balance, focus, decision making and, like a brother hitting a sister, the consequences of your own actions. Perhaps no one put it better than a Mountain Hardwear-sponsored climber at an outdoor industry seminar in Boulder, Colorado. "If I hadn't discovered climbing when I was young," the panelist told the crowd, "I'd be in juvenile school. It pretty much saved my life."

If you're not experienced, go with a guide or instructor until you're qualified to take your kids out on your own. Coming back safe and ensuring a positive experience is all that matters.

I'm not about to tell you how to set up top ropes for tykes, tie figure eights for eight-year-olds, or belay your brood. If you're not a climber, don't learn with your kids on the line. Take lessons until you're comfortable with every facet of the sport; go with a friend who knows what he's doing and who you trust implicitly; or sign up for a course that you can take together as a family.

I'm no Reinhold Messner. But I got myself into enough jams growing up in the climbing Mecca of Boulder to feel comfortable taking my own kids out on easy top rope forays. I'll also pair up with other like-minded parents so our kids have some camaraderie. Having partners helps for both kids and grown-ups.

If venturing out on your own, one of the first lessons is to pick somewhere close. You want the climb to be the memory, not the tick- and poison ivy-filled hike. Also, pick an easy spot, ideally a gently sloping rock with plenty of confidence-inspiring foot and hand holds and an easy place for you to set a secure anchor.

Despite all your car seat, burley and baby jogger practice, here's some quick advice about harnesses. Make sure they're certified—it's not the place to test a homemade invention or the latest from ACME—and that they fit as snug as a diaper. In the early years, go with a full body harness, one with slots for the legs and arms and that connects to the rope in the middle of the chest. These will help your child stay upright in the event of a fall instead of dangling upside-down like a bat.

Our kids might not realize it, but they're hopelessly spoiled when it comes to recreating in the outdoors. They can mountain bike single track from school, which also happens to pass by a perfect, kid-sized rock for climbing in Butcher Knife Creek. A couple of times a year, a few other dads and I will break away from work and set up a top rope just in time to meet them bicycling home at 3:30 p.m. They'll get off their bikes at the base of the rock, swap their Dora packs for harnesses, clip in and start climbing. One afternoon we had three ropes set up, with the older kids attacking the steeper face and the younger ones on an easier portion. Casey had as much fun swinging on the rope and pushing off from the rock with her feet as she did the actual climbing, but it didn't matter. There were no grades being passed out, and everyone made the grade by having fun.

Brooke, in particular, is especially fond of the image the sport conveys. Specifically, the chalk bag. Even when she doesn't need it, she'll make sure I clip it onto her harness, and she dips her hands into it like a pro. She'll even ask about it before the more crucial items like the harness and rope. "Did you bring the chalk bag?" she queries, not caring if we have anything else. As far as she's concerned, climbing means chalk bag and the chalk bag is too cool for school. Now she's gotten her sister Casey going on it, and both return home a white, chalky mess.

Like helping your child ride a bike, you'll yell words of encouragement that seem obvious to you, but aren't to your brood. You'll point out handholds and footholds, and tell them to use their feet more than their hands. You'll tell them to "just go higher," as if it's the easiest thing in the world. When they reach the top and it's time to lower them back down, you'll encourage them to sit back like they're going to the bathroom instead of hanging on the rope, a description sure to draw giggles. "I'm pooping," Casey says whenever I use that analogy, with lucky me standing right below her.

Like any other pursuit you do with your kids, it won't always be smooth abseiling. When I took Brooke with a few friends to a slightly more exposed spot on Seed House Road, it even backfired for a spell.

"Quit yelling at me!" she screamed when I tried to coax her up the vertical face. "Quit bossing me!"

She was obviously in over her head, but that's the nature and beauty of climbing, pushing yourself just a bit farther than you think you can go, with the benefit of a rope to make sure you do so safely. It even schooled her in the nervousness that goes hand-in-hand with the sport. "I'm scared," she said halfway up another climb. "Know how I can tell? My butt feels tweaky."

When Casey, three years younger, tried the same face, her reaction was more subdued.

"Oh, dear," she said, simply.

Then, when she regrouped and got to a comfortable ledge, she uttered one of her favorite sayings, which also involves her derrière: "Ow! I'm getting a wedgy!"

Wedgy from the harness or not, there's no hiding the sense of accomplishment they got as they worked themselves up higher. Eventually, they each persevered and had a great time, Brooke nearly reaching the top and Casey, with no ego whatsoever, content to stop wherever she wanted and pick lichen.

And they both had it easier than their pint-sized friend Bennett, who was so light that his dad had to rig another rope behind him just to pull him back down after he reached the top. Bennett simply wasn't heavy enough for gravity alone to lower him. The end result was a spider web of rope and a two-handed belay job by his dad—one hand controlling the belay device and the other reefing on the trailing rope as hard as he could to give gravity a hand.

It was his older brother, Max, who enjoyed the debacle the most. When Bennett was stuck about six feet off the ground and dangling in mid-air like a piñata, Max blurted out "Wait, let me go get a stick!" Luckily, even though he didn't have a hand to spare, his dad stopped him from swinging .

These and other climbing adventures have helped our kids reach highs and lows, both literally and figuratively. More importantly, they've hopefully imparted skills they can call upon later, whether they're climbing the altar or corporate ladder. I could tell a recent mission had an effect on Brooke when I tucked her in bed once on a Sunday night. "You're a hand-hold," she said, meaning to say "hand-full."

GEORGE, GEORGE, GEORGE OF THE JUNGLE... WATCH OUT FOR THAT TREE!

Don't have natural rock or climbing gyms around for your kids to climb? No carnivals with inflatable walls? Consider something even more plentiful that can be found in yards, neighborhoods and parks everywhere.

Though you don't see too many parents setting up protection on them, trees of all sorts—elm, pine, spruce, fir, maple, apple and more—are proven testing grounds for getting kids off the ground climbing. Most also offer the benefit of being located above grass, which cushions the fall.

Safety, however, is still paramount. While you could feasibly set up rope protection on them, not many people do. And that means kids who climb them are subject to Newton's Law of Gravity every bit as much as Newton's apple. And the gravity of succumbing to gravity can be severe.

A giant oak tree in our yard at the corner of 12th Street and Cascade Avenue in Boulder serves as a case in point—and also as a reminder not to trust trees' most customary protection: nailed-in ladder steps. Like many homes with trees, ours had a tree fort—the building of which brings up an entirely different form of recreating with kids. You climbed a rope to get up to the main platform, and from there you could ascend any number of shoddily constructed two-by-four ladder rungs ascending higher limbs. It was on one of these that my friend Chucky pulled, only to watch it pull off the tree under his weight. But we called him Lucky Chucky for a reason. While he fell a good 25 feet onto the ground, he only broke his arm, which also served as a handy excuse to get out of piano lessons.

Aside from being surrounded by grass, which helped save Lucky Chucky, trees offer several other things that rocks don't. One is the fact that they grow. Come back to the same route five years later and it will be different. Of course, your kid will have grown also, so it might be a wash; the limbs of both will be higher off the ground.

Trees also offer things like birds and squirrels to deal with, as well as fruit that often entices climbers ever upward. Some of my best tree misadventures as a kid involved climbing the apple, cherry, plum and peach trees in our yard, trying to reach that perfectly ripe morsel always just a finger-tip away. I don't know how many predicaments I got myself into, standing on ever-shrinking limbs just to nab one last cherry. It's not like I was ever hungry, or needed that plum to survive. But the thought of getting some sort of tangible reward for climbing—the plum being an actual plum, so to speak—fueled me to greater heights than any other motivating factor.

It also dished up life's lesson that the grass isn't always greener. Even if an apple looked perfect from my precarious perch on a twig, there was often a worm hole hiding on the other side.

This brings up one more thing trees have over rocks: limbs. They're the perfect hand holds—round, grippy and big, and often perfectly sized for children's hands. Instead of having to trust your entire weight to your fingers clinging to one tiny nub of rock, you can put whole arms around them to aid in your endeavor. Pick the right tree and your kids will be able to put their whole hands around certain limbs as if they were sculpted specifically for the kid-climbing purpose.

The downside is that, especially on mature deciduous trees, the lowest limbs are often out of reach of the average youngster. Casey and Brooke routinely ask me to hoist them into trees in our town parks. While that elevates them, it also elevates the risk should they fall, and the protests from my wife if she happens to be watching. Once they've established Limb One Base Camp, they're comfortable as clams (I still don't know who dreamed up that analogy). From there, they inherently seem to know their bounds, ascending higher when comfortable and calling me to the rescue when not.

As on rock, they're genuinely proud of their tree-climbing accomplishments as well. Both have yelled to me from precarious perches on limbs high above—my wife thankfully out of sight—heralding their new heights to the heavens.

Getting down, of course, is another matter. When it comes to kids climbing trees, Newton's principle doesn't always prevail. What goes up doesn't always come down without the help of a parent. So that's when you, the parent, have to intervene and call upon your own tree-climbing skills of yesteryear to lend a hand. The number one rule of tree climbing: leave the falling to Newton's apples.

Spider-like Prodigy

There are phenoms in every sport at every age; just look at Michelle Wie in golf and Freddy Adu in soccer. Rising to their same height in the climbing world could well be Sasha DiGiulian, who, at age 13 was already gracing ads in *Climbing*, *Urban Climber* and *Rock & Ice* magazines.

Sasha, who, like all kids, loved trying to climb out of her crib as a toddler, has gone to heights even she never envisioned as a child. At age 14, she became the two-time national rock climbing champion in her age group (14-15) by climbing to first place at the three-day U.S. Championships in Boston. At the same age, she also took first place at the Junior North American Championships, and won a Junior World Cup event in France.

Her career in bouldering has been just as remarkable. At age 12, she finished second at the Canadian Bouldering Nationals in the all-age women's open division, and finished first overall in the heralded Mammut Series.

"She has talent, determination, commitment and the ability to learn faster than any other kid I've ever coached," says her coach, Claudiu Vidulescu. "She has a strong personality, but is also very coachable, which makes her the perfect athlete. Who knows what else she's capable of achieving."

She carries this motivation off the rock as well. She's an A-student at home in Alexandria, Va., who friends call "one of the brightest, kindest and most humble friends someone could ever have."

As she can attest, you're never too old—or young—to start. Her first experience with it came at age 7 at her older brother Charlie's, birthday party (yes, his parents held his party at a climbing gym). She's loved it ever since. "I like the challenge of it," she says. "Mentally, it's tough knowing where to go next. You're always trying to get yourself to the next place."

Her mom vouches for her love of the sport as well. "She loves to push herself," mom Andrea says of Sasha's work ethic. "She loves to work hard at solving a problem, and climbing allows her to do that. She also loves the friendships it creates."

To make sure she stays at the top of her game, Sasha practices at a climbing gym in Alexandria, Va., and climbs five times a week. "She doesn't need a lot of supervision," adds Vidulescu. "She's determined and committed to doing well."

Sasha also realizes that her chosen outdoor pursuit offers a perfect metaphor for life. "Climbing has helped me appreciate the fine balance of our planet in that we all must work together to move forward," she says. "I try to always be positive and make people happy. I love climbing and sharing my passion—to me, there's no greater feeling than sharing my love of climbing with other people."

CLIMBING EQUIPMENT 101

Gear-wise, it's not hard to get kids started climbing. No one knows this better than former pro climber Nancy Prichard Bouchard, who has three daughters of her own, all of whom have made the jump from rocking chair to rocks. Here's what she recommends to get started.

For bouldering all kids need is a pair of climbing shoes and a chalk bag. For about $60, a child can be totally outfitted for the local climbing gym. Turn an old pair of kids' sneakers into climbing shoes by using Five Ten's Stealth® Paint™ (www.fiveten.com; $16.99). The shoes should be relatively tight (i.e. last summer's tennis shoes, or squeeze them into their younger sibling's footwear). Also consider investing in a pair of shoes made specifically for climbing. Most cost under $50 and encourage kids to stay involved because they have the right gear (for both prestige and performance).

While most climbing gyms have rentals, climbing shoes make great birthday and Christmas presents. Diaper-like Velcro closure systems like the Five Ten Mini Moc (www.fiveten.com) make putting them on and taking them off easy. The shoes also have a fairly stiff sole, so they support and protect small feet. While most kids can wear a single size for at least a couple of years—order them about a half size big. Most kids aren't initially comfortable in properly fitted climbing shoes, so this lets them grow into them as their skills increase.

When it comes to chalk bags, let your child pick out his own with a design he likes. Get one with a good closure system, like Metolius Mountain Products' colorful array of kid-friendly bags (www.metoliusclimbing.com).

If you decide to move from bouldering to roped climbing, you'll also need a kid's harness. For children 70 pounds and lighter, a chest harness is the best bet (www.petzl.com) as it keeps them from dangling upside-down like a bat in the event of a fall and fits diaper-tight. Bigger kids can usually wear an adult XS harness (www.metoliusclimbing.com). Just make sure it's always fitted properly, and that you remember to thread the belt back through the buckle for safety.

Chapter 9

FISHING WITH FINGERLINGS

"Many men go fishing all of their lives without knowing that it is not fish they are after."
—Henry David Thoreau

FISHING WITH KIDS HAS TO BE one of the all-American—and all-world, for that matter—pastimes, as bonding between you and your brood as pushing a swing or stroller or reading *Little Red Riding Hood* at bedtime. And just like *Little Red Riding Hood*, whose grandmother fell prey to the big bad wolf, or the *Three Little Pigs*, in which said wolf had a hankering for pork chops, it teaches them about the ever-present food chain: fish eat bugs and other tiny fish, and people eat fish.

Best of all, however, it goes hand in hand with many of the other activities covered in this book. You can combine it with biking, hiking, camping and even paddling to cluster your life as a gear-packing parent even more. But it's also a great form of recreation on its own, one that exposes kids to the Great Outdoors—as well as sharp hooks, slimy worms and fish guts—as well as any other activity under the salmon-egg-colored sun.

Its popularity rises from its place in human history. No one knows for sure who the first parent was who ever caught a fish. But when he or she brought it back to a waiting family, an outdoor activity was born. Parents from Africa to the Americas have untangled the lines of their loved ones ever since, taking their kids down to rivers, lake-shores and oceans to show them the art of putting food on the table. When a hook finally skewers your daughter's thumb, bear in mind that the same thing likely happened centuries before to other parents pursuing this age-old finger-piercing pastime.

Nowadays, families do it for recreation as much as for food (and it's a nice way for wives to get husbands and kids out of their hair on a Sunday afternoon). Go to any pond, lake, river or wharf on a weekend and chances are, you'll find someone wetting a line with a child who's still wetting her diaper.

This doesn't mean it's easy. It's far easier to take your kids hiking than it is to rig their rods, thread their hooks and untangle their lines. For hiking, all you do is tie their shoes. With fishing, you still have shoelaces to deal with, but also rods, lines and hooks. You'll change more lures than you do diapers at home, and untangle line just as you do your daughter's hair every morning (without the benefit of a brush).

But the rewards are worth every knot and puncture wound. Fishing gives you an excuse to get outside with your kids, and instills a food chain tutorial that they just don't get with gummy worms. It might even get them thinking about life's bigger lessons the next time they chomp into their fish sticks at school.

GETTING STARTED: WEBSITES AND PROGRAMS

Want help getting started? Every June, the Recreational Boating and Fishing Foundation (RBFF) hosts its National Fishing and Boating Week, an event designed to mobilize anglers and grow interest in fishing among our nation's youth. Its website (www.takemefishing.org) has a wealth of information on how to get your kids started, as well as pages where you and your children can post photos and stories of your adventures. A Hall of Fame page lets kids post pictures of their catch; the Big Catch story board lets kids tell fish stories like a pro; the First Fish page honors children's first-ever catches; the Best Fishing and Boating Buddy section showcases photos of parents and their offspring; and a page called Strange and Hilarious lets people post photos of the wacky situations that inevitably arise when you fish with your kids.

If that's not enough, there's a school of other websites your children can visit that also instill the fun of fishing with kids:

• www.boatingsidekicks.com: A great boating and fishing site for kids from the National Safe Boating Council, featuring cartoons, coloring pages, quizzes, word games, dot-to-dot, jigsaw puzzles and more, all presented in color animation.

• www.tu.org: This site for Trout Unlimited includes a First Cast program, designed to introduce youth to coldwater conservation through angling. As part of the organization's efforts to train the next generation of water stewards, it's revamped its entire youth education agenda. Look to the site also for the Fly-Fishing Merit Badge, established in 2002 to give Boy Scouts the opportunity to learn about fly-fishing and conservation.

• www.teamtacklebox.com: This site features interactive games, puzzles and other activities designed to introduce children to the sport of fishing. Activities can be played online or printed via easily navigable pages.

THE LARVAE YEARS

When your kids are still fingerlings themselves, it's more about you getting out for a little R&R and your kids getting out for a little fresh air than it is actually catching fish. Granted, your kids will benefit from being outside, but they're likely to gain the same appreciation of nature in the park or the backyard.

That said, what better excuse is there for you to wet a line? "Honey, I'm taking the kids fishing," is an utterance that will likely never land you in the dog house. What self-respecting, time-deprived spouse would turn that down?

Of course, like anything involving kids, it's easier said than done. Hooks, line, wiggly rods and, if you're lucky, fish, on top of everything else you need to deal with when kids enter the picture, add a new dimension of cluster to the equation.

In the early tadpole years it's not so bad. Until your kids are actually fishing themselves, you're simply bringing them with you while you pursue your hobby. All that really takes is some additional equipment in the form of a Snugli or kids' backpack (see Hiking with Kids).

But herein lies one of the first decisions you'll have to make, one that's contingent on the type of rod you're bringing. If you're fly-fishing, go with a kids' pack over the front-carrying Snugli. A Snugli gives you an easy place to attach flies you're not using, but having your kid up front makes it harder to pull out and strip in line when casting or retrieving. And a series of coils around your kid's neck, followed by a strike by a fish, isn't considered proper parenting. With a backpack, your kid is behind you, assumingly out of harm's way—at least until an errant back cast shish-kebobs him in the cheek. If you're heading out with a spin rod, Snuglis and kids' packs work equally well.

Either one will help you match the hatch when you have your own hatch along. They'll also help you score the rare-but-coveted parenting twofer: you're watching your kid and fishing at the same time.

Be forewarned, however, that fishing with brood attached compromises performance. Foremost, it's difficult to be stealthy with a screaming child on your back. Sneaking up on a rise, you'll hear a slew of coos, giggles and tantrums from behind that scare off anything within earshot. To their credit, kids don't know they're supposed to be quiet. It's not like you're in a library. You're in the wilds, where Tarzan yells. Why shouldn't they?

When I fished with Brooke on my back, I had to take the drag sound off my reel; every time she heard it, she cried, like the little girl she was, scaring fish for miles. Another time, she started crying for a different reason. I had waded out in a lake to chase a rise and, unbeknownst to me, I went in a hair too far. She didn't mind when the water reached her toes, or even her shins. But when it splashed up onto her butt, that was the last straw, and she let Dad—and every fish within earshot—know it, inches away from my ears.

You can't blame kids for fidgeting. The whole time you're fishing, they're staring at the back of your head. While you're scanning the surface for rises, they're scanning your bald spot. I'd squirm, too.

Confined and dangling like a puppet, they get bored and start fidgeting, jerking this way and that, the same way you pull a streamer through the water. Obsessed with their own squirming, they don't appreciate the fish squirming on the end of your line.

"Look, Casey, I caught one!" I once boasted to my one-year-old behind my back, only to feel a blob of cold, uncaring drool drip onto my neck, slimier than even the worm.

The good news: these fidgets and audible infractions don't last long. Like a mobile dangling overhead, the gurgling of water and lap of waves usually lulls them to sleep, leaving you with a brief moment of Serenity Now. Take advantage of the reprieve. When it happened to my kids, I'd tip-toe around shore with rod in hand and baby on back, trying to get in one more cast while the Sandman was still around.

But if they're asleep, keep an eye on your backcasts. Babies' heads have this parent-cringing habit of drooping into casting range. This is even more important if you're casting a streamer or wooly-bugger, whose hook outsizes your daughter's ear lobe. While I've never actually hit Brooke or Casey, I've come closer than I'll ever admit to my wife. Woe be the parent who has to go home and explain that their child got her ear pierced by a size 16 Royal Wulff.

"Honey, I've got some good news and some bad news. The good news is that we don't have to worry about getting Brooke's ears pierced anymore ..."

Thwack goes the rolling pin.

Another tippet: don't expect to give a fish a long chase down the bank like Brad Pitt in *A River Runs Through It*. Running over slippery, ankle-breaking rocks with a baby on your back while keeping tension on a line isn't mastered easily. And be careful bending over to change lures or release a fish; your passenger might get released also.

THE PUPAE PUPIL

Eventually, like fry evolving into fingerlings and finally a fish story, you'll grow—or rather, your kids will grow—out of the carrying phase and get to the point where they want to fish too. Knowing how much fun it is to watch someone else fish, you can't blame them. Cast, watch. Plop, watch. Reel, watch. Wheee!!! No wonder they fall asleep in backpacks so easily. From then on, the backpack days will be down the river and you'll be rigging two rods instead of just your own.

For this you'll need to gear up. At the most basic level, this simply entails getting them a rod. No need to get splashy in the early years. Rule No. 1: get a rod your kid likes. I've always forsaken casting distance for design, and eschewed specialty fishing stores for the Wal-Marts of the world. They make rods with motifs ranging from Barbie, Cinderella and Barney to Scooby-Doo, Sponge Bob and the Ninja Turtles. A Hannah Montana one is likely not far off. These rods might not win any casting derbies, but the casting of characters they employ ensures something far more important: your kids will like the equipment, and hence the sport, and not abandon it like a discarded Web Kinz.

Perhaps no other sport lends itself to such blatant child-targeted commercialism as fishing, but it's all for good reason. When I brought Casey home a Barbie rod, she was beside herself with joy, and the rod was beside her and under her pillow for days. Kids view it as a grown-up tool with kid-like character. Though I'm loath to admit it to my fly-fishing buddies, our garage is filled with six Scooby rods, thanks to a fishing derby I staged in a swimming pool at a trade show. We had the world's best kayak fishermen casting Scooby snacks—in reality, magnets—in hopes of landing metal lunkers we stashed below. There was even a special Swag Fish that netted prizes. If kids look less than professional with these poles, imagine how these grown-ups looked in front of their peers. "Rooooby, doo!"

While you can bastardize rods with Bart Simpson, you can't child-down tackle. A lure is a lure. It has to have a pointy end for catching, and flashy colors for luring. I suppose a Barbie theme could give a lure some flash—a swirl of pink bikini, blue headband and blond hair—but what's the point? It's the fish that see it, not your child. And it's not like you want your kid playing with and coveting a sharp lure, putting it in her pocket and taking it with her to bed.

Fortunately, tackling the tackle issue is also easy in the early years. You don't have to bring much. Up to age 2 or 3, you'll bring along far more in the way of snacks, diapers, changing pads, sippy cups, blankies and stuffed animals than you will in actual fishing gear. Until you're actually trying to catch fish, you won't even use a real lure. Most caricatured rods come with a tiny plastic fish tied to the end to hold the line in place. My advice: Keep that plastic fish there as long as possible. For a while, your kid likely won't even know the difference between that and a real one.

In the early days, it's not so much about catching fish, but casting. Kids like to throw things, and if a device lets them throw something farther, hallelujah. So it doesn't really matter what you're casting. Since your child's attention span is likely no longer than her rod, have her cast that plastic fish out there for as long as you can get away with it. It'll save you from untangling lines and tying on—and losing—lures just to see her drop everything and chase a butterfly thirty seconds later.

When Casey lost her little plastic fish in the heat of the moment, I tied on a tiny twig instead. It didn't make one bit of difference to her. Twig, plastic fish, lure—it was all the same. She'd cast it out and reel it in not knowing any better—which gave me time to help my older daughter really fish. It's a placebo they can use as long as a pacifier. And you don't have to feel guilty about pulling the wooly bugger over their eyes. You're not lying about anything. You're just protecting them, as well as your free time, by having something already on the hook in place of a hook.

Eventually, the gig will be up. They'll wise up, notice your lure is different than theirs, and you'll have to put on a real lure or hook.

Before you enter this arena, think through what you're going to do if you actually catch something. It's not the birds and the bees, but sooner or later it will bring up the inevitable conversation about the food chain and The Lion King's Circle of Life.

Once a hook's on the line and you're actually *trying* to catch a fish, a discussion on killing and mortality and mankind's place on the planet isn't far behind. It's the Y chromosomes that seem more inclined to kill. Get a fish on the line and boys are like that guy in Arlo Guthrie's "Alice's Restaurant," the one who got thrown in jail for being a litterbug, yelling "I want to kill, I want to kill...I want to eat dead burnt bodies, see veins in my teeth, I want to kill, kill, kill...."

Like mini-mobsters, boys have no problem wanting to whack whatever they catch. Consider the case of my friend Bill, who took his oldest son Max, 5, up to an inlet feeding Steamboat Lake one Mother's Day when the rainbows were spawning. His son caught one, reeled it all the way in to the rod's eyelet, and then walked it backwards, dragging the poor fish over hill and dale with him.

"Let's kill it!" he then said with evil sincerity .

"No, no," countered Bill, off guard.

Like never quite knowing when the birds and the bees talk will surface, Bill found himself instantly explaining why it was good *not* to kill the rainbow. Why it was better to let it live. It was one of those life lesson moments he could never have foreseen, rising when he least expected it, just like the fish he was after. Max might not have understood completely, but he complied, letting the fish go back in the water to school his own fingerlings.

You can understand a child's point of view. Why try to catch a fish if you're not going to keep it? And it's not just fish. Casey tries to keep everything she catches, from grasshoppers and crawdads to frogs, ladybugs and snakes. But the latter are pets. Most kids don't want to keep fish as pets; they want to eat them. And we all know you

don't eat pets. That's why my friend Pete doesn't name the pigs he raises every year. He doesn't want his two sons getting overly attached to Orville and Wilbur.

Pet-eating aside, there's also the finicky eater issue. Oftentimes, if you keep a fish to eat like any other food, your kids will get bored with it after one bite. It's one thing if they get bored with a can of Spaghettios. It's another if they get bored after you killed something to put on their plate.

Brooke tried to keep a tiny brook trout as a pet once, convincing me, in a way only girls can do to their fathers, to let her put it into a bike bottle filled with pond water to take home in the bike cage on my bike. I acquiesced, and after riding home a couple of miles we opened up the bottle to find it stiff as a board. Shaken and stirred, as James Bond might say. Brooke was naturally sad, and never wanted to keep another one again, and I felt bad for letting her talk me into it, not to mention the wrath I incurred from my wife, who made me clean the bottle.

Conversely, there is a time to kill. For the most part, this occurs when you're fishing for sustenance, not sport: salmon in Alaska, walleye and pike in the Midwest, tuna on the high seas. Even the occasional trout from a lake while backpacking can justify a fish in the pan. I'm not knocking anyone who keeps fish and I appreciate fish fried in oil and lemon pepper as much as the next guy. On a college-age trip in Minnesota's Boundary Waters, we once took a wrong portage and lived on lemon pepper, oil and fresh pike for three days.

I remember taking a trip to Canada with my dad and three siblings when I was a tadpole of a man myself, driving all the way from Boulder, Colorado, up to latitude 65° to visit some farmland he had bought. En route, we went fishing at some lost-in-childhood-memory lake and the guide showed me how to stun the fish with a quick stick whack on top of its head. When it was my turn to stun my catch, I couldn't find a stick and instead clubbed it so hard with a rock as to leave even Tanya Harding speechless. By the time I was done, the poor fish was smooshed to smithereens, its brain reduced to a pulp. Even the guide cringed when he saw it.

Which brings up the feelings of remorse and guilt that often come with such slayings. All kids are different. Some will be able to kill with reckless abandon, while others are more sentimental, likely to feel sorry for everything from the dandelion you stepped on en route to the lake, to the worm on the end of the line, let alone the fish. I had my lesson in my childhood when I placed a mousetrap in a field on our family ranch in Wyoming and caught a mouse, and then buried it. Angry that I had killed it in its own environment, my dad said he was putting it in that night's chili to teach me a lesson. Take this lesson home to your kids. If they kill it, they should eat it.

Even letting a fish go evokes discussions—if not of life and death, at least about pain. Oftentimes, you'll have to explain how the hook doesn't really hurt the fish, after cussing out loud because it shish-kebobbed your finger.

"Then why'd you just yell?" they'll ask, as you shake the blood from your thumb.

You'll also likely field questions, as I have, about the fish's families, including brothers and sisters and parents and uncles and aunts. Casey once even asked me about a fish's grandparents.

The best bet is to follow the advice of the Boy Scouts and be prepared for anything. Luckily, if you're fishing with your kids, you're already a parent, so you're used to odd-ball questions. Improvise a food chain speech like my friend Bill, or any other diatribe that lasts long enough for them to get bored with your answer and move on to something else.

Releasing what you catch or not, you have three options when trying to catch fish with your kids: bait, lure, or fly. I'm not going into the nuances of each approach, nor the knots you need to secure hooks to the line. There are plenty of books out there covering things like that, and I'm not the best one to impart such skills.

While I fished sporadically as a kid, I didn't take up fly-fishing until the summer after my senior year in college, while guiding raft trips in Alaska. A fellow guide nicknamed Big R took me under his wing, just as I've done with my kids and you'll likely do with yours. I was as spastic as Casey with my casts, losing flies to cobblestones and bushes, and credit Big R's parent-like patience for not throwing his hands up in despair.

That's what you'll need with your youngsters. If the Scarecrow needed a brain, the Tin Man a heart and the Lion courage, you'll need a heavy dose of patience to perform the wizardry of teaching your children to fish.

Knot, Knot...Who's There?

Most of this patience will be used for untangling knots. If you're the type who gets frustrated untangling a simple extension cord or shoelace, think twice about taking your kids fishing as a relaxing family activity. Like it or not, untangling knots is an integral part of the sport, more so than flat tires bicycling, or wipe-outs skiing.

A few other family activities, like kite flying, shoelace-tying and hair-brushing, involve untangling knots. But fishing wins the knot war. The line is thinner and clearer, and the knots infinitely more mangled. Dog leash wrapped around a pole? Child's play. Jump rope tangled? Easy street. Slinky knot? No comparison (though, admittedly, still a pain).

At first, you won't seethe over coming to the rescue—in a way, it validates your existence as a parent and makes you feel important, a grown-up yet again showing superiority over children by saving the day. Untangling knots is simply the price you pay for teaching your kids how to fish, you'll justify. "Daaaaad!" they'll whine. "This thing's all messed up!" And then you'll stroll over with a smug grin and happily fix the problem, as only parents can.

The hard part is relaxing enough to turn a blob of knots into a straight line again, all while still watching the kids. One eye on your kids (you are still watching them, after all), one on the knot, and a third eye on the hook, which will invariably skewer you whenever you're not looking. You also have to complete the task before your kids get bored with the whole operation and don't want to fish anymore.

You'll curse, you'll swear, and then you'll chastise yourself for cursing and swearing. "How the heck could it get this bad?" you'll wonder. And then you'll remember that your child was whipping it back and forth for ten minutes (while you were ignoring him), before he even called you over. No wonder it looks like a plate of spaghetti noodles. And then you'll make matters worse—again, as only parents can—by pulling it the wrong way through the only opening when you turn to deal with your child who just stepped in the water.

If it's bad enough, you'll pop out the pocket knife, sever Scooby's line and start all over again. ("Does that hurt it?" the ever-sympathetic Casey once asked about the line when I cut it.) Then it'll be smooth sailing again...for a couple of minutes, anyway, until like Bob Dylan, you're tangled up in blue all over again. And that's when you just might start pulling out your own tangled-up hair.

In a way, hair is about the only thing remotely similar to the knots you encounter fishing. But at least then you have a comb or brush to help you, or even cream rinse or Johnson's No More Tangles. Unlike your child's hair tangles, there's no magical elixir to help you sort out fishing knots, just your Rubik's Cube wits, patience, and, if it comes to it, nail clippers. And instead of your kid screaming as you smooth out her knotted, split ends, it's you screaming under your breath as you dive into the tedious, thankless task.

Spin Rods

Until they get old enough to appreciate the art of fly fishing, or have enough patience to watch a bobber floating above bait, a spin rod is likely your best bet. The reason: your kid is actually doing something the whole time.

Isn't that the age-old commandment for kids? Keep them busy? The simple art of casting and reeling can keep a kid occupied for hours, even if there's not a fish in sight. Cast, reel. Cast, reel. Parent, relax. Get a nibble or two and it's like taking the training wheels off a bike. Your kid's eyes will light up like his rod.

But we're getting ahead of ourselves. Don't expect your child to win any casting contests right off the bat. She'll likely be able to throw a stick farther than she can cast. The timing of pushing the button and letting go as you flick your wrist takes some acclimation. Sadly, Game Boy and Play Station skills help—but don't tell your kids that. It's like patting your head and rubbing your belly, only there's a sharp metal hook hurtling through the air.

The first few casts will land on their shoes, graze the dog, and hit the backpack. They'll sail hither and yonder like those whistling flying saucer fireworks that refuse to file a flight plan, errant missiles whirling out of control. And there's no safe place to hide. You'll flinch. You'll cringe. You'll throw your arms over your face for protection. Casey and Brooke's casts have hit everything from my pant legs to the picnic basket.

Eventually your kids will get it down—depress the thumb button, flick the wrist and then release. And, then, as only kids can, they'll pat themselves on the back for their prowess, commenting on their own success.

"Dad, did you see that one?" they'll ask the first time it sails even close to straight. "Look how far I got it." No matter that it barely went farther than their rod tip—they're on their way to becoming fishermen.

The reeling is easier. It's almost as if they figure this part out quickly just so they can cast again. Once they remember which way to turn the crank, they can do it just as well as most adults. It's not rocket science, after all, but a fishing reel. Sure, they'll get sidetracked by a butterfly only to see the lure sink and snag on the bottom. But eventually they'll master it, their spinners rotating just like their attention spans.

Hopefully, it will only take them a few times to learn not to reel the lure all the way up to the eyelet. Do that, they'll figure out, and it compromises the casting. There have to be a few inches of line left to launch the lure into orbit again. But it's hard to curtail the excitement of reeling, and this lesson won't sink in without some practice.

Next up is discerning the difference between a bite and a snag. "Dad, I got one!" you'll hear, only to see her reel in a lump of seaweed and a dejected look steal across her face. Then you'll take it off to a bunch of "Ooooh, slimy, gross!" comments and she'll be on her way again, errantly casting to her heart's content. (Note: perform the pretend-seaweed-is-boogers-coming-out-your-nose trick, but only if no other adults are around.)

Eventually they'll distinguish between the two when their first piece of seaweed starts wiggling. And that's when you'll be able to hear it with authority and confidence: "Dad! I got one!"

Bait Fishing

My fly fishing friends will be chagrined, but occasionally (with kids only, of course) I'll throw a little PowerBait onto an old dry fly and turn Brooke and Casey loose at a little brook trout pond near home. Doing so makes catching fish as easy as, well, taking candy from a baby.

The reason I use a fly instead of a blank hook is simple: ashamed as I am to admit it, the PowerBait sticks better to the fly's tiny cilia, like bubble gum on a brush. The fly hackles give it a little purchase. Though no self-respecting fly-fisherman would ever desecrate a dry fly like this, let alone admit to it, in the name of fishing with kids, and

SPIN-CASTING TIDBITS FOR TADPOLES

Unlike bait fishing, where kids often cast out a line and then wait around for something to happen, spin-casting keeps them busy the whole time. They cast, reel and then cast again. If there aren't any fish, they'll get bored eventually, but it gives them something to do.

- For button-depress reels, it's all in the thumb. Have them work on lifting the thumb right as they flick the wrist for the cast. At first you'll have casts going every which way of the compass, but eventually they'll narrow in on target.
- Have them practice a constant reeling motion so the lure won't fall to the bottom and get snagged on weeds. Also, teach them not to reel the lure all the way into the eyelet, keeping it a few inches away for the next cast.
- Teach them to keep an eye on both their rod tip and point where the line disappears into the water.

getting them hooked on the sport, it throws the game into turbo-drive. There's no deciding what lure to use, how fast to reel it in, or any of that rot. Simply throw a little split shot about eight inches above the newly improved power fly so the PowerBait floats off the bottom and —Bam! Get ready for action.

This isn't to say that PowerBait doesn't have its downsides. Foremost concerns your fingers. They'll turn pistachio pink from mashing the disgusting gunk up into pea-sized balls, and its tell-tale smell will follow you home from garage to bedroom (trust me, it's not romantic.) And just like fly fishing, there's an art to the PowerBait squish. You need to roll it up just so—into a tight enough ball—and mash it onto the hook hard enough so it doesn't fly off with every cast. It also has to be the right consistency. Too wet and it's slimesville. Too dry—like, say, hypothetically, after you forgot to tighten the lid all the way—and it crumbles like brown sugar. Until you get it just right, your kid's morsels will fly off the hook in a shotgun pattern, peppering the lake with pink pellets everywhere except where your hook lands.

But master these nuances and your kid's catch per capita will increase. Which brings up a drawback. The catch and release part gets trickier when a fish, especially a tiny brook trout, swallows that pink gumball whole. Like a child slurping down a malted milk ball, the hook typically beds down deeper than it does on a lure or fly, leading to more discussions on pain. "Does that hurt it?" your kid will ask as you deftly remove the fish's tonsils.

By no means is PowerBait the only bait that works, either. Worms and night crawlers teach the food chain lesson even better—and every bit as much as lures, flies and other artificial munchables—because they're real, Mother Nature-made food with earth-tone colors, not a processed, artificially pink counterfeit. The only drawback to them is that they wiggle and slime all over the place, making some kids gross out. This means you'll be the one skewering them onto the hook, which is actually a good thing as it'll save explaining the puncture wound on the tip of your kid's finger to your spouse. A key: skewer the creepy crawlie a few times, threading the hook through its seven heart compartments until it looks like a sine wave. Thread it through only once and it'll sail off and become Air Worm on the first cast, no matter how bad it is. Take it from me: a flying worm landing on your spouse watching from shore is not a good thing.

While it's easier to buy them at a store, you can increase the day's lesson by digging for worms, or even hunting for grasshoppers, in the yard beforehand. But the labor doesn't always yield fruits, and your kids might burn out and change their minds about even going fishing during the whole process.

Apart from also using salmon eggs occasionally—in which case you have to explain why fish eat their own eggs, which isn't a pretty topic—that's the extent of my bait-fishing prowess. I didn't grow up near lakes, didn't sling baitfish off a dock into the ocean, and haven't even broken out fridge leftovers for chasing catfish. But I do know this: if you really want your kid to catch a fish, make a date with bait.

Once, when I was fishing with Brooke using a fish-shaped Rapalla lure, an ambitious pike barely twice the lure's size took it halfway down. Then the light bulb struck to continue trolling with the new half-fake-half-real combo meal, and a fish the next size up took the whole enhanced enchilada. We started using a lure and ended up bait fishing—a true lesson in the survival of the fittest that Brooke related to Mom as soon as we got home.

But more often than not I go with the pink persuader, PowerBait, when fishing with kids. I feel guilty for keeping its jar in my fly-fishing vest until I hear the yell that makes all parents proud: "Dad! I got one! I got one!"

BAIT FISHING TIDBITS FOR TADPOLES

- Choose your bait and hooks based on the type of fish you're after (get hooks that will fit into the fish's mouth). Ask your local tackle shop about the hook sizing system (i.e. 6, 4, 2, 1, 1/0, 2/0, etc.). The smaller the hook (i.e., the bigger the number) the better the chance of a bite.
- There are as many baits to choose from as there are Polly Pocket accessories (worms, salmon eggs, grasshoppers, PowerBait, etc.). Purchase live bait at an angling shop, or gather it on your own. If fishing for bluegill or catfish, cut-up pieces of hot dog, cheese, dough, corn kernels and even French fries work for worm-ophobes.
- Don't completely cover your hook with the bait (the point should stick out). Worms should be put on a slightly bigger hook, taking a loop of skin on the hook and repeating.
- If the water is swift, attach weights about twelve inches above your bait. This will keep your bait about an inch above bottom. If the water isn't moving, use a bobber, adjusting the distance between the bobber and bait to accommodate the depth of the water. Shorten and lengthen the distance as necessary. Another technique: tie your sinker to the end of the line, and then attach a snelled hook (a hook with six inches of line pre-attached) a foot above the sinker. If there's no action, move your bobber deeper at one-foot intervals. You can also remove it completely to fish the bottom, holding the line

between your fingers to feel bites.

- Cast your line and wait. Watch the line or bobber, or feel the line with your fingers. If you haven't gotten a bite after 10-15 minutes, try casting again, and to different places to test different depths.

Fly-fishing

Though a self-professed hack, I pursue this type of fishing most, usually in the late summer and early fall when the rivers have cleared and it's officially time to start slinging dry flies. It's also the type of fishing I do on the rare occasions that I can actually get everything together enough—from getting the kids to the pond, rigging their rods and getting their lines in the water—to have them fishing on their own, leaving me to wet a line as well.

Doing so with kids around takes bat-like radar. Even if they're scattered about, kids have an uncanny knack of getting in the way of your back casts. Like crossing a street, they don't fully comprehend the vastness of the area involved, nor the reach of the danger. Fly rods can serve line in a far wider swath than any spinning rod powered by Scooby.

About the same time they recognize the berth to allow, they also recognize that it's a different form of fishing than what they're doing. As far as they're concerned, their Scooby rods are training wheels. They'll want to upgrade to do what Mom and Dad are doing.

They'll also quickly realize that it's more interactive, which kids are all about. They'll stare at their own rods, either at a motionless bobber or their cast-and-reel monotony, and then watch me whip the line back and forth and aim it right where they saw a trout rise to the surface. Then—Whamo! The fish will suck in the fly like kids will a plate of homemade cookies. Wanting to be like their parents (up until the teenage years, anyway), their eyes will shift from their Scooby rods to yours and back to Shaggy and they'll want to try this new form of fishing on their own.

Be forewarned: despite the proverb, "Give a man a fish and he'll eat for a day, teach him to fish and he'll eat for a lifetime," fly-fishing is tougher to teach than bait fishing or spin casting. You're adding an art to an activity, and it's a little more delicate than your average finger-painting session. Fly-fishing is a sport of subtle moves—which even wily veterans hone religiously—and kids, as we all know, aren't known for their subtlety.

It starts with the equipment. Most fly rods are three times as long as the average three-year-old. They're unwieldy, flimsy, pointy and, worst of all, fragile and expensive. None of these attributes lends itself to child's play. The first time your kid grabs your fly rod and holds it up, your natural reaction is to reach for it and say, "Whoa, careful with that!" as if he's playing with a model airplane. You can't blame a parent for this level of concern, largely for the fragile and expensive part. Giving a kid a fly rod before he's ready for it is like giving him a set of china for Christmas—right after he opened the tool kit.

You also can't show them how to cast as you did on your first romantic fly-fishing date with your spouse. They're too small for you to reach your arms around them from behind and show them the motion. You have to stoop over 90 degrees, in which case you're more worried about your back than your daughter's back cast.

Brooke lived up to my worst fears when she took my fly rod in hand for the first time and started whipping it back and forth, inches away from the boulders on shore like she was twirling a jump rope. "Whoa, careful with that!" I said instinctively, reaching for the rod. "Not like that."

I had reason for concern. A few years earlier, we took an overnight float trip on the Yampa River through Duffy Canyon (note to self: don't do that mosquito-fest ever again). Knowing the fishing was supposed to be good—and naively thinking I'd actually have time to fish while rowing the boat—I brought my fly rod and kept it rigged, tucked under some straps on the back of the raft.

I got a few casts in and caught a few fish, but my rod paid the price. At the take-out, rod, reel and rigging—including my favorite good-luck Royal Coachman—had vanished. When Brooke and her friends were riding in back, they dislodged it and it kerplunked into the Yampa like a shampoo bottle in a bathtub.

The good news is that it enticed my Dead Head brother-in-law Nino, a fly-fish-crazed Alaskan, to build me a new rod as a present over the course of the next dark winter, complete with inlaid dancing bears and a skull and crossbones end cap.

So I was as protective of this new Jerry rod as I was of my kids, as Brooke proceeded to slash it Zorro-like through the air, flirting with boulders with each swoosh. But my admonishment fell flat. When I reached down to show her the correct ten o'clock to two o'clock casting technique, her fly had already touched the water a scant two feet from where she was standing. Then—Whamo! A fish struck and she had her first trout from a fly rod on the line.

"See," she rubbed in. "I told you I was doing it right."

FISHING TIME: BASIC INFO

1. Whether they're fly-fishing, spin-casting or bait fishing, have your kids practice casting in a parking lot or grassy field beforehand. You can tape the hooks up, or even cut the hook off a fly or lure so your kid casters can get the feel of the setup without hooking themselves or innocent bystanders.

2. Choose the right location. You can do everything right and still get skunked by picking a fishless pond. It's like heading to the movies and picking a dud, minus the popcorn and Junior Mints. Do some due diligence and ask around. Also choose a location that isn't crowded (you want to catch fish, not people), and look for a pond with pan fish. Kids don't care what they catch, and are as happy with a bluegill as they are a brook trout.

3. Regulations differ state by state. Check locally to see if your child needs a fishing license, and get one for yourself. Also look for bait restrictions. Many waterways require barbless hooks and artificial lures or flies. Also know how many fish you

can keep, and their sizes, and be aware that some areas are catch and release only.

4. Don't make rigging your child's rod another home project you'll ignore for years. Have your tackle shop spool the reel for you, and don't be embarrassed to ask.

5. Invest in good line. Sure, you can always blame your knots. But that doesn't diminish the disappointed look in your child's eye when a fish gets away. Go for a two- to four-pound test for most lakes and rivers. A 200-yard-long spool is plenty.

6. If you can transport it without breaking it into smithereens, assemble your own rod—and even your kids' rods—beforehand. With children in tow, once you get to the water your hands will be tied like your fly when it comes to rigging. Just when you get the hook threaded, Junior will need to go the bathroom, show you a spider web, or cry because his foot got wet. Have your rod rigged and ready beforehand to make the process easier.

7. Be selective in where you wet your line. Try the shallows around docks, rocks and weeds, and cast below overhanging trees and in other shaded areas. Besides running around in schools, fish are a lot like kids—if it's hot and sunny, they won't be too active.

8. Bring fun food, snacks and treats. Anything fun they can associate with fishing will help bring them back for another cast.

9. The casts don't have to be gargantuan. Sometimes fish are right next to shore. Offer positive encouragement, even if a cast lands by your kids' ankles.

10. Don't push your kids for too long; leave them hungry for more. If they get bored, it's okay if they want to chase frogs; the whole point is to enjoy the outdoors.

11. Once your child is serious about it, forego Sponge Bob and invest in high-quality equipment. A good rod and reel is easier to cast than one with Daffy Duck staring you in the face, letting you spend more time fishing than untangling knots. Look for a rod in the five- to six-foot range that's lightweight and flexible. A good beginner's rod should bend freely when shaken.

12. Teach patience. If there aren't any bites, reel in and cast again, or spin-cast a lure to a different location (a technique that will come in handy when they're fishing with younger siblings).

13. If your child feels a bite, have him raise the rod to set the hook (it's often difficult to differentiate between a bite, the current and the bottom). To reel it in, have him lift the rod and then start reeling—only use the reel itself to pull in very small fish. Keep the line tight to ensure the hook stays in, and teach them how to use the rod to steer the fish to open water.

14. Regulations permitting, keep a few to take home and eat. This helps them appreciate the whole activity. But teach them to keep only what they'll eat that night and put back what they won't to catch another day. Teach them not to catch their limit, but to limit their catch (to what they'll eat).

15. If you keep a fish, have your kids watch/help with the cleaning. This will make it become part of their fishing routine and not something just Dad does. It also gives them an appreciation that they are killing a creature for their food and that they should be thankful for that, not wasteful.

16. Empty clear pretzel or cat food containers hold about 2 gallons of water and make a great holding tank so your kids can see what they've caught.

17. Be careful near water of any depth and to play it safe, make your kids wear life jackets. Ensure enough adults are present to keep all children in sight.

18. Leave No Trace. Properly dispose of monofilament line and other trash.

FLY-FISHING TIDBITS FOR TADPOLES

Younger children won't be able to grasp the concept—or the rod—of fly-fishing as well as older kids. But when they want to try—like Brooke did a few times after she saw me—following are a few pointers.

- The hardest part to teach is stopping the wrist from breaking back too far, resulting in the rod dropping too far back and opening the backcast loop. Trick: Put a thick rubber band around the reel seat below the reel and around their wrist. If they start breaking their wrist too much, it pulls the rubber band, helping them to know when to stop.

- Have them practice casting in the yard with a piece of foam on the line instead of a fly.

- When they get the feel of the rod and can cast a bit, start at a pond or lake so they don't have to deal with currents pulling at the line. Keep the leader short (7.5 feet max) until they start mastering the cast.

- Be patient. There'll be more lines in the brush and leader tangles than you ever thought possible, so bring extras. And stick to dry flies for a while. You're asking for tangle trouble with split shot, nymphs and hopper droppers.

- Explain as best you can the big three: match the hatch; casting; and drag-free float.

Chapter 10

SWIMMING WITH KIDS

"Just keep swimming!"
—Nemo, *Finding Nemo*

IF THERE'S EVER AN OUTDOOR recreational pursuit with some practicality, it's swimming. While all the others in the Great Outdoors gamut are great, swimming is something you want your kids to learn for survival's sake as much as fitness and fun.

When watching *Titanic* the other night with our kids—I know, it's a bit on the grown-up side, but my wife's great aunt went down on it, and we pointed her name out to our kids on the victim list at the traveling exhibit in Denver—Brooke asked why the people falling into the water couldn't swim. That led to a discussion about hypothermia and cold water, but also to the fact that some people simply never learned.

"I thought everybody knew how to swim," replied our budding Michael Phelps. "They should."

She's right, of course. And as well as being a sensible arrow to add to your kids' all-around quiver, it also opens the doors to a slew of other recreation possibilities, from water skiing and paddling to snorkeling, scuba diving and surfing (stop right here if you have an aversion to sand).

Unlike riding a bike, teaching your kids to swim is best left to professionals. But it's still a rite of passage parents can participate in, and you can help get the bubbles blowing and them stroking in the right direction.

Like bike riding, swimming has its consequences if you don't do it correctly. While water is softer than pavement, it comes with the baggage of that whole not-being-able-to-breathe thing. And that can burst the bubble of the most eager tadpoles trying to learn.

You'd think swimming would come more naturally to us. After all, we spend the first nine months of our lives encased in embryonic fluid. Of course, we also have an umbilical cord as a snorkel. Everything changes when lungs develop and we enter the world as living, air-breathing beings.

Parents fret about breathing more than most anything else, even when our kids are out of the water. We make sure our kids are breathing when they're sleeping, rush to the rescue when they gag at the dinner table, and have a conniption when their heads go underwater at bath time. We even worry when their noses are clogged, diligently sucking out boogers to clear blocked passages.

All these worries are for good reason. Broken bones and scrapes we can deal with, but breathing cuts to our very core. Introduce water to the equation and our comfort level is stripped like a wet diaper. Luckily, these worries ease as your children age and everyone, parents and kids alike, learns to breathe more easily about it.

BREATH-HOLDING 101

Eventually, it's time to acclimate your children to this foreign medium called water. It's not like kids are ducklings following Mallard Mom around, or tadpoles emulating Mr. Toad. They have Webkinz dolls, not webbed feet, and play with Dora, not dorsals. Nor do they have gills, like Nemo and his school. When it comes to swimming, kids are fish out of water. And the most prudent teacher is the school of hard coughs.

Luckily, children naturally know that water's not something to be taken lightly, or sitting down, for that matter. They know something down there isn't good for them. It's our job as parents to help teach them about it and get that water monkey off their backs.

Someone whose credentials I never checked once told me that the best way to teach your kid how to hold her breath is to blow in her face and then dunk her under for a nano-second. Of course, that nano-second can feel like eternity for the parent.

Your child's instant reaction after the face blow, the mysterious advisor said, is to hold her breath. So what better time to introduce her to the underworld? She's holding her breath anyway, why not take advantage of it with a little test?

Gullible grown-up that I am, I tried it. And lo and behold, it worked.

Still, despite explaining everything to her with scientific rationale, at age one Casey had little clue what was going on.

"Okay, sweetie...you're going to feel a little puff in your face and that's going to create a stimulus/response reaction where you hold your breath, and then I'm going to dunk you."

"Goo-goo, gah-gah," came the cheery, bubbly reply.

She had no idea what was coming. One second she's looking at me with her innocent green eyes and the next she's thrust downward for her first visit to the underworld. A quick blow and an even quicker donut-like dunk. Then she was back in the land of the breathing, a little wider-eyed than when she left, having survived her first visit underwater.

Not that she liked it. She came up perplexed, as if she had just discovered one of life's biggest secrets. *You can go under there without perishing.*

I didn't make a habit of such experiments—especially when my spouse was around. I did it once in our hot tub while my wife happened to be looking on, and I ended up in another kind of hot water. So from then on I did it secretly, away from other prying, parenting eyes.

STROKING IN THE RIGHT DIRECTION

Holding your breath can only get you so far. Eventually you'll either sink or swim. To ensure it's the latter requires more thorough instruction.

There are several schools of thought on this. The most questionable, obviously, is the Great Santini approach, or controversial Baptism by Water. This is where you simply chuck them in a pool or lake with a wing (not a water wing) and a prayer and tell them to swim for shore. I've never actually known any parents who have employed this technique, and certainly don't condone it. A blow and a quick dunk while they're still in your arms is one thing, an unsuspecting cannon-ball quite another.

There are better ways to have your kids figure out the mystery of swimming, the best of which is professional lessons. But even before enrolling them in a certified swimming program, you can help acclimate them to Atlantis.

Hot Tubs

Hot tubs are far more than a status symbol of the rich and famous, or a place to soothe the aches and pains of aging. They're the perfect training grounds for helping kids become accustomed to water. Once your kids become capable swimmers, hot tubs are also worth their weight in babysitting gold.

Their own weight, of course, is why we had to move ours off our deck and onto a concrete pad on the ground. While we used it to placate the saga and sagging of aging, it was making our deck do some sagging of its own.

There in its new perch it helped both of our kids earn their water wings for swimming. Even at just a few months old, Casey and Brooke visited it regularly (under our watch, of course), which helped them get acquainted with this foreign medium.

Water...these are our kids.

Kids, this is the water.

I hope you both get along swimmingly.

I'm not saying that you need to buy a hot tub solely as a water-training tool for your kids (though it's a handy excuse). But if you have one, or a heated pool, your kids will have a leg up on keeping their heads up.

While kids also learn about water with rubber duckies in the bathtub, hot tubs accelerate the acclimation process because the pools are wider and deeper. Plus, you're always in there with them, which encourages them to experiment with strokes, dunkings and, unfortunately, splashings. Kids can touch bottom in a bath tub. They can't always in a hot tub.

Our tub is where both of our kids learned to hold their breath. It's also where they learned to dog paddle and cannon-ball, skills they'd later perfect at the pool. More importantly, it also taught them to hold their bladders as well as their breath, giving them a goggle-covered head start over their friends.

Of course, it requires a complete clean-up crew after each session. Not from them going number one, but from toys. Our daughters would bring Barbies, cups, brushes, bottles, squirt guns, rafts, and other floatie-floats in with each session, making our tub look like their play room on a Saturday morning.

Speaking of floatie-floats, this also brings up the golden rule of acclimatizing your kids to water: unless they're in your bathtub, make them wear a swim diaper until they're potty trained. Save the Baby Ruths for *Caddyshack*. Swim diapers come in colorful patterns and designs, fit snugly around tiny derrières, and will do wonders to help you relax when you're in the water with your kids. Without one, you'll be on edge just thinking about the consequences.

Even with a swim diaper firmly in place, you'll still be nervous, especially when others are in the water with you—just like you are whenever you're in the company of other soaking infants. Get any parent in a body of water with someone else's child and the first thought to go through his head concerns the kid's bowel control. Consider the swim diaper an insurance policy that you hope you'll never have to use.

Back to the toys. The beauty of the dolls and things your kids cart in is that they keep them playing in the water longer. And time in the water leads to being comfortable in it. Just ask Phelps.

You'll be in the tub with them for the first couple of years (woe is you), and the next few you'll have to keep a constant eye on them. But once your kids become self-sufficient swimmers, your tub will earn its keep as well as any other babysitter—without ever bringing a tattooed boyfriend over to watch a movie on the couch.

Throughout all this, you'll experience the joys of hot tub upkeep, not unlike keeping teenagers in check. Ours was a little more temperamental than most. Funds drained from building our house and having Brooke, we got it secondhand from someone who got it secondhand from someone named Rosco. Like a teen, it was far from self-contained. Its pipes ran under the deck and into a crawlspace below our living room, where the gas motor resided. If turned on, it would heat until either boiling or someone turned it off. More than once, I ventured out with enthusiastic kids in tow, only to find it more suitable for cooking lobster than teaching swim lessons.

The only upside of this is that, in winter, I could fix matters by shoveling in snow, much to the delight of the kids whose heads the piles landed on. In summer I could cool it with the hose, to their drinking and squirting delight. Ours had so many peculiarities that for a while, I found myself most relaxed whenever it was broken. That's the only time I didn't have to deal with the dang thing.

Then there's the mad scientist mixing of chemicals. Ever since that beaker incident in high school, physics has never been my strong point, and hot tub maintenance isn't either: pH and alkalinity increasers, Bromide dispensers, and little strips of paper to measure how badly you're doing monitoring each. As with being too hot at times, other times it was too chemically. If it eats Barbie's hair off, your kids are better off in the bath tub. Combine this with the ritualistic fishing-out of creepy-crawlie bugs that work their way in (as if they, too, are eager to teach their kids a lesson) and it's not exactly maintenance-free. The bugs are all dead, of course, thanks to the toxic level of chemicals inside, but they, too, have disrupted our dips with the kids. There's something about bloated spiders that takes the pizzazz out of a pool.

But for us, all these little annoyances are worth it. Our tub got our kids used to water before taking the plunge into the deeper world of real pools. By the time they were ready for the pool downtown, they were already a rung up the ladder from their peers.

Public Pools

It happens to every parent—that first venture into a public swimming pool with your kids. Don't be nervous (especially if you have a swim diaper). Sure, the chlorine turns hair green and eyes red, making your kids ready for Halloween. And sure, every once in a while you have to flick away a floating Barbie Band-Aid. But take the plunge and you'll see that pools teach a practical skill while later serving double-duty as a babysitter.

In my younger days, it was the High-Mar club in Boulder that served this purpose. It didn't matter that we spent as much time catching crawdads in a nearby irrigation ditch as we did learning the crawl stroke. We'd kill entire afternoons there, playing such games as Sharks and Minnows and Marco Polo, belly-flopping and can-openering off the diving board, and groveling for change to get red, white and blue Bomb Pops from the snack bar. Our parents would park us there all day, leaving us to our own sinus-douching devices while they read newspapers, played tennis, chatted, and, eventually, even left to run errands or dropped us off completely.

Flash forward a few decades and we're now doing the same with our own brood. Fortunately, Steamboat has a large, natural, hot springs pool open year-round, with a lap pool for adults, shallow pool for kids, and freshly remodeled warm pools where parents can soak their tired, child-rearing bones. Settlers named the town after its springs, believing they sounded like a chugging steamboat.

But the town's namesake made it through the water a slight bit better than our kids did at first. And the steamboats certainly moved faster than we ever did in the changing room.

Before you even get to the pool you have an even bigger gauntlet to survive: braving the changing room and emerging unscathed on the other side. If it's tough for your kids in the pool, it's even harder for you to keep your head above water in the changing room. More than one parent has thrown his arms up in despair at the plight, high-tailing it home and putting plans for the pool on hold.

The first hurdle is finding an appropriate place to lay Her Squirminess down to change. The beauty of swimming is that unlike biking, skiing, fishing and other kid-friendly activities, there is little equipment involved—pretty much just a swim suit. In the early years they can even do it in their birthday suit for that matter. But you still have to get them out of their clothes and into their trunks.

Most locker room designers don't take into account the poor parents who have to lay their kids down somewhere to change diapers and clothes. You'll try everything, from the bench, where other swimmers' naked derrières have plopped, to the floor, where their athlete's feet have been. At one pool whose locker room was lacking level-ness, I even stooped so low as to use a toilet lid as a last resort. Hopefully, you can commandeer a countertop. If so, lay down a towel to make things more comfortable for the change.

Perimeter secured, it's time to get down to business. It's not so bad with just one infant or toddler in tow. You're on man-on-man coverage, instead of zone-D, with one arm, and even a foot if need be, to hold down each kicking and wiggling leg. You can also enlist the help of strangers. "Hey, mind helping me pin her down here while I get this swim diaper on?" you might ask. "It's for your own good." Then you can both All Star wrestle her to the mat, one grown-up per appendage.

Change two kids simultaneously and the workload grows exponentially. Now you have to place one child on the counter where she can't get away, and then quickly change the other, juggling clothes, swim suits, and limbs like a Barnum & Bailey performer.

Gender issue is another matter. Our pool doesn't have a family changing area, so if it's dad's turn (believe me, it's enough of a hassle that you'll trade off with your spouse) we're in with the naked fellas. It's not so bad if you have sons. That's where they're supposed to be. But we have two daughters, and once they started coming of age enough to talk, they also began noticing subtle differences in locker room anatomy.

"Big pee-pee," Casey once said to my chagrin, pointing to the gentleman next to us. I had to slap her tiny-by-comparison finger down quickly.

Another time she commented on a fellow dresser's weight, which caused more stuttering and back-pedaling. Then she blurted out something about someone's torso-covering tattoos. If I've learned anything in life, it's not to make fun of someone's torso tattoos.

It doesn't help that your kids are eye-to-derrière with the other dressers, or that the tight confines put them in literally cheek-to-cheek proximity with them. Changing a kid is hard enough in the privacy and spaciousness of your home, let alone where everyone's watching your struggles while rubbing up against you.

Eventually, miracle of miracles, you'll get them outside to the pool. Providing you still have any energy left after surviving the changing room, it's time to take them swimming. If your kids can swim on their own, great. If not, you're officially on duty all over again—which isn't as easy as it looks.

The first few times you'll basically just hold them above water, two hands under the armpits, and whirl them around while making little motor and "Whee!" noises. While the technique might look simple, one errant glance elsewhere and your child is playing Diver Dan. "Huhlooo....little help down here!" their thoughts percolate up in tiny balloon bubbles.

To them, even being just an inch under is the same as being halfway down the Pacific Trench. Luckily, finely tuned, well-oiled parent that you are, your reaction time gets honed quickly. Accidental submersion? You're there faster than a torpedo.

You'll develop just as lightning-fast a reaction time when it comes to potty emergencies. Even with obligatory swim diapers, you'll have some close calls that test both your sprinting and sinuses.

"Dad, I have to go to the bathroom," the innocent comment will come. Then, no matter where you are in the pool, you'll move Phelps fast to rectify matters. It's go-time—for both you and your kid. Back up the steps, dripping wet carry back to the locker room, and onto the toilet seat whose lid you just changed her on.

Much as I hate to admit it, pee breaks aren't as crucial. Every parent could confess to covering up a pee-in-a-pool incident at one time or another. While the practice should certainly be discouraged, it's not quite as crucial as the old number two. I remember one time when our pool was evacuated for just such an infraction (no, it wasn't from one of our daughters).

Bathroom breaks aside, the pool is where life's most basic swimming lessons surface. First you'll help them keep their heads above water. Next, you'll move on to blowing bubbles. Then you'll teach them how to avoid getting water up their noses. One accidental front flip or head tipped backwards and the tingly lesson is learned. The only sensation that compares to it is their feet falling asleep, only the tingling is right there in front where both eyes can see it.

In early years, you'll spend your time simply sitting on the steps or in the shallows where you can keep an eye and hand on them. Then you'll reach minor milestones. The first comes when they grasp the concept of treading water, which is exactly how you feel every time you're stuck at home watching them.

Kicking her feet and fluttering her arms, Casey mastered it just enough to barely keep both lips out of the water, pursed like a kissing fish to suck in air. Everything else—ears, forehead, chin—was completely underneath, save for those precious lips, as puckered-up as they ever are at bedtime. When I'd reach out to offer help, she'd tread the other way, proudly surviving and breathing on her own.

The next step is the aptly named dog paddle. While instructors don't hand out doggie treats as a reward for it, it's the most primal form of water locomotion. Kids gravitate to it like they do the snack bar. From my limited perspective, 20 million canines can't be all wrong. Plus, our kids often eat like dogs at dinner—the other night Casey slurped juice straight from the table with those same pursed lips—so why not swim like them as well?

Still, the stroke is insufferable to watch. Your kids barely move, barely breathe, and barely give you any indication that they're not, in fact, drowning. It's like they're crawling all over again, only without the living room carpet for purchase. On the bright side, it seems to come naturally and technically propels them, which is certainly better than nothing. Even Phelps didn't start with the butterfly right off the bat.

The next milestone is actually controlling the dog paddle and steering back around toward the steps rather than continuing on to the wild blue yonder. Reward this boomerang-like homing instinct with a fudgesicle at the snack bar; it shows a propensity to think rather than sink.

All these milestones often come with the inevitable piercing glare from whichever spouse is on shore. Since he or she is not on the front line with you, everything looks like a life-threatening situation when it's actually under control. Teaching your kids to swim brings up a Catch-22. They're not going to learn if they don't push their boundaries, but you don't want that boundary to be the pool bottom.

Props can help. Foremost are water wings, those inflatable armbands that leave your kids dangling in the water like they're hanging in the stocks. While they help keep kids' heads above water, they're cumbersome, restrict stroking motion, and are awkward when your kids are back on land. In a way, on shore it's a way to shackle them so they can't get into trouble. They won't be able to punch their sister, take their goggles off their head and lose them, or walk anywhere without their arms out high to their sides.

They become muscle-bound, mini-Michelin Men.

A close cousin is the inflatable tube, which goes around your kid's belly instead of his bicep. Some come with duck heads while others are just plain circles. No matter the design, they help you, the parent, relax. Your kid plops inside and dangles, arms draped over the sides. And that's about it. You can spin them, push them, tow them and even swim up underneath them. The high-tech ones have a diaper-like seat that holds their legs so they're suspended in a floating chair. If they made them for grown-ups, you'd be asking for the remote and a cocktail.

Kickboards also top the prop list, offering another form of flotation. They can also be used to learn the basics of proper kicking. Simply have your kids hold on and kick like they're throwing a tantrum. Your kids will also figure out that they can submerge them and then launch them like a missile.

Of all these props and gadgets, swim goggles are the most eye-opening. Once your kids can swim on their own, this simple device will keep them occupied for hours, becoming junior Jacques Cousteaus, exploring stairways, railings and other swimmers' hairy and shaved legs. And this helps you come up for air after watching them constantly.

For Casey, swim goggles were the magic ingredient that helped her hold her breath and discover the limits of her lungs and dad's white legs. Hint: put your child's name on them. Your budding swimmer will likely lose them every other time he uses them. They'll get taken off by the ladder, the steps, the sides, the snack bars, the locker rooms, the bathrooms and more, requiring a treasure hunt to find them. And get accustomed to seeing Dracula-like indentations around your daughters' eyes when they finally re-emerge from the depths.

Going hand in hand with goggles are throwable diving toys. Like the dogs they emulate with their dog paddle stroke, your kids will spend hours fetching any and every thing you throw. They become miniature homing submarines, locating the object, calculating the needed vector and breath-holding needed to get there, zeroing in on the target, making contact, retrieving and returning. If they had tails, they'd be wagging.

The world, or at least the pool, truly becomes your oyster when your kids can swim on their own. I realized this as soon as Casey, at age three, donned a pair of goggles and swam down to the bottom of the hot springs' deep end at eight feet. With goggles of my own on, I saw her swim puffy-cheeked to the bottom, retrieve a ring, gauge the distance back to the surface and kick away. She looked like a tiny space ship.

This led to games of submarine, her hanging onto my back while I descended and then tapping my shoulder whenever she wanted to resurface; hour-long wrestling matches, throwing both kids head over heels as they climbed all over me as if I were King Kong; games of tag and Marco Polo – where one person is "it," and shuts her eyes while trying to touch those around her; flipping them off my shoulders after rising up from a crouch below; having both kids "surf" on my submerged back across the pool; and snorkeling around the pool's perimeter as if we were in the Bahamas.

This is also the point when they started experimenting with water slides. Our pool has two, both twisty, narrow and dark. You have to be a certain height to use them, but the guard at top doesn't ask anything about your swimming ability before you plunge

THE CHILD'S PERSPECTIVE

into the pool at the bottom. Before they were big enough to go on their own, I went with them, screaming through turn after turn and then lifting them up when we were spit out at the bottom. I'd go under, while they, for the most part, would stay high, if not dry. When the time came for them to tackle it on their own (they measured up to the pelican measuring stick at the bottom of the stairs) they nervously said their good-byes and slid away, the pool at the bottom forcing them to remember everything they knew about swimming. While the surprise dunking caused a few coughs, they wasted no time in racing up the stairs to do it again and again, pausing only to measure themselves at the pelican again for good measure.

When they reach this point, they'll also start venturing to other areas of the pool,

THE PARENT'S PERSPECTIVE

most noticeably the snack bar and diving board. Like hot chocolate skiing, they'll quickly associate the snack bar with swimming (perhaps because they burn so many calories doing so). It's usually popsicles and other frozen goodies, as well as pizza and Pretzels.

When they're not diving into snacks, they're diving off the board. This is a rite of passage every bit as much as holding your breath. For years the diving board will loom at the far end larger than life, the domain of older kids who dive, flip, jump and spin off with nary a nod to parents on shore. The fear for younger kids is twofold: the first is from the board itself, perched Grand Canyon high off the surface. The second is the water's depth. The boards are always at the deep end, which kids instinctively know. There's no touching.

Depending on your pool's rules, the lifeguards might let you tread water below the board while waiting for young Evel Knievel to jump. If they do, great. Your child has someone he trusts waiting below to catch him. If not, your child has to muster the courage to jump and swim to the pool's edge himself. All you can do is offer encouragement from the side as he walks the plank toward the end, trepidation palpable with every step. His fingers will go to his mouth. He'll turn around, other kids waiting impatiently behind him. For him, it's not much different than Peter Pan be-

> ### TIPS FOR WATCHING CHILDREN AROUND WATER
>
> - Maintain constant supervision. Watch children around any water (pools, rivers, lakes, bathtubs, toilets, and even buckets of water)
> - Stay within arm's reach of an inexperienced swimmer
> - Do not rely on substitutes. The use of flotation devices and inflatable toys cannot replace parental supervision.
> - Prevent access to water features, such as small ponds and waterfalls
> - Empty kiddie pools immediately after use
> - When visiting another home, check the site for potential water hazards and always supervise your children
> - Teach children to swim by enrolling them in a Red Cross Learn-to-Swim course
> - Participate in a Red Cross water safety course
> - Learn cardiopulmonary resuscitation (CPR)

ing forced off the pirates' plank by Captain Hook.

Finally he'll do it, his fingers pinching his nose at the last second to prevent the inevitable douching, followed by a rousing kerplunk! into the pool below. With luck, he'll pop back up after a couple of kicks, rub his eyes to get his bearings, and then swim to a parent as proud as Debbie Phelps by the ladder.

LESSONS

With full props to swimming props, you can only get so far without lessons. Like piano (arrgh! don't remind me), learning to swim takes repetition and practice, which means pool time with mom and dad, but also qualified instruction. And thankfully, there are no rulers across the knuckles for missed notes.

Fortunately, there are systematic techniques for learning that are far better than daddy's depth charge drops. Look for pools that offer the Learn-to-Swim program endorsed by American Red Cross, whose programs start at Level 1 and progress on up to Level 6. You could almost relate it to depths of the pool. Level 1 and you're ready for a one-foot-deep pool. Level 6, six feet.

Except for Level 1, the prerequisite for each is the successful demonstration of skills learned in the previous level. As a special bonus, kids completing Levels 1-2 receive a free Raffy Learns to Swim cartoon booklet reinforcing what they learned; those completing Levels 3-4 receive a free Waddles in the Deep cartoon book. Androgynous as most ducks appear, Waddles and Raffy are actually brother and sister learning to swim under the guidance of a lanky-legged Miss LaPink the flamingo and a baseball hat-capped Casey Condor. The Level 1-2 book starts with a scared-out-of-her-suit Raffy hiding under a blanket the morning swim lessons start. The Level 3-4 book shows Waddles happily riding up to swim lessons on a bike.

Here's a quick breakdown as to what to expect:

Level 1 (Introduction to Water Skills): Helps students feel comfortable in the water by learning how to enter and exit, float on their front and back, open their eyes and exhale underwater, move hands and arms, and more.

Level 2 (Fundamental Aquatic Skills): Teaches the basics, including exiting via a ladder or the side, treading water, floating and gliding on the front and back, jumping in from the side, retrieving objects, breathing rhythmically, and rolling over from front to back to front.

Level 3 (Stroke Development): Builds on Level 2's skills, including jumping in the deep end; the butterfly motion; changing from a vertical to horizontal position; diving from a kneeling or sitting position; survival float; the crawl stroke; and performing reaching assists.

Level 4 (Stroke Improvement): Designed to develop more confidence, this level introduces the breaststroke, enhanced diving techniques, swimming underwater, the elementary backstroke, the scissors kick, open turns, and more.

Level 5 (Stroke Refinement): Further coordination and refinement of all six strokes; shallow, tuck and pike surface dives, front and back flip turns, survival swimming, rescue breathing, and more.

Level 6 (Swimming and Skill Proficiency): This level refines all the strokes, works on power and smoothness, and prepares students for more advanced courses, including water safety instructor and lifeguard training.

Get your children through even a few of these levels and eventually they'll graduate to the Holy Grail: swim team.

SWIM TEAM

I'm not sure if Hollywood has ever made any *Bad News Bears*-type movies centered around swim team, but it most likely could. There could be budding romances, bad- and good-guy teams, coach/athlete conflicts and a nail-biting showdown at the end.

Get your kids excited enough about swimming and there's a good chance they'll wind up on a team. That's where we are with Brooke, and I'm now officially a...Swim Team Dad.

Despite the crack-of-dawn practices that make you play Rock-Paper-Scissors with your spouse for early-morning shuttling duties, swim team is the natural progression from lessons and the best way to make your kids stronger, more confident swimmers. What kid would ever swim lap after lap by himself, without a coach egging him on? But with practices, a coach blowing a whistle and holding a stopwatch, and friends in the locker room and next lane over, there's no way your kids' technique won't improve.

Practices, of course, are just preparation for the (drum roll, please)...swim meet — that loud, screamy, cheery, splashy, frothy affair pitting your child's team against those from neighboring towns and pools. It's the swim clubs vs. *Breaking Away's Cutters*, with everyone in bathing suits instead of on bikes.

We escaped the watery havoc for eight years, but eventually time, and Brooke's ability and desire, caught up with us and we found ourselves traveling to our first swim meet in Glenwood Springs, Colorado.

My wife had long championed the fun other families always seemed to have at such meets, piling into cars on weekends and staying in hotels or camping with like-minded, pool-bound parents and kids. To me, driving four hours to swelter in the heat and burn the entire weekend to watch ninety seconds of your kid's competition didn't hold much appeal. But realizing it wasn't about my own recreation anymore, but our kids', I relented and we found ourselves driving to Glenwood the morning of the big event.

Color me reluctantly open to the ordeal. I had just read a story in *Men's Journal* on the world record run by Phelps, and had gained a new appreciation of the sport. I'd never swum on swim team myself. I was a decent swimmer, but too much of a hooligan to commit to the early morning practices. Plus, my parents would never have driven me, meaning I would've had to convince one of my older siblings to do so, ending up forever in their debt. Brooke, however, was hooked.

Pulling up late (our *modus operandi* whenever traveling with kids) to the indoor rec center, I settled into Casey mode while Denise ushered Brooke into the locker room. Her first race was at 1 p.m., with warm-ups slated for noon. Sheer mayhem permeated the pool. The entire perimeter was lined by parents screaming at their kids in the water. How the kids could tell which shrieks were directed at them, especially with ears buried by water and swim caps, was beyond me. But it didn't matter. They knew the support was there.

Fists pumping, arms circling and hands clapping, the parents, it seemed, were getting as much of a work out as their offspring. Their yells echoed off the walls, water and giant vents overhead until the entire room was a cacophony of overlapping sound waves. Swim lanes filled with splashes added to the commotion, as did high-pitched shrieks from kids. It was like being in a multi-species bird house, with various twirps, cheeps, chatters, screams and cheers all bouncing off chlorine-condensed windows and walls. It would have been a horrible place to have a hangover.

I barely recognized Brooke when she emerged from the locker room. My little girl had grown, with long sinewy, muscled legs disappearing into a tight, one-piece, black swim suit with a gold slash across the front marking her as a member of the Steamboat Lightning. Her long blonde hair was tucked neatly into a yellow swim cap, complete with ribs to help break the surface tension of the water.

It also afforded me my first look at a dad's worst fear: how'd she look with tattoos. It's customary, I found, for swimmers to write over themselves before matches. Some of it has a purpose. On her forearm was a block of letters and numbers indicating what races, heats and lanes she was in: 29, 5, 1 means Event 29, Lane 5, Heat 1. "My god," I thought shortly after digesting this tattoo nomenclature. "I have to sit through 29 races, all with multiple heats?"

I could see the rationale behind the markings. With some kids competing in up to eight events, it's hard to keep them all straight. But somewhere along the line, kids or coaches got carried away with the markers and it morphed into body art. On Brooke's shoulders were the words "Eat My Bubbles," accompanied by various cartoonish-looking fish. Another girl had the slogan "What happens on swim team stays on swim team." Great, I thought, as I continued to examine her tattoos. Is swim team going to be like Band Camp in *American Pie*? At least I might be better prepared another eight years from now, when Brooke comes home with a rose and piercings where they don't belong.

Then Brooke disappeared with her teammates into a throng of kids at the start. That's when another inherent problem of swim racing hit me: you can't tell who's who. Everyone's the same size, and is wearing matching yellow swim caps and black one-piece suits. You can't even use hair color or hair length to tell kids apart. It's like a team of kid clones.

You end up having to look down at the tattoos scrawled across their backs, which hopefully isn't construed as being lecherous.

Nope.

Nope.

Ahhh...there it is.

"Eat" in capital letters on back of the left shoulder. "My" scrawled out across the right shoulder blade. "Bubbles" spread out across the lower back. Of course, a lot of the kids had that slogan, so it alone wasn't much help. But Brooke's had the word "Please" written out in parenthesis below, adorned by my too-polite wife.

"Please?" I asked my wife later, chagrined. "No one says 'please.' Do you think Phelps had 'please' written across his back?"

Putting the "Eat My Bubbles, Please" slogan in the back of my mind, I could only hope that the swimmers in the lanes next to her would never see it. That might be all the encouragement they needed to kick her polite little butt.

Before I could give her a hug, a horn blared, signaling the start of another race. Splashes and yells quickly followed as the water whipped into a maelstrom and the pool morphed into a flurry of limbs.

Next to us in lane three, a couple screamed at their daughter as she neared the edge of the pool. The man, who I would later learn was a local father named Nate, was yelling at the top of his lungs and pumping both muscular arms up and down simultaneously as if he were pulling two train whistles at once, encouraging his eight-year-old daughter to swim even faster. The man's wife was equally loud and boisterous. Is that how I was supposed to act when it was Brooke's turn to race? I sincerely hoped not.

"Look at that couple," I told my wife. "A little aggro, don't you think?"

Shortly it was Brooke's turn and they could have said the same thing about me. The response is almost Pavlovian. Once your brood hits the water, against ten other swimmers just like her in nearby lanes, your vocal chords compete right along with them.

"Go, Brooke, go!" I yelled instinctively, the first time a little reserved but later with the passion of the other pool-cheering parents. "Hup, hup, hup!" It didn't even cross my mind that I might look as obsessed as every other neurotic parent out there. The cheering felt as natural as lifting your head above water to take a breath swimming.

Brooke's technique didn't seem to be the most efficient, arms and legs stroking wildly as she charged to the end of the lane. But it was certainly tenacious.

She did great in freestyle, her strongest event, and held her own in the relay. Unfortunately, none of the encouraging and line-sorting tattoos, aerodynamic swimsuits and caps, or cheering from the sides helped her in the breaststroke race. She DQ'd by accidentally doing a crawl stroke instead at the beginning. In her defense, it's a lot to memorize. Let's see...is it the breaststroke in Lane 5, Heat 4, Race 18, at 11:14 a.m., or the medley? She then DQ'd in another race for accidentally not touching the wall during a flip turn. No matter that the move slowed her down by eight seconds anyway, letting every other kid pass her. They DQ'd her to boot.

Some parents, obviously more into it than I, even took to videoing each and every heat for some ungodly reason. I, for one, can certainly think of better things to do back home than watching a swim race video. It's one thing if it's a piano recital, talent show or play, and even that's pushing it at times. But a swim race? You can't even see your kid's face or body—just a flurry of arms and splashes.

Between heats I shot baskets in the nearby gym, poached magazines from the aerobics room and chased Casey around the ping-pong table. When their own kids weren't racing, other parents did the same, taking over the neighboring gym and sprawling out as if they were at an airport waiting out a canceled flight. The only difference is that they came prepared with folding chairs, blankets and pillows. Some even brought tents and barbecue pits that they set up outside.

During a longer break, I left the premises and took Casey to the bike path along the Colorado River. It was a gorgeous day, and being cooped up inside a loud, chlorine-smelling room when I didn't have to be seemed sacrilegious.

We arrived back at the pool to loud-cheering Nate barbecuing on a cement deck outside. Casey and his youngest hit it off instantly. He was a regular at these meets and had the system down. He had backed his truck up to the back door, and brought his own grill, chairs and umbrella – a true swim team veteran. I earned a new respect for his fist-pumping, fatherly support when he offered me a beer and bratwurst, Swim Dad to Swim Dad.

His daughter was a great swimmer who regularly cleaned up at meets. But this was her last meet competing against seven- and eight-year olds. The next week in Grand Junction she was getting bumped up to the 9-10 age group. "We'll see how she does then," Nate said, flipping a burger. "My main role is just to yell."

RIVERS, LAKES AND OCEAN

Many aspiring and accomplished swimmers get to forsake the conformity and confines of pools for something a little more *au naturele*. When it comes to swimming with kids, lakes, rivers, oceans and other bodies of water offer every bit as good—or even better—an environment as pools, without the chlorine and Band-Aids.

Granted, visibility is usually an issue. You're not going to send your kids diving for weighted rings or have them snorkel around and look at people's belly buttons in most lakes, rivers and oceans. Visibility aside, it's also hard to beat the steps and controlled temperatures of pools. As a place to learn, pools are hard to top—especially with their proximity to lifeguards, snack bars and bathrooms.

But once your kids master swimming's basics, these other locales offer water in its natural state—not filtered, chlorinated and impounded—as well as beaches, trees and even rocks and cliffs to play on. Plus, you don't even care if they're close to a bathroom. Going number one in the Big Blue or a river isn't going to wreck anyone's day.

Most kids swimming in these mediums are beyond those days anyway, and have other things to worry about besides their bathroom needs—like remembering to let go on time off the rope swing, calculating just how far it is to that floating dock, or how powerful that ocean wave is that's about to come crashing down.

Lakes are God's gift to swimmers. You can find them car-camping, backpacking and hiking, at cabins, parks and off trails. They're what pools aspire to be, free of drains, chemicals and (except for reservoirs) artificial confines. Kids can wade out as deep as they want, plunge under, and even set goals to swim to: across a short bay, to an island, or even to floating docks. Plus, they let you catch crawdads and fish and skip rocks, as well as open the door to paddling, sailing and even motorboat-based sports.

Lakes have created a veritable Loch Ness Monster out of Brooke. She loves the things, and, unfortunately for Dad and his shrinkage problem, the colder the better. If we're hiking in the Rockies and get to a high-alpine lake, she's the first one in, and I always have to follow. When grandma offered to take her on an Elderhostel trip this past summer, Brooke chose a trip to the Sierras where she could swim in high-altitude lakes every day.

While it's not quite as good a learning environment, the ocean also has a leg up on pools, offering waves, sand, beach-combing and still the benefit of lifeguards at popular beaches. Granted, it also has things like sharks, red tide, rogue waves and jellyfish to sometimes worry about—I still remember my sister, Helen, jumping in off a dock in Australia and getting zapped (who would have thought her brother's urine would be the cure); and Brooke having one brush her leg in Mexico—but all that just makes you tougher.

Nothing beats the sight of your brood up to the waist in the ocean, playing in gentle waves. They'll duck under them, jump over them and body surf them into shore, shrieking with glee each time. You'll pick sand out of their scalps and ears for days afterward, but consider it the price of admission. Throw skim boards and boogie boards into the mix and that Play Station will become a distant memory.

As much fun as my kids have swimming at a beach, they have just as good a time running up to the waves and then running away from them, burying poor Dad up to his neck, building sand castles, and combing the beach for shells. The only two things you really have to worry about are rip tides and the sun.

Though the state used to be covered by shallow seas, in Colorado we're somewhat restricted in our natural swimming environs. As kids, we'd go to the beach at Boulder Reservoir; sketchy, clear-the-rock-while-you-jump swimming holes in Upper Boulder and South Boulder creeks; and cliff jump up at Gross Reservoir, which was technically illegal since it's a municipal water source.

Like many lifeguard-monitored lakes, Boulder Reservoir had buoys marking a swim zone, and a series of distant docks you could swim to, jump off, and use for sunbathing or to escape your younger siblings who couldn't swim that far. Like a poor man's Malibu, it even had gravelly sand where you could build moats and castle towers with Dixie cups.

The swimming holes in the creeks we went to were downright spooky. The pools were deep, but only if you landed in just the right spot, and first you had to clear an

outcropping just to get to the water. The same held true at Gross Reservoir, only while the lake was deep everywhere, you had to jump in from forty to sixty feet high. I still remember my sister freaking out midway through a gainer, legs flutter-kicking her straight to a belly flop. I don't condone this type of recreating with your kids.

We have a safer alternative in Steamboat. Now that Casey and Brooke have developed a modicum of skill, I take them down to the local swimming hole in the Yampa River, a block away from our house. We wait for runoff to drop so the current won't drag them like nymphs down to the bottom, and when it does, usually by early July, it teaches lessons in current, eddies and even flotsam. "Look at this," said Brooke one day, holding up an inner tuber's flip-flop.

In the early days, I'd load Brooke on the trail-a-bike, put Casey, the dog and a pack-n-play in the Burley behind it, and head down to the D-hole, named for the Dream

Island trailer park just downstream. Then I'd shackle Casey inside the pack-n'-play on the beach while practicing with Brooke.

Before venturing into the deeper pool, where there was still a bit of current moving downstream, she'd start in an eddy. With me positioned upstream, she'd hike downstream to its bottom and then jump in on her stomach and float to me like Superman. When she reached me, I'd grab her between my legs and swoop her up, only to start the cycle all over again.

The first few attempts involved lifejackets. Only when they got better would I let them go without. But I still remember the day Brooke swam across the river on her own, emerging beaming and dripping on the far bank. It was the first time she had applied the skills she had learned in lessons to an obstacle outside of the controlled nature of a pool, and she's been happily cannon-balling in ever since.

In the dog days of summer the kids now look forward to this more than even our dog does. From my perspective, it's a way to cool off, have fun and instill a life skill, all while earning babysitting points with my spouse.

AMERICAN RED CROSS WATER SAFETY TIPS

- Always swim with a buddy; never swim alone
- Read and obey all rules and posted signs
- Swim in lifeguard-supervised areas
- Take extra precautions, such as wearing a U.S. Coast guard-approved lifejacket when around the water
- Watch out for the dangerous "too's" – too tired, too cold, too far from safety, too much sun, too much strenuous activity
- Set water safety rules for your family based on swimming abilities (i.e. staying in water less than chest deep)
- Be knowledgeable of the water environment you're in and its potential hazards (i.e. deep and shallow areas, currents, depth changes, obstructions, etc.)
- Know how to prevent, recognize and respond to emergencies
- Use a feet-first entry when entering the water (enter headfirst only when the area is clearly marked for diving and has no obstructions)
- Don't mix alcohol with swimming, diving or boating.

SNORKELING WITH KIDS

While swimming can open your kids' eyes to the watery world around them, with a little help from technology it can also open their eyes to the world beneath the surface. As a scuba diver, and knowing their infatuation with Nemo, Sponge Bob and Arial, I couldn't wait for Casey and Brooke to become proficient enough swimmers to go on a real snorkeling trip.

The chance came when Brooke was seven and Casey three and we took them for spring break to Akumal, Mexico. The Mexican Riviera, they call it, and while we had long ago shelved any notions of romance on the trip, we had replaced them with the satisfaction our kids would get snorkeling. We'd taken the kids on beach vacations before, but this was our first attempt at a destination specifically to introduce them to the underworld.

They took to it right away, especially after they figured out that "snorkel" rhymes with "dorkel." Casey also enjoyed the fart noises she could make when blowing out through her nose while it was still in the mask.

While Cancun is Ft. Lauderdale on steroids, Akumal, seventy miles south, is tranquilo and out of the college-crazed meat market. Most importantly, it offers world-class snorkeling right out your door. Pop off the PJs, pull on the mask, and you're soaring above sea grass, turtles and rays before your morning coffee. With a kid-friendly national marine park at the end of the bay, schools of fish easily took their minds off school back home.

While swimming in the ocean can be intimidating, the right gear makes things far easier. This comes in the form of fins for propulsion, a diving mask for visibility, and a snorkel for breathing. But there are still pitfalls. Your kids' hair will get pinched in the mask strap while other strands will ruin the seal, they'll swallow water through the snorkel and come up coughing, and they'll complain about the fins rubbing the tops of their feet. Don't fret. These annoyances come with the territory. Soon they'll be playing Junior Jules Verne.

Unfortunately, none of this high-tech equipment helped Casey during her first foray into moray country. She was quite at ease donning swim goggles and diving to the bottom of the pool back home. We had also practiced with snorkel gear beforehand, which saw her diving between unsuspecting swimmer's legs (and Brooke clear snorkel water onto strangers' heads). It was another story, however, in the quiet, world-class lagoon at the end of the bay, which was the perfect depth and clarity and teeming with brightly colored fish. Feeling confident, we geared her up with the mask and then had her sit on the end of the dock and hop in. But there was an unseen enemy lurking below that we hadn't counted on: salt.

"Yecchhh!" she spat, coming up instantly and rubbing her lips.

It's the last thing I would have suspected, her being scared of salt. She puts it on her eggs, sees us pour it into our soccer-ball-shaped ice-cream maker, and once even threw it over her shoulder for good luck. But we weren't having any luck getting her to swim in water contaminated by it. No amount of coercing could convince her to go back under the rest of the week. With some of the best snorkeling in the world just inches away below the surface, she was having nothing to do with it. We tried ice cream, late bedtime, videos, braided dreadlocks, every bribe we could think of, to no avail.

At least we weren't alone in our predicament. Another parent was trying to teach her son how to snorkel in the hotel pool, with similar results. Only stubbornness was to blame instead of salt. The child just wasn't able to grasp the concept. He kept plugging his mouth with his fingers when he went under water, instead of his nose. He'd go under, pinch his lips with thumb and forefinger, and for some inexplicable reason still get water up his schnoz.

Perhaps he might have been a candidate for another training wheel device: the old see-through kick board. Some friends of ours—you might recognize him from earlier in the book, Edge—tried this with their daughter, Abbi, on a trip to Hawaii when she was six. They went into K-mart and bought her a kickboard with a see-through window. No itchy goggle straps around the head or getting caught in your hair, no fog-ups and no water seepage stinging the eyes. Simply grab on, flutter kick behind it, and watch Nemo pass by below. Of course, if you drop the thing you're toast, both in terms of flotation and visibility. But they reported she did fine, and that she even didn't want to give it up to big brother Stuey.

Fortunately, we fared better with Brooke, who took to snorkeling instantly.

In the marine park, she'd venture out for hours, mesmerized by her first real-life, up-close-and-personal encounter with ocean life. She'd point out fish to me and then give chase, following them into nooks. She also began following me through "secret passages," just like skiing through trees at a resort or discovering side-trails on the bike path. I'd swim through a tunnel that looked doable, she'd query me with the underwater "OK" sign, and I'd signal back if it was good to go. Such passages sometimes hurt her ears a little, but no more than mine from her belting out "I'm a Barbie Girl" in the backseat of our car. The only thing we had to watch out for was her back getting sunburned (which we cured with a rash guard), and the goggle indentations on her forehead.

A few days later we took her in the less protected bay in front of our hotel. First thing in the morning we'd swim straight from the beach, flying over sea turtles and rays. It was a longer swim to reach the reef, but it didn't matter. She hardly even knew she was swimming. "Did you see that turtle?" she asked when we returned. "It was just like Dude."

Casey's breakthrough came when we visited a fresh water cenote. While there weren't as many fish, there also wasn't any salt. So she opened her eyes and became a convert. Nemo's dad himself couldn't have been any prouder.

On a later visit, she put her fear of salt behind her for good. She snorkeled the lagoons and rivers of Xelha and Xcaret (natural water parks that should be on every family's travel hit list), attacking the activity with the same gusto as her favorite granola back home. If she wasn't comfortable with how deep it was, she'd charge ahead in her lifejacket, mumbling "Dad, follow me!" through her snorkel. When we finished one such session, she pulled her snorkel out and blurted, "That fish looked just like a disco ball!" While I'm not sure what that says about her above-water influences, she then placed her snorkel back in and kicked away.

You don't even have to fly anywhere exotic to pursue the pastime. A closer-to-home chance for our kids came through a program offered by the Denver Aquarium, with others like it scattered throughout the country. They let you and your kids don mask, fins and snorkel and hop in the tank, right alongside sea turtles, grouper, eels and even a couple of nurse sharks.

If our kids were wiggly with excitement during the behind-the-scenes tour beforehand, they were also too wiggly to get their wetsuits on. But as soon as they settled down, the guides fitted them with gear, walked them to a perch on a "rock," and then turned them loose.

The buoyancy of the wetsuit and salt water turned even Casey into a star, and she grabbed me constantly, pointing and then swimming away. The guides even let her have an etch-a-sketch board, on which she wrote "I love you" to grandma watching on the other side of the glass. The only thing she didn't get the hang of was talking, which she repeatedly tried through her snorkel in vain.

"Mrmmmphhh!" she'd cry, her eyes as bugged as the fish. "Mrmph! Mrmphhh!"

While water magnifies the size of fish, it also does so for kids. More than once I grabbed Casey, thinking she was Brooke, to get her to follow me through a passage. But she was often busy, just as interested in performing for the people watching from the glass tunnel below as she was seeing any of the fish. The visitors had never seen anyone wave so much from a fish tank before.

Technically, we weren't allowed to go under the surface as it disturbs the fish. But that didn't stop Brooke from hamming it up and performing a back flip for the crowd when the guide wasn't looking. Another demerit came when she accidentally sat on a turtle, thinking it was a rock.

During the car ride home, Brooke admitted to another transgression. "I hope the alarm didn't go off when I peed in my suit in the tank," she said, sheepishly.

But they both had a great time and are eager to do it again. "The only thing I don't get," continued Brooke, "is that the sharks were sleeping the whole time we were in there."

"They must have stayed up late at a sleep-over," chimed in Casey.

SCUBA DO!

Brooke fell for scuba diving as readily as she did the *Twilight* book series, only rather than reading about Edward sucking blood, she was now enticed with sucking air.

While you have to be ten years old to get certified by PADI, she first tried it as a nine-year-old at a friend's birthday party in the deep end of our town pool. Like Bella to Edward, she loved it at first breath, from drain to the diving board.

Her first oceanic venture into the breathing-underwater club wasn't scuba (Self-contained Underwater Breathing Apparatus) at all. It came in the Sea Trek program offered by Delphinus, a dolphin training facility at Mexico's Xelha Park near Playa del Carmen. You put a helmet over your head and descend into the depths like Diver Dan. Sampling it at the dolphin training facility, it let her interact with Flipper four fathoms down.

The next step up from snorkeling is a new program called Snuba. While still not self-contained, it offers more freedom than Sea Trek technology, with participants swimming with mask, fins and regulator attached to a communal air tank housed in a small raft above. The tube length and pressure ramifications keep you to about 25 feet deep, but in reef country that's plenty to whet one's appetite for Atlantis. You have to be eight years old to participate in this program, which left Casey, age six at the time, fending for herself on the beach while Brooke, her mom and I Snuba'd alongside each other, marveling at eels and plant-stalk-eyed flounder.

But both of these were small fry compared to the Real McCoy. Even if not certified, at age ten you can take part in a Resort Dive or Discover Scuba program at an accredited facility. We found ours at the Scuba-Du dive shop outside the Presidente-Intercontinental hotel in Cozumel.

When she found out that she could go, Brooke was giddy with excitement all night—even more than for a sleep-over or the next *Twilight* book from the library. The next day at 2 p.m., we met our instructor, Carlos, who first gave us a chalk talk on the beach. Encouragingly, Brooke was an astute, polite student, much different than the "Where-do-you-plug-her-in-at-night?" pupil Mr. Miller told us about at her parent-teacher conference. Whether it was about ascending slowly, using the octopus valve, gaining neutral buoyancy, or clearing her ears, she listened, asked questions and nodded when she understood.

Next, Carlos took us from the beach into the water to practice five basic tasks: breathing, finding our regulators, clearing our masks, adjusting our buoyancy-control devices (BCs), and checking our depth and pressure gauges.

When Brooke finished her first underwater task successfully, Carlos held up his hand for a beneath-the-surface high-five. Instead of accommodating him, she recognized the flat palm as a signal we had gone over and fumbled for her pressure gauge (this from a girl who usually high-fives everything). Only when Carlos grabbed her hand, high-fived it, and followed with knuckles, did she understand the ceremony. To her credit, while I was as rusty as the sunken ship we would soon explore (it had been a few years since I had dived), Brooke passed with the flying colors of the fish around us.

From there, we kicked off, Brooke's eyes as wide open as the double "OK" signs she flashed. She'd tap me to show me something, fiddle with her BC when needed, and even folded her arms across her chest like Carlos to conserve heat.

Surprisingly, she didn't experience any ear problems at all—a far cry from her not hearing me yell when it's time for dinner or to pick her towels up off the bathroom floor. She pinched her nose like she does when suffering her sister's flatulence and equalized them with equal aplomb.

Since you can't talk underwater, the scuba experience also exposed another benefit. When diving, kids are forced to contain their excitement and save their exclamations for afterward. They can't blurt something out immediately, as Mr. Miller said she often does in class. It teaches listening—or in this case, watching—and not interrupting, which is as good a practice for school as it is the dinner table at home.

It was also comforting to see our communication reduced to sign language—pointing, the "OK" sign, thumbs-up, and the something's-fishy hand wiggle. If only communicating with kids was always so easy and straight-forward. No reading into things, no sulking, no hidden meanings. Are you okay? Yes. Want to go up? No.

Mom was waiting with the camera as we emerged onto the beach like the creature from the black lagoon about 45 minutes later. Having never been quiet that long in her life, Brooke's pent-up blabbering started immediately: "Did you see that?" "Mom, we saw..." Five minutes later I had to tell her that she could take her mask off.

The barrage continued on the taxi ride to dinner. "Did you see that one thing?" "What was your favorite?" "What was that wiggly thing?" "That one fish was so cool." Beneath the surface of these comments was an activity that opened her eyes to a new world, one that Nemo or Arial could never upstage.

SURFING

I'll admit it. Who along any coast, or with any surfing background whatsoever, is going to take pointers on getting your kids surfing from a nose-pearling, over-the-falls-dropping, long boarding landlubber from Colorado? (Why do you think I put this section at the *end* of the chapter?)

Frankly, I don't blame you. I'm a hack, my wife's a hack, and our kids are hacks. Always have been, always will be. You could say it runs in the family, not because we're necessarily uncoordinated, which we most certainly are, but more because we simply haven't had the opportunity to Kelly Slater it as we'd like to.

If you're a surfer, skip right through this section as you won't learn a thing. If you're not, stick around if you want to, but you likely won't learn anything either—except, maybe, that it's next to impossible to expose your kids to every sport under the sun.

Still, our kids love it. Crouching down low and extending their arms, they both surf the train aisles and moving walkways at Denver International Airport, surf the kids' slides at school, and even occasionally surf the coffee table at home. They even surf my back when I go underwater at the local pool. Humor me, then, by putting up with a few accounts of our first forays surfing with the offspring.

While I'm a decent enough long boarder to escape to a Corona-filled surf shack off the tip of Baja every few years with buddies, I've yet to bring the kids along on one of these surf-only outings (why bring your own urchins when you're avoiding the spiny kind?). Foremost, I use these trips as a way to *escape* the duties of parenthood. Secondly, while my children enjoy beach vacations as much as the next kid, there's not a whole lot to do on a crashing beach without any shade if you don't surf.

That said, on an earlier camping outing to Baja my friend Edge and his wife decided to tote young Stuey along. But they only did it once, if that tells you anything about the success of the mission. From then on, we learned to only bring toddlers along on a surf trip when there's a roof overhead. Sand in pacifiers, scorpions in salad bowls, flip-flops pierced by cactus, and shade only in sauna-like tents doth not a happy child make.

In a way, however, surfing is the perfect sport for parents of newborns. You're up at 6 a.m. anyway, so one of you might as well hoof it out to the glassy, pre-dawn surf break. If you're staying beachside, handoffs are easy, and kids can build sand castles while you're riding the line.

Once they're decent swimmers, it's time to take them out in the water with you. After our Baja era, we began hitting a slightly more developed break in Sayulita, Mexico (yes, staying in rooms with bathrooms). While Brooke, age six at the time, could swim in a pool well enough, as with Casey snorkeling, the ocean's turbulence and saltiness didn't particularly suit her when it came to surfing.

Your best bet: find the longest, foamiest, floatiest board you can for their first few times out. More importantly, find the right break. I doubt even Laird Hamilton's daughters— Reece Viola, Izabella and Brody Jo—got their start on the Banzai Pipeline. Don't worry so much about getting your surfing protégé a barrel or even on the green the first time out. Pick an easy, slow-breaking shore break where everything's under control. Wade out with her until you're waist to shoulder deep, put her atop the board, and then wait for the wave to come. Then give the board a shove toward the beach and have her either ride it out on her stomach or, if she's feeling confident, pop up to standing (have her go through the motion on shore beforehand). Then swim/run after her both to see the smile on her face from her first stand-up ride, and to pick up the pieces from the biff afterward.

That's about as far as we've made it with our kids surfing, which is a shame because both are as blond-haired and blue-eyed as Gidget, love water, and are adventurous, all of which are traits made for enjoying the surf. I have buddies, Mark and Missy, who take their daughters Keala and Mahlia (Hawaiian surf names, of course) to Australia for four months every year, and they and their kids have it dialed. But they also happen to have a dad who grew up with the sport.

All I know is that it's a sport I want my kids to get better at than I am—just as long as they don't drop in on my wave.

Chapter 11

JUST THE STATS MA'AM

"Look deep into nature, and then you will understand everything better."
—Albert Einstein

I'**M NOT THE ONLY ONE PREACHING** the benefits of recreating outdoors as a family. Everyone from Oprah to Obama has espoused upon the importance of keeping youth active—and that doesn't mean chasing your kids around at bedtime with their toothbrushes. Though my message might not reach quite the same number of people as theirs (unless, ahem, Oprah invites me onto her show), its point is the same: getting your kids outdoors with you will keep you, and them, healthy, wealthy and wise.

Okay, maybe not the wealthy part. Your kids will probably have so much fun that you'll have to buy more equipment for them. But it will keep them, and you, healthier, which will likely pay dividends in the long run.

And maybe not the wise part, either. Oftentimes, when you look at parents recreating with their kids—dealing with tantrums, mounds of awkward gear and a pace on par with snails—they seem like the most frustrated, dimwitted people on the planet. Why didn't they just get a sitter and leave their whiney kids at home? But it's a wise man who knows his own kids, and wiser still who encourages them to frolic outdoors.

If nothing else, do it for your house's sake. Ushering your kids out the door will enable them to wreak havoc on the Great Outdoors instead of your great room. They'll trash grass instead of carpets, mark-up sidewalks instead of walls, and ransack yards instead of their rooms. But more importantly, it will keep them active simply because there's more room to run around. Sure, they might suffer a few more cuts and bruises along the way, and subsequently up your Band-Aid bill, but in the long run, it's well worth the worn-out knees on their jeans.

National Public Radio recently conducted a survey of orthopedic surgeons, finding that doctors are treating far fewer broken bones among today's youth and more repetitive motion injuries. Not that I'm crusading for more broken bones, but they at least mean your kids are getting after it, and most likely doing so outside. You don't hear about too many broken arms from playing video games. Broken records and highest scores, maybe. But not broken bones. You kids should be getting their repetitive motion outside.

Of course, my own parents might see repetitive motion injuries as a blessing, and preferable to what they endured with the six Buchanan kids running roughshod over the neighborhood. We had the most dangerous trampoline in the county—a tiny, torso-sized rectangle with no pads covering the metal frame and springs that went sproinging every which way every third jump—which was largely responsible for several doctors' pensions. My parents would likely have preferred a case of GameBoy wrist over trampoline femur any day. And I still remember our neighbor Mark McCadden's broken arm from sliding into third base, which doubled as a rock in our yard.

But today, it seems, many children would rather play electronic games inside than hide-and-seek outside—or fake it with a rousing game of Wii. And that's the root of a spate of health problems with far more long-lasting consequences than broken bones.

Not to numb you with numbers, but this chapter paints the bleak picture of how many kids are and are not getting outdoors today, and examines a few surveys addressing the issue. On the bright side, the trend shows increased interest in getting kids active. By default, most of the solutions mean getting them outdoors.

Boulder, Colorado's Outdoor Industry Association recently released its *Getting Youth Active Toolkit*, designed to improve the health of youngsters in America. Its sister association, the Outdoor Foundation, also debuted its *Getting Americans Active* database, which highlights 100 different outreach organizations designed to get youth active (www.outdoorfoundation.org).

But who in Tom Sawyer's day would have ever thought that we'd need associations to help kids get active outdoors? What happened to afternoon-long games of tag, spud and capture-the-flag? When I was a kid, teachers had to force Ritalin down kids' throats to accomplish just the opposite. It's different today. From Ipods and Wii to FaceBook to video games, today's inactive distractions (though some would say Wii is active) are keeping our children inside.

There's good reason to keep kids full of zip. The main one is the rise in childhood obesity. According to the International Obesity Task Force, 22 million of the world's children under the age of five are overweight or obese. (Obesity is defined as total body weight exceeding 25% fat in boys and 32% in girls.) This equals 13% of all children in the United States. Another alarming statistic: according to the Kaiser Family Foundation, kids spend an average of 44 hours a week with TV, computers and video games. It's no wonder you can't get a tyke to hike.

Carrying it further, a U.S. National Health and Nutrition Examination Survey estimates that 16% of children ages 6-17 are overweight, and more than 10% of preschool children aged 2-5 are overweight (up from 7% in 1994). More disturbing: a Center for Disease Control report says that the percentage of overweight children ages

6-11 has almost doubled since the 1980s, and the percentage of overweight adolescents has risen nearly three hundred percent. To combat this, the Center recommends that children participate in at least sixty minutes of moderate physical activity daily—easily accomplished outdoors.

The implications of the above statistics are startling. Studies show that 60% of overweight children already have a risk factor for heart disease, and 25% show early signs of Type 2 diabetes, which is associated with obesity (up from 4% in 1990).

Don't get me wrong. I used to enjoy a Hostess Ding Dong as much as the next kid, and would even trade baloney sandwiches for them at school. But I counteracted this by staying outside every night until the dinner bell rang, which, thankfully, was the latest of every household in our neighborhood.

I'd venture that none of the kids in our neighborhood fell into the overweight categories. If anything, they skewed the Bell curve and scales down. It's hard to gain weight when you're mired in pine cone wars. But it's doubtful that any of the study's overweight kids actively participate in outdoor activities.

Nudging them in the right direction is easy; you don't have to drop your kids off atop the Eiger to get them exercising outside. Simply encouraging them to play outside will do wonders for their health. And the more you can do outside together, the better.

Parents have a huge effect on their children's hugeness (just look at Augustus' dad in *Charlie and the Chocolate Factory*). Nutrition expert Anne Collins maintains that parents have a big influence over their children's weight, citing adopted children studies that show genes account for only 33% of a child's weight, with the balance due to environmental factors. While diet is a big part of it, "environmental factors" also refer to actively recreating outside. Collins advises parents to get active with their kids, and to have fun doing so. "Take them to the pool, play ball, go fishing, go hiking," she advises. "Teach them to appreciate the outdoors by taking them camping, even if it's only overnight."

Even higher-ups in government recognize the importance of a fit constituency. After a lackluster U.S. showing in the Rome Olympics in 1960, President John F. Kennedy penned a piece called "The Soft American" for *Sports Illustrated* saying, "Our struggles against aggressors throughout our history have been won on the playgrounds, corner lots and fields of America. In a very real and immediate sense, our growing softness, our increasing lack of physical fitness, is a menace to our security. Physical fitness is as vital to the activities of peace as those of war, especially when our success in those activities may well determine the future of freedom in the years to come."

More recent presidents also recognize this, with Clinton taking morning jogs,

George W. dusting body guards on his mountain bike, and Barack Obama driving to the lane shooting hoops. They're setting an example the rest of the country should follow.

For families, it's a game of Monkey See, Monkey Do. Parents who are active in outdoor pursuits themselves will have an easier time convincing their children to be active too. Eat chips and burp on a couch, and little Junior will likely be belching right next to you.

It also helps to get them started early. A fitness survey of 6,000 adults found that 25% of those who were considered active at ages 14 to 19 were also active adults, while just 2% of those who were inactive at ages 14 to 19 were said to be active adults. So push your kids out the door, and they won't be pushing the scales at the doctor's.

Luckily, there's a decent-sized population already jogging down this recreation road. According to the Outdoor Foundation's Outdoor Recreation Participation Study, more than 138.4 million Americans age 6 and over participate in at least one of twenty-two active outdoor activities. That's 50% of the population, taking a total of 11.37 billion outdoor outings every year. Nearly 60 million of these take vacations specifically to participate in an outdoor activity, whether it's wildlife viewing in Yellowstone or climbing Yosemite's El Cap.

All this shows that there are plenty of people already interested in outdoor activities, and many of these are parents. Census statistics show that there are 45 million children age 8 and under in the U.S., meaning there are as many as twice that number of parents open to recreating with them.

The Outdoor Foundation calls the ever-important youth market the Millennials. They're not the Generation Xers or Yers, or even Baby Boomers, but their own. These are the 100 million people or so born between 1981 and 2000, as well as the 50-million-strong group of 6- to 17-year-olds, who are redefining what it means to be active. Today's teenagers have vastly different interests than they did twenty years ago. Instead of pursuing nature-oriented sports, they're into sports that require low time commitment and achievement.

The sad truth is that they have less opportunity to get to the outdoors. Faced with tighter budgets, schools are scrapping sports and field trips. Some feel the government's No Child Left Behind academic program is leaving the outdoors behind for these kids by emphasizing academics over activities. This pushes the burden of recreation from schools and onto family and community-based groups.

Thanks to a collaborative effort between the Outdoor Foundation, Sporting Goods Manufacturers Association, National Golf Foundation and SnowSports Industries America, there are now concrete numbers identifying youth activity trends.

TIPS FOR GETTING YOUR KIDS STARTED

As a parent, you have an important role in shaping your children's physical activity attitudes and behaviors. Following are a few tips experts recommend to encourage your children to be more physically active.

- Set a positive example by leading an active lifestyle yourself. Make physical activity part of your family's daily routine, such as designating time for family walks or playing active games together.
- Provide opportunities for children to be active by playing with them. Give them active toys and equipment, and take them to places where they can be active.
- Offer positive reinforcement for the physical activities in which your child participates and encourage them as they express interest in new activities.
- Make physical activity fun. Fun activities can be anything the child enjoys, either structured or non-structured. They may range from team sports, individual sports, and/or recreational activities such as walking, running, skating, bicycling, swimming, playground activities, and free-time play.
- Ensure that the activity is age appropriate and, to ensure safety, provide protective equipment such as helmets, wrist pads, and knee pads.
- Find a convenient place to be active regularly.
- Limit the time your children watch television or play video games to no more than two hours per day. Instead, encourage your children to find fun activities to do with family members or on their own.

The Outdoor Foundations's Next Generation of Outdoor Participants Report targeted more than 60,000 Americans ages 6 and older and 114 different activities. Its bottom line isn't surprising: the best way to get kids involved in the outdoors is to take them there. Ninety percent of today's active adults, it says, were introduced to their favorite activities before the age of eighteen. Younger children are introduced to the outdoors by their parents and family, while teens are also influenced by mentors and groups.

The good news is that youth participation numbers are relatively high, and that participation by all ages has been steady over time. This is especially true in the five "Gateway" outdoor activities which attract the most outdoor participants: Bicycling (any type), Camping (backyard, car, or RV), Fishing, Hiking, and Running/ Jogging/ Trail running.

In tracking 40 outdoor activities, the study found that nearly 75% of youth ages 6-17 participated in one or more outdoor activity per year. Bicycling tallied the highest ranking, showing 37.5% of this youth group participating, followed by fishing at 32%, hiking at 34.2% and camping at 30.7%. These are the same Big Four "gateway" activities as the last ten years, and the results are the same when adults were polled. (Note: you can skew the curve by biking with your kids to a trailhead, and then hiking in to go fishing, scoring a trifecta.) Showing the changing interests of these Millennials is the fact that skateboarding is not far behind, at nineteen percent.

The problem is frequency. How often do these kids pursue these activities? Is once a year enough to hook them for life? The study finds that the average number of days spent pursuing outdoor activities falls sharply with age, from 135 days per year for 13- to 17-year-olds to 73 for people over 25. More than half of today's youth participate in an outdoor activity less than once per week (34.6% for 6- to 12-year-olds and 39.9% for 13- to 17-year-olds). This number, too, drops as children age.

Two other categories shed more light on this enigma. Forty percent of today's youth participate in some sort of indoor fitness activity, while 56% participate in a team ball sport. There's also a direct correlation between enjoying the outdoors and fitness. Eighty-six percent of youth who do an indoor fitness activity also do some sort of outdoor activity. While young adults (18-24) are less likely to do ball sports, the top sports they want to learn are outdoor sports. The top four? Surfing, skateboarding, snowboarding and wakeboarding (and get this: skateboarders are twice as likely to bicycle than those who don't skateboard).

The problem boils down to retention. Participation in outdoor activities declines with age. While 78% of kids 6-12 participate in outdoor activities, this number falls to 69% for the 13-17 age group and 55% for the 18-24 sector. The variety of activities also decreases with age. Six- to 12-year-olds participated in an average of 3.4 outdoor activities per year, while 13- to 17-year-olds tried 3.2 and 18- to 24-year-olds, three. This means that, with the exception of eating vegetables, the younger your kids are, the more open they are toward trying new things.

Gender rears its head next. Boys participate in outdoor sports longer than girls do. While the numbers are similar for the age 6-12 bracket, 73.5% of boys aged 13-17 participate in outdoor sports compared to only 54% of girls the same age. For whatever reason, pre-teen and teenage girls are finding other things to do in these impressionable years. They also turn to indoor activities at a younger age than males.

I sincerely hope you're not numb from numbers. And I won't be bummed if you skimmed through these baseball-like statistics. I preach all of this altruistically. I don't necessarily want the rivers, trails and slopes that my kids and I recreate on to become crowded, but I'd rather that than not giving other children the chance to experience the rewards of outdoor recreation.

RESOURCES

Want help getting your children's outdoor activity schedule off the ground? Try one of the following websites, dedicated to just that:

- **www.outdoorfoundation.org**: A non-profit established by the Outdoor Industry Association, designed to inspire and grow future generations of outdoor enthusiasts by introducing youth to outdoor recreation through nationwide programming, and producing research quantifying youths' participation in outdoor recreation.
- **www.scouting.org**: The Boy Scouts of America provides a program for young people that builds character, trains them in the responsibilities of participating citizenship, and develops personal fitness.
- **www.cdc.gov/healthyyouth**: A listing of educational and interactive websites especially for children and teens, discussing the need to be active and offering ideas on how to get youth moving.
- **www.bam.gov**: BAM! (Body and Mind) is a website designed for kids 9–13 years old, providing this age set all the information they need to make healthy lifestyle choices.
- **www.cdc.gov/powerfulbones**: If your kids are going to be recreating outside, strong bones certainly help. This site educates and encourages girls aged 9-12 years to establish lifelong, healthy habits that build and maintain strong bones.
- **www.verbnow.com**: No, this is not a site for enhancing your child's vocabulary. It takes a social marketing approach toward youth 9-13 to encourage tweens to be physically active on a continued basis.
- **www.smallstep.gov**: Even the government is getting into the recreation action, running a series of TV ads enforcing the stay-active message. My favorites: the one showing kids finding a bloated, buried stomach on the beach, a dog mistakenly playing with an obviously non-active butt.
- **www.presidentschallenge.org**: This program lets you and your kids track activities by states, fill out activity logs, and earn awards through fitness calculators to help families get started.

Whatever else you may have gotten from this book, take this home if nothing else: kids grow up quickly and won't always want to do things with you. So take advantage of getting outside with them while you can. It will make the world a better place.

GETTING GREEN WITH YOUR KIDS

Except for broccoli and Brussels sprouts, most kids like all things green, from the grass stains they wear on their clothes like badges of honor to M&Ms and mint chocolate chip ice cream cones.

While all these things are considered cool (especially the grass stains), so, too, is getting green another way – by practicing etiquette that leads to a healthier Mother Earth.

Global warming, pollution and diminishing natural resources are just a few of the worldly issues you can teach your brood through recreating outdoors. Skiing with your kids? Point to the cars in the parking lot and explain that their own children might not enjoy the luxury of snow. Snorkeling or swimming? Describe how oil spills, plastic bags and other pollution are devastating marine life. On your next hike, explain the plight of the Amazon rainforest, and how trees are disappearing faster than a bowl of Count Chocula.

Of course, the best teacher is Mother Nature herself. There's no better way to encourage your kids, who represent our planet's future, to protect the environment than by taking them outside and instilling a love for it. Get bitten by the bug – figuratively, not literally – and they'll be more inclined to preserve the planet for future green-living generations.

Parents can encourage their kids to become more environmentally friendly in a variety of ways, from talking at the dinner table to having children take part in recycling bottles, cans, cardboard and plastic. There are even websites that can help. A favorite is www.treadlightly.org, which calls upon all kids to tread lightly through its squirrel mascot, Lightfoot. It also has a free Kids' Club to help kids reduce their impact on nature.

Even when treading lightly, getting kids' feet dirty outside can instill a lifelong lesson. Recreating outdoors helps you appreciate the earth, which encourages you to protect it. Kids might not understand the phrase, but appeal to their social consciousness and they might be more inclined to open the front door. Instilling a green attitude in your brood is also one of the best things you can do for the environment as a parent.

You can only do so much in one lifetime. Get your offspring involved in the cause, however, and it means someone will be following in your earth-saving footsteps.

It shouldn't be difficult. Experts maintain that kids are quick studies when it comes to life changes that have far-reaching ramifications. Your kids will likely grasp the green concept faster than they can grasp the green frog they find by the pond.

"Children are able to learn new habits far better than adults, and so they're the ideal audience for learning how to live in a more environmentally sensitive way," maintains child expert Virginia Bentz, Ph.D., author of *Quick Guide to Good Kids*. "And since today's kids will one day have to face what previous generations have done to our Earth, they should learn alongside grownups how to reverse or minimize some of the damage."

Bentz says that there are countless ways to help kids contribute to a greener planet, but that the changes must include an overall lifestyle adjustment that gets kids off the couch. "Parents must find ways to pull the plug on the TV and computer and encourage outdoor activities along with proactive approaches to conservation," she says.

Following are a few of her pointers on doing so:

Model and reward responsibility. Make conserving a normal part of family life by practicing what you preach. Turn out all lights and televisions or radios when you leave a room. Close the outside door each time you enter or leave the house. Turn off faucets while you brush your teeth and take quick showers. "When kids see the whole family taking these steps, they'll grow up showing care and responsibility for their planet," says Bentz. "Kids learn what they live. But if they need a little boost to get started, you can reinforce these lessons with a star chart. For every day your kids conserve water and power, they each get gold stars. At the end of each week, you can reward them with a small prize to further instill green habits into their daily lives."

Find your family's footprint. A carbon footprint is the level of impact each person leaves on the environment in terms of the amount of greenhouse gasses he or she creates. While kids don't directly affect the environment as much as adults do, it's never too early to teach them about reducing their footprints. Visit a website with a carbon footprint calculator (www.conservation.org) to determine how much you collectively impact the planet. "Kids can grasp concepts more easily when they have hard numbers in front of them," she says.

Green your bookshelf. Invest in a field guide to trees, plants, birds and animals in your region, so you can pull it out and learn about your children's collections along the trail. As well as providing information through pictures and brief blurbs, field guides are also perfect for kids' limited attention spans.

Bring green to school. It costs more, but stock your children's school bags with supplies made of post-consumer recycled materials. Recycled paper and pencils are easy to find in any school supplies store, and retailers are starting to offer bags and totes made of 100 percent organic cotton. Your kids will love the trendy new styles, and that it's great for the environment.

Get growing. Teach your children that a garden is a great way to provide yummy fruits and vegetables without purchasing produce that has been shipped and jetted all over the world. It also gets them outside. Supply spades and other tools and let the kids dig holes in the dirt and mud. Teach them how to drop seeds into the holes and make sure they spend time in the garden watching the seeds grow into plants.

Create a compost pile together. Who needs fertilizers when garbage can create a compost heap? Designate a corner of your yard as your compost pile and teach children which items are best candidates for the heap (again, encouraging visits outside). Ask them which foods and waste products should be added. Teach them about how grass clippings, fruit peels, dead house plants, old hunks of veggies, and other foods can be mixed with the soil to create a nutrient-rich blend to fertilize your garden.

Make yard work a family affair. Round up a wheelbarrow, rake, and shovel and host a family yard cleanup. The kids can help pull weeds and rake grass clippings and leaves to add to the compost pile. This provides bonding time, teaches responsibility and appreciation of the natural world, and provides fresh air and exercise. Hint: put the money you'd save on hiring it out toward a family vacation.

Show kids that dirt doesn't hurt. Don't despair over dirty hands and clothes after a fun afternoon outdoors. Clothes and kids are washable (sometimes at the same time) and the lessons they learn from getting grubby will last far longer than any stain. "Too many 21st century kids lead sanitized, sedentary, indoor lives," says Bentz. "How will they ever be motivated to save the environment if they're afraid of its realities?"

Give boredom the hiking boot. When kids get bored, don't pop a bag of popcorn and sit them in front of the television. Instead, head out to the nearest park for some nature appreciation. If you lead the way and set an example, they'll follow.

Draw your kids' attention to the wonders of nature. When you go on a family hike, encourage your children to watch the ground for interesting things they can collect along the way: an unusual heart-shaped stone, a twisted branch, a dark pine cone, a fallen leaf. Provide a plastic baggie for each child marked with his or her name so these discovered treasures can be compared and admired later.

Connecting Youth with the Outdoors.

The Outdoor Foundation is a national not-for-profit organization established to inspire and grow future generations of outdoor enthusiasts and environmental stewards. The recognized charitable partner of Outdoor Industry Association and more than 250 outdoor companies, The Foundation has emerged as a top leader working with the public and private sectors to spur a massive increase in outdoor recreation, particularly among youth. Thanks to generous donor support, The Foundation and its partners are ensuring a healthier future for the outdoor community – its people, places and prospects.

The Outdoor Foundation at Work

The Outdoor Foundation focuses its efforts on three core areas: ground-breaking research, high-impact convening and broad-based outreach and education. Through this inter-related work, The Foundation has emerged as an influential organization that is mobilizing a diverse coalition – from outdoor companies and public agencies to grassroots organizations and passionate individuals -- to spur a mainstream movement that connects young people, of all ages, with the outdoors.

Research: Identifying Best Practices and Trends

Since 2004, The Outdoor Foundation has produced a dozen specialized reports exploring the trends and impact of outdoor activity across the country. Areas of research range from outdoor-related economic impact to minority and youth engagement to overall participation.

Outreach: Engaging New Audiences

Demographic and geographic shifts across the country will profoundly impact the outdoor community, especially participation trends. To engage and inspire new audiences, The Foundation creates and manages innovative outreach initiatives that are often national in scope, local in impact.

Convening: Fostering Collaboration and Action

In a range of action-oriented convening events – from high-powered gatherings to large-scale festivals -- The Outdoor Foundation brings together top public and private leaders, nonprofit executives and youth activists to foster greater collaboration, investment, impact and results.

Join Us

The Outdoor Foundation is building a powerful coalition to reconnect young people, of all ages, with the outdoors. We hope you will consider joining this growing movement by making a financial contribution to The Foundation. Together we will inspire the next generation of outdoor enthusiasts and ensure a healthier future for the outdoor community – its people, places and prospects.

For more information on its action-oriented, results-driven work, visit The Outdoor Foundation online at www.outdoorfoundation.org.

The Outdoor Foundation
4909 Pearl East Circle, Suite 200
Boulder, CO 80301
303.444.3353
www.outdoorfoundation.org
info@outdoorfoundation.org

™The Outdoor Foundation is a trademark of The Outdoor Foundation.

Special Thanks to:

GOLD SUPPORTERS

Adventure 16 .... www.adventure16.com
Boy Scouts of America .... www.scouting.org
Campmor .... www.campmor.com
Coast Mountain Sports .... www.coastmountain.com
Eastern Mountain Sports .... www.ems.com
Go On and Get Lost .... www.goonandgetlost.ca
Grand River Kayak .... www.grandriverkayak.ca
Jenda Paddlesports .... www.jenda.com
MEC .... www.mec.ca
NRS .... www.nrs.com
Outdoor Kidfitter™ Co. .... www.outdoorkidfitters.com
Paddling.net .... www.paddling.net
Philmont Scout Ranch/Tooth of Time Traders .... www.toothoftimetraders.com
REI .... www.rei.com
River Sports Outfitters .... www.riversportsoutfitters.com
Rutabaga .... www.rutabaga.com
The Trail Store .... www.louisvilletrailstore.com
Wilderness Tours .... www.wildernesstours.com
Winded Bowhunter .... www.windedbowhunter.com

SILVER SUPPORTERS

Adventure's Edge .... www.adventuresedge.com
Alberni Outpost .... www.albernioutpost.com
Austin Canoe and Kayak .... www.austinkayak.com
Boutique BoréalDesign .... www.boutiqueborealdesign.com
Diamond Brand Outdoors .... www.diamondbrand.com
Ecomarine Ocean Kayak Centre .... www.ecomarine.com
Escalante Outfitters .... www.escalanteoutfitters.com
Kano & Kajak Butikken .... www.kajak.dk
Molehill Mountain Equipment, Inc .... www.molehillmtn.com
Nantahala Outdoor Center .... www.noc.com
Pelee Wings Kayaks & Canoes .... www.peleewings.ca
The Outfitters Shop at ZOAR Outdoor .... www.zoaroutdoor.com/store
Thorncrest Outfitters .... www.thorncrestoutfitters.com
Trailhead .... www.trailhead.ca
US National Whitewater Center .... www.usnwc.org
Utah Office of Tourism .... www.travel.utah.gov
White Squall Paddling Center .... www.whitesquall.com

SUPPORTING ORGANIZATIONS

American Hiking Society .... www.americanhiking.org
American Park Network .... www.ohranger.com
Bechtel Family National Scouting Center .... www.scouting.org
Boy Scouts of America .... www.scouting.org
Bureau of Land Management .... www.blm.gov
Children and Nature Network .... www.childrenandnature.org
chooseoutdoors.org .... www.chooseoutdoors.org
Colorado Mountain Club .... www.cmc.org
Hydro Flask .... www.hydroflask.com
Kids in the Valley, Adventuring! .... www.kidsadventuring.org
KOA .... www.koa.com
Kona Bikes .... www.konaworld.com
Level 6 .... www.levelsixinc.com
LittleLife .... www.littlelife.com
Molehill Mountain Equipment, Inc .... www.molehillmtn.com/
Mountain Mama .... www.mountain-mama.com
National Ability Center/DiscoverNAC .... www.discovernac.org
National Parks Conservation Association .... www.npca.org
Nielsen Business Media/Outdoor Retailer .... www.outdoorretailer.com
SmartWool .... www.smartwool.com

BOOK TOUR SPONSORS

INDEX

The Essential Guides

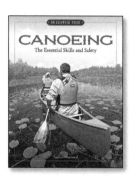

Canoeing
The Essential Skills and Safety
By Andrew Westwood

For all levels of paddlers, providing beginners with the skills they need to maneuver a canoe effectively on flat water, and offering more experienced paddlers expert advice on how to hone their skills.

$19.95 · 144 Pages

Canoe Camping
An Essential Guide
By Mark Scriver

This comprehensive guide by senior guide and World Champion paddler Mark Scriver makes canoe camping fun and safe for both new and experienced canoe trippers.

$16.95 · 112 Pages

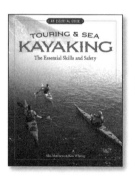

Touring & Sea Kayaking
The Essential Skills and Safety
By Alex Matthews and Ken Whiting

This guide provides beginner and experienced kayakers with the knowledge and skills necessary to safely and comfortably enjoy sea kayaking.

$19.95 · 120 Pages

Easy Campfire Cooking
75 Recipes and Family Fun Activities for the Great Outdoors
Edited by Peg Couch

Whether you are heading out on a camping trip or simply enjoying a backyard bonfire, this book will satisfy your appetite and provide hours of entertainment for the whole family.

ISBN: 978-1-56523-724-7
$12.95 · 128 Pages

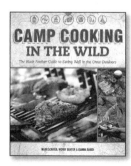

Camp Cooking in the Wild
The Black Feather Guide to Eating Well in the Great Outdoors
By Mark Scriver, Joanna Baker, and Wendy Grater

Camp Cooking can help you create a menu, set up a kitchen in the woods, and teach you new techniques and recipe ideas whether you are a beginner or a more experienced camper.

$19.95 · 216 Pages

Grilling Gone Wild
Zesty Recipes For Entrees And Side Dishes That Really Turn Up The Heat
Edited by Peg Couch

Use the instructions inside this book to serve a perfectly grilled, yet simple entrée or side dish... or turn up the heat and go wild!

ISBN: 978-1-56523-725-4
$12.95 · 128 Pages

Recreational Kayaking
The Ultimate Guide
The Ultimate Guide
By Ken Whiting

This easy-to-read guide makes paddling fun and safe for both new and experienced paddlers looking to broaden their horizons.

$19.95 · 192 Pages

Kayaking for Fitness
An 8-week Program to Get Fit and Have Fun
By Jodi Bigelow

This is the essential guide to achieving and maintaining physical fitness and body tone through kayaking.

$19.95 · 160 Pages

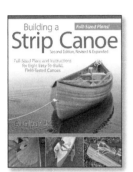

Building a Strip Canoe, Second Edition, Revised & Expanded
Full-Sized Plans and Instructions for Eight Easy-To-Build, Field-Tested Canoes
By Gil Gilpatrick

Paddle along with an expert outdoorsman and canoe builder as he shares his experience in guiding both novice and accomplished woodworkers in building a canoe with easy step-by-step instructions.

ISBN: 978-1-56523-483-3
$24.95 · 112 Pages

The Paddling Chef, Second Edition
A Cookbook for Canoeists, Kayakers, and Rafters
By Dian Weimer

Paddler Dian Weimer shows hungry readers how to pack, carry, and cook outdoor meals that help make water borne trips memorable—for all the right reasons.

$16.95 · 184 Pages

Big Book of Whittle Fun
31 Simple Projects You Can Make with a Knife, Branches & Other Found Wood
By Chris Lubkemann

The whittler extraordinaire, Chris Lubkemann is back, with 31 fun and rewarding new whittle projects in his latest guidebook, *Big Book of Whittle Fun*.

ISBN: 978-1-56523-520-5
$12.95 · 128 Pages

Winter Backpacking
Your Guide to Safe and Warm Winter Camping and Day Trips
By Ben Shillington

Backpacking in the winter months can be exhilarating, refreshing, and-with the help of this book.

$19.95 · 160 Pages

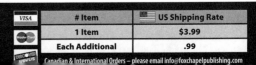

Natural Wooden Toys
75 Easy-To-Make and Kid-Safe Designs to Inspire Imaginations & Creative Play
By Erin Freuchtel-Dearing

Learn how to make safe, colorful, and irresistible imagination-building wooden toys with a stay-at-home mom turned woodworker! Step-by-step instructions show you how to make 75 charming designs, and how to create natural, non-toxic finishes.

ISBN: 978-1-56523-524-3
$19.95 · 184 Pages

Getting Started in Pinewood Derby
Step-By-Step Workbook to Building Your First Car
By Troy Thorne

Follow Dash Derby, your Pinewood Derby guide, on an adventure through the seven easy steps to building your first Pinewood Derby race car.

ISBN: 978-1-56523-617-2
$12.95 · 96 Pages

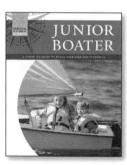

Junior Boater
A Hands-On Guide to Teach Your Kids About Boating
By Skills Institute Press Editor, John Kelsey

Designed for the 8–15 year old who is interested in boating, this is a great guide for young people who are ready to be crew, not just passengers.

ISBN: 978-1-56523-700-1
$19.95 · 144 Pages

Woodcarving (Kid Craft Series)
By Everett Ellenwood

Perfect for children or anyone learning to carve—includes basic carving skills and projects for a fun croaking frog, a snowman ornament, whistle, arrowhead, eagle's head, and a name plaque for your bedroom door.

ISBN: 978-156523-366-9
$14.95 · 121 Pages

Woodworking (Kid Craft Series)
By John Kelsey

Discover the fun of woodworking with 10 projects that only require ordinary lumber and simple hand tools. Learn to build a bird nesting box, tool box, and much more.

ISBN: 978-156523-353-9
$12.95 · 104 Pages

Leathercraft (Kid Craft Series)
By Linda Sue Eastman

Learn 5 basic leatherworking skills that you can use to create a carrying case for your GameBoy, a cell-phone case, moccasins and more with just a simple set of tools.

ISBN: 978-156523-370-6
$14.95 · 128 Pages